this food that wine

Wine and food pairing made easy

Angie MacRae **Stacey Metulynsky**
Chris Knight

McArthur & Company
Toronto

First published in 2007 by
McArthur & Company
322 King St. West, Suite 402
Toronto, ON
M5V 1J2
www.mcarthur-co.com

Library and Archives Canada Cataloguing in Publication

Knight, Chris, 1960-
This food, that wine / Chris Knight, Angie Macrae, Stacey Metulynsky.

Includes index.
ISBN 978-1-55278-684-0

1. Cookery. 2. Wine and wine making.
I. MacRae, Angie II. Metulynsky, Stacey III. Title.

TX714.K543 2007   641.5   C2007-905231-2

Design by *Mad Dog Design Connection*
Printed in Canada by *Transcontinental*

Louis Jadot label courtesy Lifford Wine Agency

The publisher would like to acknowledge the financial support of the Government of Canada through the Book Publishing Industry Development Program (BPIDP) and the Canada Council for our publishing activities. The publisher further wishes to acknowledge the financial support of the Ontario Arts Council for our publishing program.

10 9 8 7 6 5 4 3 2 1

Contents

Cold Thai Shrimp Salad	Gewürztraminer	111
Roasted Asparagus with Caper Mayonnaise	Chablis	114
Butter lettuce with Oranges, Goat's Cheese, Toasted Walnuts and Shallot Vinaigrette	Fumé Blanc	116
Spring Salmon Salad	Sauvignon Blanc	118
Mushrooms on Toast	Oaked Chardonnay	121
Savoury Squash Onion and Feta Tart with Creamy Yogurt Sauce	Viognier	122
Roquefort and Green Apple Tart with Walnut Crust	Riesling (off-dry)	124
Crispy Scallop and Potato Sandwiches	Viognier	126
Grilled Squid with Chilis	Albariño	128
Mussels in a Dijon and Saffron Sauce	Pinot Gris	130
Grapefruit and Lobster Cocktail	Fumé Blanc	131
Pan Seared Maple Trout with Apple Turnip Compote	Vidal	133
Whole Trout Pan Fried with Sage and Pecans	Riesling	134
Arctic Char with Vegetable Confetti and Brown Butter Sauce	Fumé Blanc	136
Linguini with Pesto and Cherry Tomatoes	Sauvignon Blanc	139
Salmon with Curry Coconut Sauce	Viognier	140
Poached Halibut with Provençal Vegetables and Basil	White Rhône Blend	143
Seafood Pad Thai in a Spicy Tamarind Sauce	Gewürztraminer	146
Baked Trout en Papillote	Pinot Blanc	148
Angel Hair with Fiddleheads, Smoked Salmon and Lemon Vodka Cream Sauce	Pinot Grigio	150
Good Ol' Roast Chicken	Oaked Chardonnay	153
Chicken and Lemon Pot Pie	Unoaked Chardonnay	155
Chicken Roulade with Apricots and Tarragon	White Rhône Blend	158
White Chicken Stew with Garlic	Pinot Blanc	161
Spring Poached Chicken	White Bordeaux	163
Jerk Chicken Sweet Potato Salad with Coconut	Viognier	165
Pork Tenderloin with Tomatillo Pesto	Albariño	168
Pork Chops with Apples, Grain Mustard and Cream	Sémillon	171

Foreword

After 10 years and almost 400 half-hours of television I'm still amazed at the process. Making a television show is kind of like trying to paint Van Gogh's "Sunflowers" by committee. Give everyone a paint brush with a different colour and a different part of the canvas to work on and then have them all go at it at once. Furious activity ensues and then we all stand back and look at what we've created. It's a crazy, zany, intense, pressurized roller-coaster ride and not recommended for those who enjoy sleep, weekends off, normal work hours or anything that vaguely resembles structure and routine.

Inevitably a great TV show starts with great hosts, and we got lucky – very lucky – when we found Stacey Metulynsky and Angie MacRae to host *This Food That Wine*. Angie and Stacey were selected from hundreds of applicants after an exhaustive nationwide audition. We knew we needed both a chef and a sommelier but beyond that we were keeping our options open. As we narrowed the candidates down we began pairing up potential hosts in on-camera auditions and that's where Angie and Stacey met for the first time. The chemistry between the two of them was immediate, fun and infectious. We knew right away we were on to something. Angie is an amazing chef and Stacey runs her own wine consulting business (www.groovygrapes.com) but we wanted to take them out of chef's whites and rarified wine circles and put them in an "everyday" setting that the average viewer could relate to.

What makes "The Girls" so good on camera is not only the fun they have with each other but also the way they put on-camera guests at ease. Having "civilians" as part of a show is always a risky thing and they innately knew how to make people feel comfortable and relaxed (as comfortable and relaxed as one can be on a TV set with 30 people running around and cameras in your face) from the get go.

It has been a pleasure working with them and I have made two fast friends in Stacey and Angie. Oh yeah, and they're stubborn, headstrong and opinionated . . . wait a minute, that's what they say about me.

Let me give you a water cooler synopsis if you haven't seen *This Food That Wine*. In each episode we meet the "guests du jour," real people who have an event (a birthday, anniversary, etc.) to plan and come to Angie and Stacey for menu advice and the perfect wine pairings. The ladies work with the guest on the menu, show them how to cook the meals and explain why certain wines work with the dishes they've selected. Then they send the guest on their merry way to pull off the perfect soirée.

A typical television show is broken out into four acts separated by commercial breaks. On *This Food That Wine* each act deals with a specific wine type and matching recipes. Act 1 is always nibblies and snacks with a variety of wines. Act 2 is always white wine and Act 3 concerns itself with the reds. In Act 4, Angie and Stacey show up to the party for dessert and Stacey brings along the right wine pairing.

So we decided to break the book out into four acts as well: nibblies, whites, reds and dessert. Almost all of the photos were taken by the very talented Vanessa Poirier-Ogg, a valued member of our television production team

The spine of this book lists the three of us as co-authors. The truth is all the heavy lifting was done by Stacey Metulynsky and Angie MacRae and I really just tagged along for the ride. All the recipes herein come from Angie and reflect her passion for quality ingredients and her understanding that great food doesn't have to be complicated or chi-chi. You'll find her directions not only informative but also fun and accessible. These are recipes you'll go back to time and again.

The wine information and pairings is all Stacey all the time and man, is there a lot of it. Stacey writes about wine with infectious enthusiasm and passion. She cuts through the pretentious snootiness that is so often associated with fermented grape juice and speaks of wine in a voice that is easily understood by the most tentative beginner while being of interest to a discerning collector.

So there you have it. The brief story of how we got to here. I know you're going to love this book and envy you the read you're about to have. Now if you'll excuse me there's a glass of Zin with my name on it . . .

– Chris Knight

Food & Wine Pairing – The Basics

"A meal without wine is like a day without sunshine."

—JEAN ANTHELME BRILLAT-SAVARIN, *THE PHYSIOLOGY OF TASTE*

My favourite part of being a sommelier is figuring out great wine and food matches. The idea is to pair a wine with food so that they taste better together than they each did on their own. The possibilities for wine and food matching these days are endless – there are so many different styles of wine, and shops and restaurants are filled with flavours from around the world. Some people get intimidated by all the choice. Here are a few basic tips to get you started in putting together your own delicious pairings – these are the principles that I go back to again and again when pairing wine with food. And remember, there is no absolute right or wrong, so do what tastes good to you. Wine and food matching is both an art and a science . . . keep these tips in mind and let your taste buds do the rest.

BALANCE – you don't want your wine to overpower your food, but you also don't want the flavours of your food to be too intense for the wine. Complicated? Not really. Consider both the flavours and the textures of your food, as well as the wine when trying to find a balance. For instance, steamed lobster is a rich, buttery meat with a subtle, sweet flavour that's delicate enough for a white wine, but because the texture is so rich, the white wine should also be rich and full bodied. An oak-aged Chardonnay is the perfect pairing.

DOMINANT FLAVOUR – determine what the most dominant flavour in your dish is, then match your wine to that flavour. Often, this is the sauce or seasonings used in the dish rather than the meat. Let's say you're making chicken (light, mild flavoured) with a big, spicy barbeque sauce. The sauce would be more important in choosing a wine than would the chicken because it's the dominant flavour. Think of a fruity, medium bodied red (like a Gamay or a Grenache).

MIRRORING – one way of creating a delicious match is to mirror the characteristics of the food in the wine you chose. A jammy, berry flavoured red Zinfandel with a rich meat and a berry sauce works so well because the flavour of the wine is mirrored in the flavour of the sauce. And here's a little tip – add a splash of the wine you are serving to the sauce for a foolproof match!

CONTRASTING – this is the opposite of mirroring. Sometimes when you contrast the characteristics of the food with those of the wine you can end up with an entirely different but delicious pairing. Stilton and port is a classic example – Port is a sweet, rich wine that perfectly contrasts the strong, pungent, salty cheese to create an amazing taste sensation.

THINK REGIONAL – ever wonder why a bottle of Chianti tastes so good with a bowl of spaghetti with a rich, tomato meat sauce? Because they were made for each other! Chianti winemakers would go home at night and chow down on pasta – so it's only natural that the foods of the region influence the winemaking styles of the same region. Regional wine styles developed over the years to complement the cuisine of that area, so when in doubt, try a regional wine pairing for your dish.

CONSIDER ACID AND SUGAR – these are both key components in wine that need to be considered when choosing your wine match. Acidity in food can make a wine without much acidity taste bland or flabby. Take tomatoes for example – they are packed with acid and need a wine with enough of its own to balance it out. Try a light to medium bodied red from Italy (such as Chianti, Valpolicella, or Dolcetto) or a zesty white such as Sauvignon Blanc. Sweetness in food also needs to be balanced. If you are serving a dessert or even a savoury dish that has a sweet element (such as a mango salsa on fish or candied nuts in a salad), pick a wine that has a touch of sweetness to balance it off. For desserts, your wine should always be at least as sweet as your dessert.

PAY ATTENTION TO TANNIN – tannins are a component of wine that comes from skins, seeds, and stems of grapes. They are found mostly in red wine and leave an astringent feeling in your mouth (much like strongly brewed tea). It's easy to tame the tannins – simply pair your tannic wine with a dish high in protein. A classic example is Cabernet Sauvignon with a big, juicy steak. The protein in the meat coats your mouth and makes the tannins in the wine seem soft and smooth, which makes it easier to taste the flavours of the wine.

DON'T FORGET THE ALCOHOL – the alcohol content in wine can have a big impact on how it tastes with the food, especially when the food you are serving is spicy. Alcohol intensifies spice, so unless you love blow-your-mouth-off heat, avoid serving high-alcohol wines with your spicy dishes. A great alternative is an off-dry wine, which just means that it has a bit of sweetness in it. The alcohol level in these wines tend to be lower, and the sweetness cools down the heat of the spice.

ACT 1

Act 1 is all about beginnings. The first glass of wine at the end of a busy day, or a well-earned treat before you sit down to dinner. The wines in this section all fit into the category of *apéritif*, something cool and refreshing to rouse your taste buds, perfect for drinking with Angie's deceptively simple recipes for little nibbles and snacks to spark your appetite. You'll find three different styles of wine in this section – sparkling, rosé, and drier styles of sherry, plus a couple of whites thrown in for good measure.

Sparkling Wine

"It's like drinking the stars!"

—BENEDICTINE MONK DOM PERIGNON

I love sparkling wine! But I love it not for its traditional place at a special event, but for the fun it can bring to everyday. For most people, bubbles say party, romance, celebration. Bubbles make you feel good, and not just because you usually drink it when you're already having a good time. Those tasty, tiny bubbles actually zip around inside of you faster, increasing testosterone and raising your blood alcohol level, giving you a rush. But that's not where the magic of the bubbles ends. The fruity fizz of sparkling wine makes it super food-friendly, especially with spicy, salty, or smoky flavours. Why? Well, the bubbles keep the wine light and refreshing, so it quenches your thirst and cools off your taste buds, making you ready for another bite. And that's why I love bubbly so much. It just doesn't seem right to save the fun of the fizz for special occasions alone.

But Stacey, you're thinking, it's an indulgence, too expensive for everyday. A sad misconception. Yes, the Cadillac of sparkling wine, Champagne, does tend to be on the pricey side. But read on to find out about sparkling wine from around the world that tastes just as good as French champers without breaking the bank. I always keep a bottle or two of bubbly around the house – it's perfect for unexpected guests or an unexpected thirst, and it's great with everyday meals.

HOW TO POP THE CORK ON A BOTTLE OF BUBBLY

Sure it looks fun and festive to pop the cork and let the fizz spill all over the place . . . but do you really want to waste all that yummy wine? Here's how to pop the cork on a bottle of bubbly like a pro. Remove the foil, and loosen the wire casing. Once you've done this, make sure to keep a firm grip on the cork at all times. There's a lot of pressure inside the bottle and the cork can pop at any time. Make sure the bottle is pointed away from anything breakable (including yourself and your friends!), put a cloth napkin or tea towel overtop of the cork, and keeping a firm grip on the cork, slowly twist the bottle and not the cork – this is the trick so that you've always got control. You'll start to feel it loosening, and voila! The experts say you should only hear a little sigh when the cork comes out, but I like to hear the pop – it's a sure sign the party's about to start!

SPARKLING WINE SERVING TIPS

Keep it cool – the best way to chill your sparkling wine is in an ice bucket – fill it with half ice, half water, and pop in your bottle for about 20 minutes. Also a great way to keep the wine cold as you're enjoying your first couple of glasses. Don't have an ice bucket? Fill your sink with ice and water for a good substitute. Your fridge will work too, but let it chill for at least an hour before serving. And if you're in a rush, put your sparkling wine in the freezer but don't forget about it – you don't want a bubbly-sicle!

Get the glassware – wine glasses come in all shapes and sizes but when it comes to sparkling wine be sure to stick to flutes. They're deep and narrow which keeps the bubbles concentrated so they last longer. See page 132 for more on glasses.

Mix it up – welcoming your guests with a glass of bubbly is a sure way to make them feel special and set a celebratory mood. But why not try a sparkling wine cocktail for something extra-special? A few drops of cassis topped with bubbly makes a Kir Royale, or pour sparkling wine over a dollop of fresh fruit purée to make a Bellini. Be creative and make your own signature cocktail. Our very own Chris Knight serves up a "Knight Cap" – vanilla-infused cognac and Framboise topped with bubbly.

Champagne

"I drink Champagne when I'm happy and when I'm sad. Sometimes I drink it when I'm alone. When I have company, I consider it obligatory. I trifle with it if I'm not hungry, and drink it when I am. Otherwise I never touch it – unless I'm thirsty."
—MADAME LILY BOLLINGER

I said before that I love sparkling wine for everyday . . . well, this is the one you save for special occasions. Champagne is *the* classic sparkling wine, and it has a hefty price tag compared to other sparkling wine. It's made in the Champagne region of France, hence the name, which is the most northerly wine making region in France and one of the coolest in the world. It's made from three grapes – Chardonnay, Pinot Noir, and Pinot Meunier – in a range of styles from light and citrusy to rich and toasty to berry-flavoured and pink-tinged, depending on the blend of grapes, how long the wine has been aged, and the winemaking techniques used. Generally speaking though, the bubbles are always tiny and long-lasting, which keeps the wine crisp and refreshing and very food-friendly (and of course, very celebration-friendly). There's lots of lingo on a Champagne label so here's a rundown.

Blanc de blanc – literally "white from white," a light, dry, crisp style of Champagne which by law can only be made from one grape variety – Chardonnay

Blanc de noirs – "white from black," made from the red grapes Pinot Noir and Pinot Meunier. The grapes are crushed and the skins immediately removed so there is little, if any, colour added to the wine. This style tends to be fuller in body and more golden in colour than Blanc de blanc.

Rosé – "pink" wines made from any or all the Champagne grapes, and definitely my all-time favourite. The skins of the red grapes are allowed some contact with the juice which adds the pink colour and berry flavours to the wine. So delicious, and extremely food-friendly.

Extra brut, Brut, Extra-Sec, Sec, Demi-Sec, or Doux – these terms refer to the sweetness of the wine, *Extra Brut* being the driest and *Doux* being the sweetest. The most common style is Brut which is quite dry and a great choice for drinking champers on its own. The other style you'll see more often than the others is *Demi-Sec*, a sweet style of Champagne that pairs well with desserts and rich foods like *foie gras*.

Non-Vintage (N.V.) or Vintage – you'll see N.V. on a Champagne label most often, meaning that the wine in the bottle is a blend from various vintages. This type of Champagne is usually less expensive than Vintage and represents the producer's "house" wine which tastes about the same every time they make a new batch. Vintage Champagnes are only made in certain years when the producer feels they had an exceptional harvest. They are made only from grapes of the year on the label and are pricier. For an extra-special occasion (especially if you're commemorating a certain year), it's worth the extra money to splurge.

Aromas & Flavours
Fruit flavours ranging from light, tart citrus to ripe berry flavours
Toasty, yeasty, and nutty aromas
Spicy, cinnamony baked apple aromas

Food Ideas
Scallop ceviche
Salmon tartare or smoked salmon
Caviar
Lobster bisque

My recommended regions for Champagne are:
Champagne, France – this is the only place Champagne is made

Cava

In my house, bubbly is on the menu several times a month, and as much as I'd love it to always be Champagne, that would be a bit rough on the pocketbook. So Cava has become one of my go-to sparkling wines. Made in the same way as Champagne, Cava is from Spain and produced from indigenous Spanish grapes (Parellada, Macabeo, and Xarello, sometimes with some Chardonnay blended in too). It's light, crisp, and refreshing, with lots of tiny bubbles to cleanse your palate, and fresh, fruity flavours of citrus, pear, apple, and melon. These ripe fruit flavours can make the wine seem almost a touch on the sweet side. That, combined with the bubbly freshness of Cava, makes it a perfect party wine because it pairs with all sorts of snack foods, including salty, smoky, or spicy flavours. Most Cavas on the market are at a way lower price point than Champagne – usually $15 or less, and you can pick up just about any Cava off the shelf and know it's gonna be good.

Aromas & Flavours
Fresh, ripe fruity flavours of citrus, apple, pear, and melon
Tiny bubbles and medium body
A subtle touch of yeastiness

Food Ideas
Roasted spiced nuts
Shrimp cocktail
Nachos with salsa
Smoked salmon

My recommended regions for Cava are:
Anywhere in Spain, the most common region is Penedes

Prosecco

Prosecco – another one of my go-to bubblies – delicious, cheap, and fun. Prosecco is from the Veneto region of northern Italy and is named for the grape used to make it. Usually it's made using the Charmat method, whereby the bubbly wine is made in a sealed tank then bottled under pressure to preserve the bubbles. The aromas and flavours of this wine are amazing – somehow light and fresh yet concentrated at the same time, Prosecco has intense aromas and fruity flavours. Think lemon, pear, peach, and sweet spring flowers with just a touch of sweetness, and because of the bubbles it's the perfect thirst-quencher. Compared to Spain's Cava, it's a bit lighter and fruitier, but it's still another great everyday wine and perfect for entertaining as well.

Aromas & Flavours
Fresh, ripe fruity flavours of citrus, apple, pear, and melon
Tiny bubbles and medium body
A subtle touch of yeastiness

Food Ideas
Prosciutto wrapped figs, melon, or pear
Hard, salty cheeses like Parmigiano, Grana Padano, or Romano
Spicy Asian-inspired cuisine or sushi
Antipasti such as olives, pickled vegetables, and charcuterie

My recommended region for Prosecco is:
Veneto, Italy

Sparkling Shiraz

If you haven't tried Sparkling Shiraz before, drop everything and run to the store right now to pick up a bottle! Seriously, this is yummy stuff and is just what the name implies. Everything you love in a Shiraz – ripe berry fruit flavours like blackcurrant, blackberry, cherry, and strawberry with a peppery kick, and a subtle richness like dark chocolate – but it has bubbles and a pretty pink mousse. Sparkling Shiraz is a creation of the Aussies (using the traditional Champenoise method), and it's usually slightly sweet in style, best served chilled, and is super-versatile. This is a very fun welcome drink if you're having guests over, especially during the holiday season. But it's even more fun as an after-dinner drink, served on its own or with chocolate or fruit desserts . . . so good. It's also a great brunch wine, the perfect partner for pancakes, berries, and maple syrup.

Aromas & Flavours
Ripe berry fruit flavours like blackcurrant, blackberry, cherry, and strawberry
Rich dark chocolate and peppery flavours
A touch of sweetness

Food Ideas
Chocolate desserts
Fresh fruits and berries
Baked brie with berry topping
Duck or other robust meat dishes

My recommended region for Sparkling Shiraz is:
Australia

Other Notable Bubblies

Sparkling wine is made everywhere around the world. Experiment with the bubblies made locally in your area, or from your favourite wine region. Some more regions and styles that I love are:

California, U.S.A. – especially from Carneros and Anderson Valley, where some Champagne houses have actually set up wineries to create sparkling wines that rival their French counterparts.

Canada – both Niagara, Ontario and Okanagan Valley, British Columbia are producing world-class sparkling wines that are high quality, affordable, and delicious.

Australia – besides Sparkling Shiraz, the Aussies also make the more traditional white and rosé styles of bubbly. Check out the ones from the cool climates in Yarra Valley, Victoria or Tasmania.

Other regions of France – Champagne isn't the only French region that produces sparkling wine. Look for Crémant d'Alsace, Crémant de Bourgogne, Blanquette de Limoux, and bubblies from the Loire Valley for some great values.

Rosé

"Wine gives great pleasure, and every pleasure is of itself a good."
—SAMUEL JOHNSON, *BOSWELL'S "LIFE OF JOHNSON"*

Rosé is my absolute favourite summertime, patio-sipping wine. It's like red wine in white wine's clothing, with the berry and spice flavours of red wine but drunk chilled down like white wine. It's crisp, refreshing, fruity, and easy-drinking – perfect for picnics, barbecue, and just about all summertime foods. Not to say that you can't drink it in the winter too – I certainly do! Rosé is food friendly because of all the things it isn't – it's not as heavy as reds, and it's not as light as many whites – it's a happy medium, delicious, and affordable to boot.

Rosés, however, tend to be overlooked by wine snobs. A lot of people automatically think of the sweet and simple White Zinfandel – this stuff has given rosé a bad name (I'm sure most of us can recall a White Zin hangover sometime in our youth). But what I'm talking about are the dry yet fruity, refreshing yet interesting pink wines made around the world, especially those of Mediterranean regions like southern France and Spain. Canada and Italy make some delicious rosé as well.

There are two ways that wine becomes pink. First, you can make a white wine and add a splash of red. Or you can make it only from red grapes. As I explained earlier, red grapes are actually just red on the outside – the flesh and juice inside is white. When red wine is made, the grapes are crushed and the skins left in with the juice, usually at least for a couple of weeks. This is called maceration. During this time, the skins add colour, flavour, and texture to the wine. So to make rosé, the skins are left in with the juice for only a short period of time to extract just a bit of colour and flavour, leaving the wine a rosy pink hue with ripe berry flavours.

My favourite regions for rosé are Spain and the southern part of the Rhône Valley in France. Spanish rosé is called Rosado, and the French name theirs after the region in which it's made (including Tavel, Bandol, and Côtes-du-Rhône). Both countries use Grenache as the main grape in the blend, also throwing in some Syrah and Cinsault (in France) or Tempranillo (in Spain). The wines are quite full in body with ripe strawberry and raspberry flavours, and crisp, refreshing acidity. In Canada, you often see grapes like Cabernet Sauvignon, Cabernet Franc, Merlot, or Gamay used in their rosés. They are still fruity, but slightly lighter and tarter in style then the

Mediterranean versions. Italy's rosés (sometimes called *rosato*) are made from a wide range of grapes, but my favourite style is Chiaretto which is made in the Bardolino region of Italy using the same three grapes used to make the well-known Valpolicella (Molinara, Corvina, and Rondinella). Chiaretto di Bardolino has a vivid salmon colour, bright berry fruit flavours, and a characteristic bitter tang on the finish.

Aromas & Flavours
Berry aromas and flavours like strawberry and raspberry
Crisp acidity and medium body

Food Ideas
Grilled seafood, fish, or light meats
Tapas
Rare or raw tuna
Mediterranean-inspired cuisine

My recommended regions for Rosé are:
Various regions in the southern Rhône, especially Tavel and Bandol
Spain, especially Penedes, Navarra, and Rioja Alta
Italy, especially Chiaretto di Bardolino, but also Tuscany, Piedmont, and some southern regions

TIP

What's the difference between blush and rosé?

Blush, rosé; tomato, tom*ah*to – the two terms are inter-changeable. The truth about blush and rosé though, is that blush tends to be related to the sweeter, low-alcohol styles of rosé like White Zinfandel. It's like the lower-end version, whereas rosé is the more respectable stuff. In fact, dry rosé wines are as common as the sunshine in the Mediterranean, where people crave something cool and refreshing when it's hot out, but still want something in the red wine family. Rosé is the perfect solution.

Sherry

Trust me on this one – sherry is NOT just your grandma's wine anymore. I know that sherry has an old-fashioned reputation, but it's actually one of the most modern wine trends, especially with the current tapas bar craze (tapas and sherry are best friends so with tapas becoming more popular, sherry follows suit).

Sherry is constantly bombarded with misconceptions. First is the "grandma wine" thing. Sure, lots of our grandmothers drank it, but they also drank Merlot and Chardonnay and these wines are still pretty cool. Next is that it's a rich, sweet, deeply-coloured wine. Sure, some sherries are made in that style (like Cream or sweet Oloroso) but many are light, crisp and food-friendly. So sherry has a hard time fitting in right out of the gate.

The other tricky thing is that explaining how sherry is made and how it tastes is complicated. So bear with me while I try to simplify. First, sherry comes from Spain – the town of Jerez to be exact, and a few neighbouring towns. The three styles of sherry I'm going to talk about in this section are all dry, light wines and are the perfect partners for tapas, seafood, and other Spanish delights – they are Fino, Manzanilla and the dry style of Amontillado. For now we'll forget about the other sweeter styles.

All these wines are made from the Palomino grape, which makes pretty bland white wines, but once made into sherry develops lots of personality. Winemakers in Jerez, and especially in its neighbouring coastal town of Sanlúcar de Barrameda, found that the cool, fresh air encouraged a thick coating of yeast (called flor) to grow on the surface of the wine while it was fermenting. This flor seemed strange at first but they soon realized that it created a protective coating for the wine, keeping it fresh and light in colour. Without the coating, the wine oxidized, taking a deep amber colour and "cooked" aromas and flavours, all familiar qualities that appear in the sweeter, more commom styles of sherry. The flor also added a pleasant almond flavour to the wine.

This new style of sherry was the perfect seaside accompaniment – light, refreshing, and dry, but with enough body and flavour to complement the seafood and other local cuisine. Sherry was already a favourite across the ocean in Britain, so they began to ship this new style of wine overseas. But unlike its heavily fortified siblings, Fino didn't survive the journey well. Winemakers quickly realized that this crisp, fresh wine needed to be consumed within six months of bottling. Tourists visiting the Jerez area loved it there, but back at home it was heavy and heady, and not nearly as food-friendly.

As winemaking technology advanced, sherry producers learned how to fortify and stabilize Fino sherry at about 15% alcohol without losing its refreshing qualities, making it easier to ship and allowing them to grow their export market. And now we consumers have the opportunity to taste, appreciate, and enjoy these unique wines.

Now, be warned – sherry is not the usual flavour profile we are used to from other wines. Fino, and its seaside sister Manzanilla, are both clear, light, and very dry. They have nutty aromas and flavours like almonds, and a distinct salty/briny quality to them. Not your average sipping wine. But you HAVE to try them with food. Especially seafood, salty marinated olives, or sushi. This is the perfect example of how the right food can bring out the best in a wine.

Amontillado sherry can range from dry to sweet. In its drier versions, it is nuttier, slightly richer, and with just a touch of sweetness in comparison to Fino. It has also undergone aging and a bit of oxidization, which you'll see from its golden colour. I find it a bit more people-friendly, but again it shines with food. I love it with Manchego cheese, Chorizo sausage, and spiced nuts.

Palo Cortado is another dry style of sherry – it's pretty hard to come by but definitely something to try if you happen to come across it. And one last tip – the neighbouring town of Montilla makes sherry-style wines very similar in flavour, but much less expensive – keep an eye out for these at your wine store.

Aromas & Flavours
Light, crisp, and dry with salty/briny notes
Nutty flavours like almonds

Food Ideas
Black olives and tapenade
Sardines and other fish tapas
Consommé
Roasted spiced nuts
Manchego cheese and Serrano ham

My recommended regions for dry Sherry are:
Jerez, Spain for Fino and Amontillado
Sanlúcar de Barrameda for Manzanilla
Montilla, Spain for dry sherry-style wines

DUCK POT STICKERS WITH PLUM SAUCE

If you live in an urban centre, you can avoid having to cook a whole bird for this beautiful nibbly by heading down to Chinatown and picking up one of those Peking ducks hanging in store windows. All you have to do is shred the tender meat off the bone. While you're there you can buy some five-spice powder or make it yourself. It's even amounts of Szechuan pepper, cinnamon, cloves, fennel seeds and star anise. **Makes 24**

Pot Stickers

1 cup (250ml) Napa cabbage

1 teaspoon (5ml) kosher salt

2 teaspoons (10ml) sesame oil

2 scallions, finely chopped

1 teaspoon (5ml) five-spice powder

1 tablespoon (15ml) dry sherry

1 tablespoon (15ml) light soy sauce

1 lb (454g) cooked duck meat, finely shredded

Pepper to taste

24 round pot sticker (dumpling) wrappers

3 tablespoons (45ml) vegetable oil

2 cups (500ml) warm water

2 teaspoons (30ml) white vinegar

Plum Sauce

1/2 cup (125ml) good quality red plum preserves

1/4 cup (60ml) rice wine vinegar

1 tablespoon (15ml) fresh ginger, peeled
    and grated

1/3 cup (90ml) finely chopped scallions

Pot Stickers

- Rinse the cabbage under cold water and chop into very thin slices (around 1/8-inch thick). Put the cabbage in a colander and season with salt. With clean hands, toss it to combine. Let the cabbage sit for about 10 minutes, the salt will help to draw out any extra moisture from the cabbage.

- After 10 minutes, put the drained cabbage into a clean kitchen towel and squeeze over the sink to extract any excess moisture.

- Heat the sesame oil in a skillet over medium heat. Toss in the ginger and cook until it's really fragrant, about 15 seconds. Stir in the cabbage, scallions, five-spice powder, sherry and soy sauce. Cook until the cabbage wilts, about 30 seconds. Transfer from skillet to a bowl and allow to cool for 10 minutes.

- Stir the duck meat into the cabbage mixture until it is evenly combined. Give it some salt and pepper to taste. Cover with plastic wrap and pop in the fridge for a minimum of one hour.

- To assemble the pot stickers, line a baking sheet with parchment paper. Work on one dumpling at a time, cover the remaining wrappers with plastic to keep them from drying out.

- Place 2 teaspoons (10ml) of filling in the middle of the wrapper. Using your fingers, moisten the edges of the wrappers with water. Fold the wrapper in the middle to form a triangle shape and squeeze the edges together to seal the dumpling while pushing out any air. Pinch small pleats along one side of the sealed edge, continuing to wet your fingers to help seal the edges.

- Place the filled pot stickers on the baking sheet and cover with plastic wrap. Repeat until all of the wrappers are filled.

- Heat 1 1/2 tablespoons (22.5ml) of the oil in a medium sized non-stick skillet over medium-high heat for 1–2 minutes. Arrange half of the pot stickers, pleat side up, snugly together in the heated pan. Cook, shaking the pan once, until the dumplings are deep golden brown on the bottom, 1–2 minutes.

- Carefully add 1 cup (250ml) of warm water and 1 teaspoon (5ml) of vinegar to the skillet, cover partially, and cook for 4–5 minutes. Reduce the heat to medium and cook until the bottoms of the pot stickers are dark brown and very crisp and all the water has evaporated, approximately 5–6 minutes.

- Slide a spatula under the pot stickers to loosen them from the pan. Place them on a baking sheet and loosely cover with foil.

- Wash and dry the skillet and repeat with the remaining oil and pot stickers.

- Serve hot with plum sauce.

Plum Sauce

- Put the plum preserves, vinegar and fresh ginger into a saucepan. Set the saucepan over medium-low heat. Bring the mixture to a simmer.

- Reduce the heat to low and allow the mixture to simmer for 10 minutes, stirring now and then.

- Pull the saucepan from the heat and allow sauce to cool slightly. Stir in the scallions.

- Serve the sauce warm with the pot stickers.

WINE MATCH – **Sparkling Shiraz**

Duck is rich and flavourful, and in this dish it has sweet, spicy, and savoury flavours with the Chinese five-spice powder. The perfect contrast is the sweet berry goodness of Shiraz and the sparkling version is a unique choice. If you'd like something a bit lighter, try a Spanish rosé that has intense berry fruit flavours.

LEMON CHICKEN LOLLIPOPS

These little lollipops are a kitschy twist one of my childhood favourites, the mighty chicken finger. To bring them into the adult world of parties and sophistocado, I've made them smaller, and dressed them up with a zingy sweet-and-sour peach dipping sauce and perched them on a very stylish bamboo skewer. Instead of traditional bread crumbs I prefer to use panko, which is a Japanese bread crumb you can find in most grocery stores these days. Makes 30

Lemon Chicken Lollipops

3 lb (1.5 kg) boneless skinless chicken breasts,
   cut lengthwise into 30 strips 1/2-inch wide
1 cup (250ml) all purpose flour
1 cup (250ml) panko bread crumbs
2 eggs lightly beaten
Salt and pepper to taste
3 tablespoons (45ml) grated fresh Parmesan,
3 tablespoons (45ml) vegetable oil
Juice of 2 lemons
24 short bamboo skewers

Peach Ginger Dipping Sauce

1 1/4 cups (375ml) good quality peach jam
2 teaspoons (10ml) finely chopped ginger
2 teaspoons (10ml) finely diced jalapeno,
   with seeds removed
1 tablespoon (15ml) rice wine vinegar
1 tablespoon (15ml) Dijon mustard

Lemon Chicken Lollipops

- Preheat oven to 200F (110C)

- Put the flour in one bowl, the breadcrumbs and grated Parmesan in another, and the eggs in a third bowl. Give the eggs a whisk until they are frothy.

- Sprinkle the chicken pieces with salt and pepper.

- It's now time to gussy up the chicken. Start by lightly tossing them into the flour. Shake off any excess and then dip into the egg mixture to coat. Finish by tossing the chicken into the panko/ Parmesan bowl and coat evenly, shaking off any excess. Lay each piece onto a tray lined with wax paper. Repeat until all the chicken is coated.

- Place a large skillet over medium-high heat. Add your oil and give it a minute to heat up to the just-before-smoking point.

- Put about 4 or 5 chicken pieces in the skillet and allow them to cook (try not to touch them) until they have a golden brown crust, about 1 minute. Flip them over and cook other side to the same golden brown stage.

- Add 1 tablespoon (15ml) of lemon juice to the pan and toss.

- Pull the chicken from the pan and onto a cookie sheet. Pop the chicken into the pre-heated oven to keep warm and to continue cooking the chicken through the middle.

- You're going to keep repeating this process until all of the chicken is cooked and lovely.

- To serve, place one piece of chicken on each bamboo stick.

- Serve it up with your peach ginger dipping sauce.

Peach Ginger Dipping Sauce

- Put all ingredients into a small saucepan and place over low heat.

- Cook it all together for about 10 minutes, giving it the occasional stir.

WINE MATCH – **Gewürztraminer**

Gewürz both contrasts and mirrors in this match – the ripe tropical fruit flavour in the wine mirrors the sweet apricot in the dip while also contrasting and cooling the jalapeño and ginger spice. The medium body of the wine is also in balance with the chicken, complementing the crispy coating without being overwhelmed. Of course, if you are serving this nibbly along with a bunch of other party food, you could also go with some nice, refreshing bubbly – Prosecco would be my choice for this dish.

CRISPY CRAB CAKES WITH MUSTARD ARTICHOKE AIOLI

Oh, the classic crab cake. No party is complete without them, really. The secret to a killer crab cake is the panko. Panko is a Japanese bread crumb which will forever replace regular bread crumbs for me. It makes for a crispier coating and you can keep a bag in your cupboard to have on hand at all times. Aioli is traditionally garlic mayonnaise. You are switching it up here to make it even more interesting with artichokes and mustard. The tangy mayo against the crispy little crab cakes will blow the taste buds off all your guests. I suggest making more than one per guest. **Makes 15**

The Crab Cake

2 tablespoons (30ml) olive oil

1/2 cup (125ml) finely diced red bell pepper

1/2 cup (125ml) finely diced yellow bell pepper

1/2 cup (125ml) finely diced red onion

1 cup (250ml) 35% cream

1 tablespoon (15ml) finely chopped chives

1/2 tablespoon (8ml) roughly chopped dill

1 teaspoon (5ml) Creole spices

1 large egg, lightly beaten

1/2 cup (125ml) panko bread crumbs

1 1/4 lb (525g) crab meat, drained and picked
    over carefully (for bones or shell)

Crab Cake Coating

1/2 cup (125ml) panko breadcrumbs

1 tablespoon (15ml) vegetable oil

1/2 tablespoon (7.5ml) unsalted butter

Mustard Artichoke Aioli

1 cup (250ml) canned artichokes, drained

1 tablespoon (15ml) Dijon mustard

Juice of 1 lemon

1/2 cup (125ml) mayonnaise

Salt and pepper to taste

Crab Cakes

- Add the olive oil to a medium sized skillet and warm it over medium-high heat until hot but not smoking. Add to your peppers and onions and sauté until they're tender, about 3 minutes.

- Remove the peppers and onions from the skillet to a large bowl. Allow them to cool.

- In a small saucepan heat your cream over medium-low heat and reduce it until there is 2/3 of a cup (180ml) left. Remove the pan from heat and allow the cream to cool as well.

- Add the cooled cream to the bowl of cooled onions and peppers. Toss in remaining crab cake ingredients. Mix this all together gently until well combined. Season the mixture with salt and pepper to taste. Now would be a good time to fry off a little piece to see how it tastes and to make sure you are happy with the flavour.

- Form your crab cakes into 1-inch rounds with a 1/4-inch thickness. Set them aside on a parchment paper-lined tray. Pop into the fridge for 30 minutes to allow the cakes to firm up.

- To coat the cakes, pour panko bread crumbs into a large shallow dish. Place the formed crab cakes into the bread crumbs. Coat evenly with the panko. Put them back on the tray as you finish them. (If you wanted to you could freeze them at this point for a party later, just thaw them out before cooking.)

- Heat a skillet over medium-high heat.

- Add your oil and butter to the skillet. Once the butter is melted and the pan is hot, carefully add crab cakes to the pan. You don't want to crowd them, they should be about two centimetres (almost an inch) apart.

- Cook for about 2 minutes per side, or until golden brown and crispy.

- Remove the crab cakes as they are done and pop them onto a paper towel-lined tray to drain them. If you are not going to be serving them right away, put them on a cookie sheet to reheat in a 350F (180C) oven (just until they have warmed to the touch; about 5 minutes).

- Serve these fellas hot with Mustard Artichoke Aioli

Aioli

- Put the drained artichokes in a blender and purée until artichokes reach a smooth consistency.

- Add the Dijon, lemon juice and mayonnaise and purée again until all ingredients are evenly combined.

- Season to taste with salt and pepper.

WINE MATCH – **Pinot Blanc**

There are a few flavours in the food world that stress out us sommeliers – mustard and artichokes just happen to be two of the toughest (thanks Angie!). But I'm always up for a challenge. This dish needs a few things in a wine. First, the wine must have enough body to stand up to the rich crab meat and the crispy coating. Then it needs enough acidity to balance off the tanginess of mustard and artichokes and a nice fruity but somewhat neutral flavour that won't taste funny with these tricky ingredients. So I'm going with a Pinot Blanc, which fits the bill in all respects.

SHRIMP TWO WAYS:
HONEY LIME MARINATED SHRIMP

An easy way to take the pooper out of the shrimp is to cut down along the back with a knife and slide a toothpick along to slowly lift it out. Or . . . buy them already cleaned. Tiger prawns are the larger of the shrimp. Usually shrimp are classified by a number which seems like a code but it's pretty simple. Tiger prawns are usually about 6–10. That means you get about 6 to 10 shrimp in a pound, which makes it easy to order from your fish guy when you know how many shrimp you need. Makes 12

12 large tiger prawn shrimp, peeled and deveined

1 small shallot, finely diced

Juice of 2 limes

2 tablespoons (30ml) chopped fresh cilantro

1 tablespoon (15ml) honey

2 teaspoons (10ml) finely chopped Thai red chili

1 tablespoon (15ml) peanut oil

Salt and pepper to taste

1 tablespoon (15ml) vegetable oil

Fresh cilantro sprigs for garnish, optional

- Toss the shrimp into a non-reactive bowl.

- In a separate bowl, mix the shallot, lime juice, cilantro, honey, red chili and peanut oil. Pour this lovely little mixture over the shrimp. With your hands or a big spoon give it all a big toss to make sure all the shrimp are treated fairly with the marinade.

- Cover the bowl containing the shrimp with plastic wrap and toss in the fridge for 30 minutes to marinate.

- Pull the bowl from the fridge and unwrap. Season the shrimp with salt and pepper.

- Place a large skillet over high heat and give it a minute or two to get nice and hot. Add your vegetable oil, give it a few seconds to heat up and toss in your shrimp in all their marinade glory.

- Cook these fellas for about 1 minute per side or until they are bright pink. You need to cook them all the way through, if in doubt pull one out and tear it open, no one will know.

- When they're ready, pour them out of the hot pan onto your serving platter. Garnish with the cilantro if you like and serve 'em up.

ORANGE CHIPOTLE SHRIMP

To me, shrimp are one of the most perfect party foods. If you leave on the tail, you have something to grab hold of. They go with so many different flavourings and generally the peeps love 'em. They can also be whipped off in a heartbeat which is always a dream when you're expecting company. Although fresh shrimp is always the ideal, I usually keep a bag of cleaned frozen shrimp in the freezer, just in case I'm caught with unexpected guests. Chipotle peppers are found in cans, usually in the Mexican food section of your grocery store. They are smoked jalapenos, packaged in adobo sauce, which add a smoky heat that snuggles up to the sweetness of the orange perfectly. Makes 12

12 large tiger prawn shrimp, peeled
  and deveined

1 tablespoon (15ml) chopped chipotle chili

Juice of 2 fresh oranges, seeds removed

3 tablespoons (45ml) cilantro leaves, roughly
  chopped (plus save some cilantro sprigs for
  garnish if you're into that kind of thing)

1 tablespoon (15ml) grapeseed oil

Salt to taste

- Throw your cleaned shrimp into a non-reactive bowl.

- Pull out a second bowl. Remove one chipotle chili from can and dice it finely. Put this in your empty bowl. Juice the orange over the bowl onto the chopped chipotle. Add chopped cilantro and grapeseed oil. Mix everything together well and pour over the shrimp. Give them a couple of good stirs to ensure they all get a good coating.

Leave marinating shrimp in the refrigerator for about 30 minutes.

- Preheat a cast iron grill pan over high heat for 3 minutes (or if you don't have one you can use a cast iron or heavy bottomed skillet.)

- Pull your fully marinated shrimp out of the marinade. You can get rid of the marinade now.

- Add a little oil to your hot pan just before you are ready to cook your shrimp. Place the shrimp in the pan without overcrowding them. Cook them for about 1 1/2 minutes. Give them a flip when they start to turn pink and have caramel char marks (unless you are not using a grill pan, then just look for them to be turning pink.) Once you've flipped them repeat the same thing for the other side.

- Remove cooked shrimp from the pan onto a plate or platter and garnish (if you like) with fresh cilantro sprigs.

WINE MATCH – **Pinot Grigio**

These two shrimp dishes share some similar elements. The first is sweetness – honey in the first and orange in the second. Next up is spice – chili and chipotle respectively, and finally, some tang that comes from the citrus in both dishes. So in a wine, I am looking for something that will not only balance off the acidity of citrus, but will also cool spice while mirroring the sweet flavours. Pinot Grigio works perfectly, and I love the floral notes in the wine that play off the citrus zest flavours in the food. A slightly off-dry Riesling would also be a good pick.

MARINATED OLIVES WITH ORANGE AND FENNEL

I love the look of a bowl of olives on a table, especially when surrounded with other beautiful snacks. To me, olives fall in the same category as the cocktail hour, Frank Sinatra, mellow social engagements with an easy going hint of class, and living the good life. Yes, one little recipe for olives can do all that. This makes good buddies on a table with the Farinata and the Smoky Eggplant Dip (see page 49) Makes 2 cups (500ml)

1/4 cup (60ml) olive oil

2 teaspoons (10ml) sherry vinegar

2 tablespoons (30ml) orange juice

2 teaspoons (10ml) grated orange rind

1 teaspoon (5ml) chopped garlic

1 tablespoon (15ml) fresh basil

2 teaspoon (10ml) fennel seeds,
    slightly crushed

1/4 teaspoon (1.25ml) chili flakes

2 cups (500ml) mixed olives (of your liking
    like kalamata, picholine, etc), drained

1/2 cup (125ml) thinly sliced fennel,
    cut into 1-inch lengths

- In a medium non-reactive bowl, throw in everything except the olives and chopped basil. Mix together really well and add olives. Mix together again. Cover the bowl and pop into the fridge. Allow the olives to marinate for one to three days before serving them. You'll want to give them a stir now and then during this time. For serving, bring the olives to room temperature and garnish with basil.

WINE MATCH – **Amontillado Sherry**

Sherry comes to life when paired with the right food. Olives are the perfect choice, with their briny, salty flavour and rich, oily texture. Amontillado is medium in body with a nice nutty flavour which matches the flavour of olives. It has big enough body to not be overpowered by the olives, and the fresh orange and fennel flavours contrast with the rich nuttiness of the wine. If you're serving this with a table full of nibblies, you could also pair this dish with Cava, the Spanish sparkling wine. Its refreshing bubbles clean up your taste buds after each bite, and its fruity, fresh flavours are an excellent pairing for salty snacks.

SMOKED SALMON ON CORN BLINI WITH WASABI CREAM

A blini is a traditional Russian pancake, generally served with caviar and sour cream. We're putting a spin on it, and turning it into a sweet crunchy corn pancake, which when topped with tender smoked salmon and a peppery wasabi cream is pretty dang delish. Wasabi is a Japanese horseradish and should be added with a very light hand, using very small amounts to start – a little goes a very, very long way. Makes 24

Corn Blini

1 1/2 cups (375ml) all purpose flour

1 tablespoon (15ml) granulated white sugar

2 teaspoons (10ml) baking powder

1/2 teaspoon (2.5ml) salt

1 egg

4 tablespoons (60ml) vegetable oil

1 cup (250ml) milk

1/2 cup (125ml) corn kernels, fresh or
   canned, drained

1 tablespoon (15ml) finely chopped chives

Wasabi Cream

1/2 cup (125ml) sour cream

1/2 to 1 teaspoon (2.5-5ml) wasabi powder
   to taste

Juice of 1/2 a lemon

Salt to taste

Smoked Salmon

20 pieces (approximately 350g) of prepared
   smoked salmon, thinly sliced

1 bunch of fresh cut chives (optional garnish)

TIP

What's the difference between old world and new world?

"Old world" wine refers to wine made in Europe – France, Italy, Spain, Germany, and other European countries that have been making wine for centuries. "New World" wines are those that come from the rest of the world, mainly South Africa, the Americas, and Australasia – regions where winemaking is a relatively newer practice. These terms are also used to describe certain styles of wine. New world wine styles are typically more crowd-pleasing – lots of easy-to-enjoy fruity flavours, full-bodied, smooth, and also often higher in alcohol than old world styles. They are mostly meant to be drunk within a few years of the vintage, have simpler labels, and are also usually great "cocktail" wines – tasty on their own without food. Some old world wines are now being made in a new world style – especially warmer climate areas in France, Italy, and Spain who are capitalizing on the popularity of new world wine characteristics, including making their wine labels easier to understand.

- Start by making your wasabi cream. In a small bowl, mix together the sour cream, lemon juice and wasabi powder. Make sure to give it a taste to adjust the amount of heat from the wasabi you would like.

- In a large mixing bowl sift together the flour, sugar, baking powder and salt. In a second bowl, whisk together the egg, 2 tablespoons (30ml) of the oil, the milk, the corn and the chopped chives. Add the wet mixture to the dry mixture and stir until just combined, don't worry if you have a few lumps, we all do from time to time.

- Heat up a non-stick skillet over low heat. Add the other 2 tablespoons (30ml) of oil to the pan when it's warm and let it heat up for a minute. Using a soup spoon, drop about a tablespoon worth of batter into the pan, making little pancakes. Repeat until your pan is full but not crowded. When the pancakes start to have little bubbles appearing on the top and sides of the cakes and have lost their shiny appearance, flip them and cook on the other side until golden brown. Remove them from the pan and keep going until you've used all of the batter. Set them aside.

- Lay out your blinis onto a serving platter. Top each one with a piece of smoked salmon and a little dollop of wasabi cream. If you feel fancy, garnish with fresh cut chives and serve.

WINE MATCH – **Unoaked Chardonnay**

This is a tasty little app and I love it paired with a fresh, fruity unoaked Chardonnay. The dish needs a wine that can stand up to the richness of the smoked salmon, while also complementing the sweetness of the corn in the blini and cooling the heat of the wasabi. Chardonnay does all of these things, and the acidity of the wine also cleans up your taste buds, getting them ready for another bite.

TOMATO AND PARMESAN TARTS

I have a fairly serious love affair with puff pastry and even more so now that I have let myself off the hook from making it from scratch. There are some great pre-made puffs on the market. The trick to finding a good one is to read the ingredients list and make sure there is butter in the first three ingredients. It makes a big difference. Makes 4 tarts

Tarts

10 oz (280g) of puff pastry, thawed

8 large, ripe plum tomatoes

2 tablespoons (30ml) balsamic vinegar

2 tablespoons (30ml) olive oil

1 tablespoon (15ml) chopped fresh parsley

2 oz (56g) Parmesan, shaved with a swivel peeler

4 oz (112g) watercress, cleaned and torn into bite-sized pieces

1–2 tablespoons (15-30ml) classic vinaigrette

Sea salt and freshly ground pepper

Vinaigrette

1/2 (125ml) cup grapeseed oil

3 tablespoons (45ml) lemon juice

1 teaspoon (5ml) finely chopped lemon zest

1 shallot, minced

1 teaspoon (5ml) minced fresh thyme

1 tablespoon (15ml) honey

1/4 teaspoon (1.25 ml) salt

1/4 teaspoon(1.25 ml) cracked black pepper

1/2 cup (120ml) extra virgin olive oil

- Over a super light dusting of flour, roll out your puff pastry to about 1/8 of an inch thick.

- With the open part of a glass or a circular cutter, cut out four rounds about 5 inches in diameter.

- Place your circles on a heavy baking sheet (if you have thin baking sheets, double them up). Pop these guys in your fridge for about 20 minutes.

- Now would be a good time to put together your vinaigrette. In a bowl or in the bowl of your blender, add all the ingredients except the oil. Start either whisking or blending while slowly drizzling the oil in a super thin stream until it has been fully incorporated. This should prevent your vinaigrette from splitting. You won't need all the vinaigrette for this dish, so keep the rest in your fridge for up to a week.

- Preheat the oven to 400F (200C). Pull the pastry out of the fridge and bake for 10 minutes, then place another baking sheet on the top to press the rounds down and keep them flat. Bake for a further 8-10 minutes until just golden. Remove to a wire rack to cool and crisp.

- Put some parchment paper down on one of the baking sheets. Slice your tomatoes evenly and arrange them in four overlapping circles about the same size as the pastry rounds (no larger).

Contd . . .

- Brush with the balsamic vinegar and oil, season with salt and pepper and sprinkle with the chopped herbs.

- Place your shavings of Parmesan on top of the tomatoes. You want to give the tomatoes a nice covering of cheese because when the Parmesan melts it will hold the tomato slices together, which will make your life much easier in a few minutes.

- Preheat the broiler. When it's really hot, place the tomatoes under the broiler near to the heat. Don't be tempted to multitask here, your tomatoes need you to focus as the cheese will start to melt almost as soon as it's in the oven, we don't want the cheese to get brown, just to melt and bind our little tomatoes together.

- Remove from the broiler. Carefully grab your delicate puff pastry circles and plate.

- Using a spatula transfer each round of tomato onto a pastry round.

- In a separate bowl, lightly dress your watercress with the vinaigrette and taste to see if it needs any salt or pepper. When you are happy with it, grab a small bunch and pile it on top of each one of your tarts. Serve immediately.

WINE MATCH – **Prosecco**

What a way to impress your guests! This recipe is simple but makes an impact with its range of flavours and textures and the pretty presentation. So you might as well make it even more special and serve some sparkling wine with it. These ingredients have an Italian flair (with the tomatoes and Parm) so Prosecco is the perfect match. It has enough tartness for the tomatoes and the vinaigrette, and the bubbles do a great job at cleansing your palate after each bite.

SALMON TARTARE & SCALLOP CEVICHE

Peppery endive makes a great edible holder for both the smooth fatty tartare and the super fresh ceviche making them a pretty healthy snack. Tartare however is also fantastic with plain chips that have a ridge or texture if you feel like something more naughty. It is very important to use only Sushi grade tuna when making tartare as it is ultra fresh. It won't smell or taste fishy at all. Ask your fishmonger to be sure. **Makes 12 endive spears**

Salmon Tartare

8 oz (250g) fresh sushi-quality salmon fillet,
belly, pin bones and skin removed
(tell your fish guy what you are using it for)

2 teaspoons (10ml) of the best quality olive
oil you have

1 1/2 teaspoons (7.5ml) lemon oil

2 teaspoons (10ml) fresh chives, finely chopped

1 tablespoon (15ml) shallots, finely chopped

1 teaspoon (15ml) sea salt (add more
if you think it needs it)

1 full bulb fresh Belgium endive

Fresh chives for garnish (if you like)

- Using a sharp knife, mince the salmon until very fine (don't use a food processor for this, it will turn it to mush).

- Place the minced salmon in a non-reactive glass bowl. Stir in the olive oil, lemon oil, chives, shallots and salt.

- Put the bowl in the refrigerator and chill for 20–30 minutes.

- Use a sharp knife to remove the hard base from the bottom of the endive. Pry apart the leaves, trying to make sure they are whole and intact, you don't want to boobie trap people.

- Spoon 1 tablespoon (15ml) of the tartar onto the rib of the endive leaving the top yellow section of the leaf unfilled. Garnish with chives if you like.

- Serve cold with scallop ceviche (see next page).

TIP

As mentioned, another way to serve this is to place the tartare on ridged plain potato chips in the same fashion and platter if you are going fancier, or put the tartar in a chilled bowl with either chips or endive leaves beside and let people spoon some of their own for a more casual dinner.

SCALLOP CEVICHE

Ceviche is a traditional Latin American appetizer. It consists of raw firm fish which has been marinated in citrus juice. The acids in the juice "cook" the fish which firms up the meat and turns it opaque. The end result is a delicate and really fresh tasting scallop. You need to ensure that your scallops are good and fresh. Again talk to your fishmonger, who you should make your new best friend. When in doubt, you can tell by smelling it. If it doesn't smell like the sea, get rid of it!
Makes 12 endive spears

5 oz. (150g) large sea scallops

Juice of 1 lime

1 tablespoon (15ml) freshly squeezed
orange juice

1 tablespoon (15ml) grapeseed, canola,
or other mild, flavourless oil

1 tablespoon (15ml) roughly chopped fresh basil

Sea salt and black pepper to taste

1 slice of fresh fennel, paper thin

1 full bulb of fresh Belgium endive

- Slice the scallops through the centre horizontally into three equal disks.

- In a small non-reactive glass bowl add lime juice, orange juice, grapeseed oil, basil, salt and pepper and thinly sliced fennel. Mix until all ingredients are evenly incorporated. Add scallops to citrus mixture and toss to coat. Place bowl in the refrigerator allowing mixture to marinate for 30 minutes.

- Using a sharp knife remove the hard base from endive. Pry apart the endive leaves, using your hands, ensuring leaves are whole and intact.

- Spoon a tablespoon of ceviche on each rib of endive leaving the top yellow section of the leaf unfilled.

- Serve cold.

WINE MATCH – **Champagne**

First, if you're going to go all fancy-shmancy, you might as well do it for both the food and the wine. So this pairing is easy – it has to be Champagne. Champagne is very food friendly, especially because of its refreshing, palate-cleansing bubbles. It has enough body to stand up to the richer salmon tartare but the bubbles keep it light enough to not overwhelm the delicate texture and flavour of the scallop ceviche. The bubbles and acidity also refresh your taste buds after each bite and the citrusy flavour mirrors the lemon oil in the tartare and the citrus juice in the ceviche. If you can't afford Champagne, go for any other sparkling wine made in the Champenoise style, like Cava.

TIP

Champagne – what's in a name?

Most of us refer to any sparkling wine as Champagne, but did you know that a bottle of bubbly can only bear that name if it's actually made in the region of Champagne, France? Others are just called sparkling wine, or they might be labeled with another regional name such as Cava from Spain or Prosecco from Italy.

VEGETABLE TEMPURA

One of the secrets to avoiding a nervous breakdown while making tempura for your loved ones is to have all your ingredients ready. Chefs call this *mise en place* or "everything in its place." It really works. Have your dipping sauce made, oil heating up, vegetables cut, paper towel-lined plate or tray beside your hot oil, a little bowl of salt beside your lined tray, etc. Hitting the vegetables with some salt as they come fresh out of the oil rather than after they have cooled is one of those little tricks that makes a huge difference to the flavour of anything deep fried. Thing is, if you are going to eat tempura, it better be good and these little scrumptious veggies will truly not disappoint. **Serves 6**

4 cups (1 litre) of vegetable, canola, or
peanut oil for deep frying

The Batter

1 large egg, lightly beaten

1 cup (250ml) cold sparkling water

2 tablespoons (30ml) dry white wine

1 cup (250ml) all purpose flour

1/2 teaspoon (2.5ml) salt plus more for
sprinkling the freshly deep fried
vegetables as they come out of the fryer

The Vegetables

Use a nice variety of vegetables. Think about
different textures, shapes and colours.

1 Japanese eggplant, cut in 1/4-inch thick
slices (6mm)

12 snow peas

1 red pepper cut into 1/2-inch strips (12mm)

1 cup broccoli florets

7 shitake mushrooms (only use the tops)

12 baby carrots, cut in half lengthwise

The Dipping Sauce

1 cup (250ml) soy sauce

1/2 cup (125ml) packed brown sugar

4 scallions, whites only, sliced thinly

To make the dipping sauce

- In a small saucepan, gently heat soy sauce and brown sugar on medium-low until sugar has dissolved. You'll need to stir it. Pull from heat and allow mixture to cool. Meanwhile finely chop the white parts of your scallions. Once the soy mixture has cooled, add your scallions and set aside in the bowl you want to serve it in. If you are concerned about double dipping or if your friends are animals when it comes to this type of thing, put sauce in individual ramekins for each person's plate.

To make the Tempura

- In a medium bowl, beat the egg and add the sparkling water and the dry white wine. Add the flour and salt and whisk until just mixed. The consistency of this stuff should look like a loose pancake batter. Add more sparkling water if necessary to thin it out.

- Fill a deep thick-walled pan (a wok would be perfect) with oil of choice until 2 inches deep. You'll need a deep fry thermometer for this (thermometers are generally pretty inexpensive and make the average cook incredibly empowered – it's worth it), and you're going to heat the oil to 395F (201C). Now is a good time to put a paper towel-lined tray and a little bowl of salt beside your oil.

Contd . . .

- Using your fingers, dip the vegetables into the tempura batter and slowly add them one at a time to the pan. Only add a few vegetables at a time, if you overcrowd the pan the temperature of the oil will go down and your tempura will be soggy and greasy.

- Remove the vegetables with tongs when the batter is crispy and has a really light golden hue, 7–8 minutes. Test the first cooled one or two by eating them and you'll get it. Put the rest of the done vegetables on your paper towel-lined tray and immediately sprinkle them with salt.

- If this is all taking you a long time, or you've taken on a larger project than you realized, then you can keep them crisp for a short period of time in an oven at about 200F (94C). But serve the tempura as soon as you can, with dipping sauce, to avoid any sogginess.

WINE MATCH – **Grüner Veltliner**

Okay, don't get me started gushing on how food-friendly Grüner Veltliner is. When we experimented with this dish, I loved how the Grüner had enough body to stand up to the richness of the batter. But its acidity also cuts through the oil of this deep-fried dish and it balances out the natural acidity of the veggies. A perfect match. If you can't find Grüner, Riesling is a good substitute.

WARM MIXED NUTS

I have a bit of an obsession when it comes to mixed nut recipes. There are so many out there you begin to feel a little like Goldilocks. Some are too sweet, some are too spiced, but these ones, my friends . . . these ones are just right, mixing sweet, savoury, salty, and a little bit of heat. Feel free to play with the ingredients to create your own or just tell everyone that you did and never show them this recipe.   Makes 4 cups (1 litre)

1 tablespoon (15ml) ground cumin

1 tablespoon (15ml) ground coriander

2 teaspoons (10ml) kosher salt

2 tablespoons (30ml) brown sugar

1/2 teaspoon (2.5ml) ground black pepper

1 teaspoon (5ml) chili flakes

2 large eggs, the whites only

4 cups (1 litre) of your favourite raw nuts,
   mixed such as almonds, cashews,
   pecans, hazelnuts, Brazil nuts, etc.

- Preheat your oven to 300F (150C).

- Line 2 rimmed baking sheets with parchment paper. (Trust me, this will save your pans and a lot of time scrubbing later.)

- In a small bowl combine cumin, coriander, salt, sugar, pepper and chili flakes. Set aside.

- In a medium bowl, beat the egg whites with a small whisk until frothy. Whisk in the reserved dry spice mix. Stir in the nuts and toss to ensure all the nuts are coated evenly with the mixture.

- Spread the nut mixture in a single layer onto one of the baking sheets. Place into the preheated oven. Allow the nuts to bake for around 10 minutes and give them a stir. Bake them for another 10 minutes (until golden brown and dry in texture). Remove the nuts from the oven and transfer them onto a clean sheet of parchment paper. Allow them to cool for approximately 20 minutes and either serve or store in an airtight container.

WINE MATCH – **Cava**

Angie and I share an obsession with spiced nuts, but I think it's mostly just a really good excuse to drink bubbly. Cava is a great choice for salty or spicy snacks because the bubbles refresh your taste buds and make you ready for more. It's very fruity, which contrasts with the smoky spiciness of the nuts, and because it's served chilled, it's even more cooling after spice. Nuts are a pretty rich snack, and the Cava is light and bubbly – the perfect contrasting pairing.

FIG ARUGULA PROSCIUTTO ROLLS

This may be one of the easiest and cutest hors d'oeuvre to make. You can whip these off the morning of your party, just lay them down on their backs and cover them tightly with plastic so the prosciutto doesn't dry out and become impossible to chew. **Makes 24 rolls**

1 bunch arugula, washed

12 slices of prosciutto

12 ripe figs

- Lay a slice of prosciutto on a clean surface.
- Top with a few leaves of arugula; be sure to have leaves coming out of both sides of the prosciutto, kind of like a little flag.
- Top with two halves of fig peaking out just a little at each end. Roll up tightly. Slice in half.
- Tuck in any of the extra prosciutto on the bottom to create a flat surface.
- Either lay on their backs and wrap tightly with plastic wrap or stand up on a platter like soldiers.

WINE MATCH – **Prosecco**

These little appetizers are perfect for a cocktail party, so why not serve them with the perfect cocktail – bubbly. I love Prosecco with these tasty bites because the fruity touch of sweetness in the wine not only matches the sweetness of the figs, it also contrasts with the saltiness of the prosciutto. And of course the bubbles are great for cleansing your palate. If you're serving a bunch of appetizers, you can't go wrong with some bubbly, and Prosecco is a great affordable choice.

TIP

What puts the bubbles in bubbly?

So how exactly do those magical little bubbles get into a bottle of bubbly? Here's a quick science lesson to explain . . . when wine is made, a chemical reaction called fermentation takes place. Sugar (which is naturally in the grape juice) + yeast = alcohol + carbon dioxide (aka CO_2). The alcohol is the part the winemaker is trying to get, and for most wines, the CO_2 bi-product is allowed to escape. To make the bubbles, wine with some leftover sugar in it is bottled and some extra yeast is added. This starts a second fermentation and this time the CO_2 is trapped inside the bottle to create the bubbles. This is the traditional or Champenoise method of making sparkling wine (it gets its name from the Champagne region, where this method is used). Another common style used is known as the Charmat method – where the second fermentation takes place in a large sealed tank, and the bubbly wine is then bottled under pressure so the bubbles aren't lost. It's cheaper and simpler to do it this way, so you'll see this method listed on wine labels a lot. The least expensive way to get the bubbles into bubbly is to inject the CO_2, much like the way soda pop is made. And let me tell you, you'll taste the difference – the bubbles are bigger and harsher instead of tiny and smooth like the other methods produce.

BAKED BRIE

I'm pretty sure this was once served to the Greek gods as an appetizer. Cheese on its own is a pretty great thing, but when you prick some small holes in the top to let all the flavours you've added leak in while you warm it . . . you end up with gooey brie scented lightly with wine and gracefully perfumed with rosemary. It makes you feel you feel like loved royalty . . . or a god.   Serves 6

2 four-inch rounds brie cheese

1 sprig fresh rosemary, roughly chopped

3 tablespoons (45ml) oaked Chardonnay

The fine zest of two lemons

2 teaspoons (10ml) finely chopped garlic

Breads, crackers, and sliced apples and

   pears for dipping

- Preheat the oven to 375F (190C)

- Place both brie rounds on a parchment-lined baking tray.

- Stab your fork into the top of the brie in several places.

- Sprinkle rosemary, garlic and lemon zest evenly over both rounds. Drizzle the wine over the brie gently and give it time to soak into the cheese a little.

- Place both rounds into your hot oven for 15 minutes or until the cheese is warm and melted.

- Serve warm with bread, crackers and fresh sliced pears and apples

WINE MATCH – **Oaked Chardonnay**

This is a perfect example of mirroring the flavours and textures of wine and food. The brie is rich and creamy, and the oaky Chardonnay is rich and creamy so they are in balance with each other. The refreshing, fruity flavours of the wine clean your taste buds after the richness of the cheese, and the toasty flavours of the wine are a nice match to the savoury rosemary and garlic. And to top it all off, since the same Chardonnay is poured right on the cheese, it can't help but be a great match!

VEGETABLE GRILL PARTY

These three recipes are pretty impressive on their own. As a trio – should you be up to the task – they're a really exciting way to kick off a summer patio party. The three dishes provide surprising and varying textures, flavours, and colours. If you're not lucky enough to have a barbecue, all of these dishes can be roasted in your oven.

Eggplant Fritters with Smoky Red Sauce

This smoky red sauce is also excellent over enchiladas. It's one of those sauces you may as well make a double batch of and freeze some just to have on hand. **Makes 20 fritters**

For the fritters

2 eggs

2/3 cup (180ml) milk

Salt

1 1/4 cup (310ml) medium ground cornmeal

1 good pinch smoked paprika

1 teaspoon (5ml) dried oregano

1 1/4 cup (310ml) flour

2 medium to large eggplants

For the red sauce

2 teaspoons (10ml) olive oil

1 cup (250ml) minced onion

1/2 teaspoon (2.5ml) salt

1 1/2 teaspoon (7.5ml) cumin

2 teaspoon (10ml) chili powder

3 cups (750ml) chopped tomatoes
   (4 to 6 medium sized ones)

1 cup (250ml) chicken stock or water

1 chipotle pepper, minced

6 cloves garlic, minced

Black pepper and cayenne pepper to taste

- To make the red sauce, heat the olive oil in a medium sized saucepan. Add the onion and salt, and sauté over medium heat for about 5 minutes, or until the onion is translucent but not browned. Add the cumin and chili powder, and sauté about 5 minutes more, if the spices start to stick to the bottom of the pan, add a tablespoon (15ml) of water to loosen it up.

- Add the chopped tomatoes and water or stock. Bring to a boil, partially cover, and lower the heat. Simmer for 15 minutes. Add the garlic, black pepper and cayenne, and continue to simmer for another 15 minutes. Let cool.

- Purée the sauce and pop it into a bowl.

- Now for the eggplant. Beat the eggs and milk together with a pinch of salt and put them in a shallow dish. In a second bowl, stir together the cornmeal, paprika, oregano and a large pinch of salt. Put the flour in a third bowl.

- Cut a slice off each end of the eggplant and discard. Slice the rest of the eggplants into rounds about 1/2-inch thick.

- Toss some of the slices into the flour to coat evenly. Shaking off any excess flour, dunk the eggplant slices in beaten egg, and then into the cornmeal, coating each fully. Place on a plate or tray and repeat the process for all the slices.

- Heat a large skillet or your barbecue to medium heat. Brush the surface of the skillet with the olive oil and pop the eggplant slices on it for about 5 minutes. Brush the pan once again as you turn them to prevent sticking and cook them for the same amount of time until the outside is crispy and golden and the inside of the eggplant is cooked. Serve, with the smoky red sauce for dipping.

Roasted Red Pepper Rolls with Spinach and Pinenuts

These tender little packages require fresh red peppers; sorry, but no pulling them out of the jar here. The color of this dish is what really gets me as well as the honest flavour of the vegetables highlighted with a little Parmesan cheese and some smoky pinenuts. I suggest you use basil-based pesto as a garnish. You can make your own which is always nice or you can easily use a quality store bought pesto and call it your own. No one will know. **Makes 10 rolls**

5 large red peppers

2 lb (900g) spinach, washed and stems removed

3/4 cup (180ml) pinenuts

1 cup (250ml) grated Parmesan cheese

Salt and pepper to taste

1 tablespoon (15ml) or more olive oil

Basil pesto for garnish

- On the flame of your barbecue, roast the peppers whole (you're going to try to keep them whole so we can wrap them a little later in one piece) until the skins on all sides are charred and blistered. You'll have to turn them with long tongs to achieve this, or, if you don't have a barbecue and you are doing this dish in a grill pan, preheat your oven to 400F. Rub the peppers with some olive oil and a little salt and pepper. Pop them in the oven on a baking sheet, again turning them as each side begins to blister. Once the peppers are charred put them into a bowl, cover the bowl with plastic wrap and allow to cool (about 20 minutes) and sweat off their skins. Remove plastic wrap and peel off the skin. Carefully slice the peppers lengthwise into 2 halves and scrape out seeds carefully without breaking the peppers.

- Wash your spinach but don't dry it. In a sauté pan, heat a little olive oil. Add your damp spinach and keep turning it until the spinach has wilted but is still a nice bright green. Season with salt and pepper and pop into a colander to drain. Once the spinach has cooled wring it out with your hands to get rid of any extra moisture, then chop finely.

- Toast your pinenuts in a dry skillet on medium-low heat watching them carefully, until they are a light golden colour. Chop coarsely and stir into the spinach, adding the Parmesan, some salt and some pepper. Give the filling a taste and make any necessary adjustments.

- Place a good sized tablespoon of the spinach-pinenut mixture along one length of the roasted pepper and roll up the pepper tightly, making sure it's well packed. Repeat until all the filling and peppers are used up.

- To cook the rolls, brush them lightly with olive oil and cook them on a barbecue, in your oven, or on your stovetop in a grill pan until the peppers have a little brown colour and are heated through.

- Serve with a basil pesto drizzled over top.

Grilled Mushrooms with Blue Cheese

Think grilled cheese sandwiches, only with meaty tender portobellos instead of bread. If you aren't a fan of blue cheese, sub in a cheese you do love. If you aren't a fan of mushrooms . . . well, turn the page. Two tricks to make this task easier. When you crumble any cheese it's always a million times easier when the cheese is cold. If you're cooking on the barbecue, soak your skewers for 30 minutes before you use them, to help prevent them catching fire. You're ready. Makes 4

8 smaller portobello mushrooms
  (try to get them around the same size)
2 cloves garlic, chopped
2 teaspoons (10ml) chopped fresh thyme leaves
6 oz (168g) soft blue cheese, crumbled
4–5 tablespoons (60-75ml) extra-virgin olive oil,
  for tossing and some extra for brushing
Salt and freshly ground black pepper

- Preheat the barbecue grill to medium high or preheat your oven to 400F (200C).

- Gently pull the stem out of the mushroom. With a spoon scrape out the gills under the mushroom and throw them out. Put mushrooms in a nice big bowl. Drizzle with a decent amount of olive oil, toss in the chopped garlic and thyme and season with salt and pepper. Give them a gentle toss until each mushroom looks nicely coated.

- If you are doing these on the barbecue, oil your grill. Lay each mushroom top-side down over the heat. Once you have some lovely grill marks, about 2–3 minutes, turn your mushrooms over and turn your heat down to medium. Cook each mushroom through, about 10 minutes.

- If you are roasting these in the oven, lay the mushrooms flat, top-side down, on a baking tray. Slide into the oven and roast for 10–15 minutes (depending on the thickness of the mushrooms) until the shrooms are tender and you can slide a knife into them easily.

- Turn your grill down to low. Fill half of the mushroom caps (top-side down) with 1/4 of the cheese. Toss another mushroom on top making a sandwich and stab it in the middle with a toothpick or a skewer. Place the mushroom sandwich back on the grill and pop the lid down for approximately 2 minutes to melt the cheese. Serve immediately.

WINE MATCH FOR VEGETABLE GRILL PARTY – **Rosé**

Rosé is the quintessential summertime patio wine. It's perfect in so many ways – satisfying enough with its berry fruit flavours, light and refreshing enough with its crisp acidity, and chilled down to keep you feeling cool. It works with these three recipes for much the same reasons. First, with any luck, you are enjoying these little treats in your backyard or on a sunny patio somewhere, so a cool, refreshing wine is just what you need. You need something with lots of acidity to balance off the roasted red pepper and eggplant. Rosé is very versatile with flavours and textures, so when you've got a lot going on in the food, it's a great choice. These recipes have a distinct Mediterranean feel to them, so a rosé from southern France or Spain fits as a regional pairing as well.

MINI SAMOSAS WITH TAMARIND DIPPING SAUCE

Samosas, fun to eat, a pain to make. Or so you thought! I've created the easiest possible route to a crunchy butter pastry (without having to make it), a high-flavoured filling, and a simple, tangy dipping sauce. It's important when you make any food to taste as you cook; that's how you learn and that's how you create. This is doubly true when it comes to making anything with a filling. The flavour needs to be slightly more intense since it's going to be hidden under a buttery layered blanket of puff pastry. The other exciting part of these snacks is that you can make a bunch ahead and freeze them. When you are ready for them, pull them straight from the freezer and into the oven. Just add an extra 5–10 minutes to your baking time.

Let's talk about one more thing. Tamarind. It's a sweet-and-sour-flavoured pulp that's found in the pods of the tamarind tree. It's technically a fruit but you can buy it in paste form at some grocery stores and Asian food markets. **Makes 48 little samosas**

1 package of frozen pre-rolled puff pastry,
   thawed
1 egg, beaten

The Filling

2 large potatoes
1 tablespoon (15ml) unsalted butter
1 cup (250ml) finely minced onion
2 medium cloves garlic, minced
1 tablespoon (15ml) freshly grated ginger
1 teaspoon (5ml) mustard seeds
1 teaspoon (5ml) ground coriander
3/4 teaspoon (3.75ml) salt
3 tablespoons (45ml) lemon juice
Pinch or two of cayenne pepper to taste
1 1/2 cups (375ml) uncooked green peas
   (frozen works well)

- To make the filling, bake the potatoes whole at 400F (200C) until a knife inserts without resistance, about an hour. Allow baked potatoes to cool slightly, then cut in half, scoop out the potato pulp, mash and set aside. Discard the skins.

- Over medium heat, melt your butter in a heavy skillet. Add your onion, garlic, ginger, mustard seeds, coriander, and salt. You might want to add a little more olive oil or butter to make sure the mixture doesn't stick and burn in your pan. Sauté for about 8–10 minutes, or until the onions are very soft, but not browned. Mix this into the mashed potatoes, along with the remaining ingredients except the peas. Mix well and taste for seasoning. Once you are happy with the filling, gently fold in the peas trying not to break any (don't sweat the odd squished one). Cool the mixture before filling the pastry.

Contd . . .

Tamarind Dipping Sauce

1/2 cup (125ml) tamarind purée

Pinch of cayenne pepper

1 tablespoon (15ml) white sugar

1 teaspoon (5ml) ground roasted cumin seeds

Salt

Water to thin the sauce

- Meanwhile, preheat the oven to 350F (180C). Fill a little bowl with water. Cut each sheet of puff pastry into 4 strips and then each strip into 4 squares. Put about 2 teaspoons (10ml) of the filling into the centre of a square. Dip your finger into the water and draw around the edges of the square to moisten. Fold to form a triangular pouch, pressing the edges lightly to seal them. Put all the pouches in a single layer on a lightly greased baking tray and brush them lightly with the beaten egg. Bake for 15–20 minutes, until the tops are golden and the puff pastry is cooked through. Transfer to a platter and serve with the tamarind dipping sauce.

Tamarind Sauce

- To make the tamarind sauce, toss all of the ingredients in a small bowl. Whisk in 1–2 tablespoons (15–30ml) of water to loosen up the tamarind and get a saucy consistency, taste and serve.

WINE MATCH – **Prosecco**

There's something so satisfying about a spicy, rich bite of food followed by a sip of fruity, bubbly wine like Prosecco. Not only do you have the richness of both the potato and the puff pastry, you've also got some exotic spices going on. The bubbles are refreshing and cleansing, and the slight sweetness of Prosecco balances the big flavours in these little bites. If you'd rather try something non-bubbly, go for a Gewürztraminer that's a smidge off-dry, it'll work just as well.

FARINATA

Farinata is a thick Italian crepe made of chickpea flour. It's the easiest snack to whip up. Add it to your dinner table or use it as a starter serving it alongside some olives (see page 26) and smoky eggplant dip (see next page). Play with the flavourings as well. I've given you a basic recipe but you can throw some olives into the batter, or sage, rosemary, sliced garlic or onions. Go crazy! If you do decide to spruce it up, add your flavorings to the batter just before you slide your pan into the oven. I'm a sucker for any warm bready type thing so would be inclined to serve it immediately. You can also serve the farinata at room temperature and your guests will still be pleased. Makes 12 wedges

2 cups (500ml) chickpea flour

1 1/4 teaspoon (6.25ml) salt

3/4 teaspoon (3.75ml) ground pepper

1 3/4 cups (430ml) water, room temperature

1/4 cup(60ml) plus 4 tablespoons (60ml)

olive oil

- In a large bowl, whisk together the chickpea flour, salt and pepper. Add the water and the 1/4 cup (60ml) of olive oil. Whisk this all together until the batter is smooth. Cover and let stand at room temperature for 1 hour.

- Preheat the broiler. Thoroughly coat a 12-inch diameter ovenproof skillet (cast iron is perfect) with 2 tablespoons (30ml) of olive oil. Pour in half the batter, tilting to spread evenly. Broil until golden brown, about 4 minutes. Remove pan from the oven and reduce the oven temperature to 450F (230C).

- Return the skillet to the oven and bake the farinata until a knife inserted into the centre comes out clean, about 3 minutes. To loosen the farinata run a spatula around the sides of the skillet. Slide it out onto a cutting board and cut into 6 wedges. Repeat with the second half of the batter.

Contd . . .

WINE MATCH – **Cava**

When it comes to snacky, nibbly food, I love pairing refreshing sparkling wine. You just can't beat how the bubbles cleanse your palate between bites of salty, smoky, or spicy food, and in this case, the dip has smoky, nutty flavours that beg for a glass of something cold and refreshing. If you can find it, go for a sparkling rosé (you can get affordable rosé Cava from Spain in most liquor stores) – it has more body and flavour than white versions, which will stand up even better to this flavourful snack. Your taste buds will thank you.

Smoky Eggplant and Walnut Dip

Barbecuing the eggplant gives it a smoky intense flavour that takes this dip to a whole other level. If it's the dead of winter or you're not blessed with a barbecue you can roast the eggplant and the pepper in your oven at 400F (200C) until the skins are black and blistery. **Serves 6**

2 eggplants, 3/4 lb (350g) each

1 green bell pepper

2 garlic cloves

1 cup (250ml) chopped walnuts

1/2 teaspoon (2.5ml) salt to taste

3/4 cup (180ml) ricotta cheese

2 tablespoons (30ml) extra virgin olive oil

1 1/2 tablespoons (22.5ml) sherry vinegar

Salt and freshly ground black pepper

2 tablespoons (30ml) chopped parsley

- In a skillet on stovetop, toast walnuts carefully over a medium heat for 3–5 minutes. Set aside to cool.

- Stab the eggplants with a sharp fork in 3 places (to avoid an eggplant explosion). Pre-heat barbecue on a medium-low gas flame. Set your eggplants as high as you can get them on a V-shaped roasting rack if you've got one, or directly on the grill if you don't. Grill for 15 minutes each side until the eggplants are completely soft and the skin is black and blistery.

- Once the eggplants have caved, pull them from the grill and set them aside until cool enough to handle. Pull away the skin and pull out the pulp. Give a little squeeze to loosen some of the juices and mash it all up with a fork.

- You need to blacken the bell pepper too, so pop it on the grill and turn it once each side has blackened. Allow to cool until you can handle it without swearing. Pull off the skin, pull out the seeds and lose the core. Chop this little pepper up finely and mix it into the eggplant mash.

- In a food processor or blender, blend the garlic, salt and half of the walnuts until it forms a paste. Now you can add your ricotta, your olive oil and your sherry vinegar, blitz everything again.

- In a bowl, mix together the garlic-walnut-cheese mixture with eggplant-pepper mixture. Stir well, season with salt and pepper. Make sure to taste it to be sure that you are happy with the seasoning.

- Just before serving add your chopped parsley and the other half of the walnuts.

- Serve with the farinata or with warmed pita bread.

MINI LAMB BURGERS

People – myself included – love burgers! *Passionately*. So why not give them burgers even if you are making something else for dinner? Make them little, call them a snack and you still have room for other things, that is, if you don't eat more than one. These earthy, funky, adorable burgers will be hard to stay away from – especially with this sauce. Frankly, what else could you serve with a lamb patty if not tzatziki?! The thick tangy yogurt sauce with a twist of feta has a fresh salty tang that lifts this burger to the high heavens. If mini burgers don't work with your menu turn these into meatballs and serve them with the tzatziki for dipping. **Makes 8 burgers**

The Burgers

1 1/2 lb (675g) ground lamb

*1/2 cup (125ml) chopped fresh Italian
    flat leafed parsley*

1/4 cup (60ml) finely chopped red onion

1/4 cup (60ml) Dijon mustard

*2 ripe plum tomatoes, seeded and cut
    into 1/4-inch dice*

2 egg yolks

2 teaspoons (10ml) dried oregano

1 teaspoon (5ml) freshly ground black pepper

1 teaspoon (5ml) kosher or sea salt

For the Burgers

- Preheat your barbecue to 375F or medium high.

- Combine all of the burger ingredients in a bowl. With dampened hands, shape into 8 2-inch thick little burgers. Place these on a tray and pop them into the refrigerator until you are ready to grill them.

- Lightly oil the grate on your barbecue and grill each burger for about 4–5 minutes per side or until cooked all the way through.

- Pop each into its own pita or little bun and top with a spoonful of your tzatziki. Add other toppings or leave it just as it is and serve.

Contd . . .

Feta Tzatziki

1 cup (250ml) plain yogurt, a good thick
    Greek style yogurt if you can find it

1 English cucumber

2 cloves garlic, finely minced

Juice of 1/2 lemon

1 tablespoon (15ml) chopped fresh dill

Sea salt and freshly milled black pepper to taste

1 1/2 oz. (42g) crumbled feta cheese

Mini pitas or small buns

Any toppings your heart desires such as
    fresh tomatoes, onion, lettuce, etc.

- Cut your cucumber in half the long way. With a small spoon scoop out the seeds and discard. Put a clean kitchen towel down on a cutting board and grate the cucumber onto the towel. Once you have about a cup grated, pull up the edges of the towel around the cucumber and over the sink squeeze out all the extra liquid. This will keep your tzatziki nice and thick. In a medium bowl mix all of the ingredients together. Taste for salt and pepper and set aside.

WINE MATCH – **Rosé**

This dish has two important elements – the rich, earthy flavour of lamb and the tart but creamy tzatziki. And the absolute perfect pairing for these two contrasting flavours is a nice, dry rosé. The fruit flavours and body are big enough to stand up to the lamb, and the acidity in the wine balances the tzatziki. All you need now is a warm breeze and a comfy patio chair.

GRILLED POLENTA WITH CHARRED PEPPERS AND ANCHOVIES

This might be one of my favourite appetizers. I love good food that you can make ahead and both elements for this snack can be made the day before. For years I was one of those people who generally avoided canned anchovies and anything to do with them but I have to tell you, they make this dish extraordinary. Anchovies, when used properly, have superhero powers which can make a dish so much better without you actually realizing they are there. Caesar salad dressing is a great example and they do the same thing here, they help to showcase the peppers and other flavours without taking all the credit for themselves. Aren't they nice?

Polenta is cornmeal mush with class. You can add herbs, different cheeses, etc., if you like, don't be afraid to play around. For this app, I like to leave it plain so it won't compete with the peppers. One thing to watch with the polenta – it spits hot liquid at you when cooking. Don't be scared, just keep your eye on it and use a long spoon. **Makes 12**

Polenta

4 cups (1 litre) chicken or vegetable stock

1 cup (250ml) cornmeal

1 tsp (5ml) salt

2 tablespoons (30ml) unsalted butter

1 cup (250ml) grated Parmesan cheese

Flour for dusting

Olive oil for frying

Charred Peppers with Anchovies

6 red and 6 yellow peppers

5 tablespoons drained capers

4 oz (112g) salted anchovies

4 garlic cloves, peeled and cut into slivers

A handful of fresh basil

Freshly ground black pepper

Extra virgin olive oil

To make the polenta

- In a heavy bottomed saucepan, bring the stock to a boil.

- Remove from the heat and slowly sprinkle the cornmeal into the hot stock while stirring with a whisk. Cook over low heat. As the polenta starts to thicken, switch to a wooden spoon for easier stirring. Keep stirring constantly, for about 10 to 15 minutes, until thickened and bubbly.

- Off the heat, stir in the butter and Parmesan. Pour into an oiled 9 x 13 baking sheet. Smooth the top with a rubber spatula. Cool first, then into the fridge for 3 hours or overnight until firm and cold.

- Cut the chilled polenta into 12 squares. I like to cut the squares into triangles — whatever shape gets you going. Lift them from pan with a spatula and lightly dust with flour. Heat 1 tablespoon of butter and 1 tablespoon of olive oil in a large sauté or grill pan and cook the triangles in batches over medium heat for 3–5 minutes, turning once until browned on the outside and heated on the inside.
  If you are doing these up ahead of time you can pop them on a cookie sheet to be reheated in your oven at 350F (175C).

Contd . . .

To make the peppers

- If you are using a grill, turn it on to medium high heat. Grill the whole peppers on all sides until the skins are entirely black. If you are using an oven, turn your oven on to 400F (200C). Cut your peppers in half the long way and pull out the seeds. Lay the peppers down on a parchment paper-lined baking sheet and roast until the skins are black and blistery (about 15 minutes). Once peppers are charred, pop them into a bowl, cover with plastic wrap and let cool (sweating peppers will help remove the skins).

- When the peppers have cooled, remove the blackened skin by tearing the pepper apart by its panels and just rubbing it off with your fingers. If you left the peppers whole and grilled them, remove the seeds and the cores as well.

- In a bowl, toss together the peppers with the slivers of garlic, capers, anchovies, basil, black pepper and a good amount of extra virgin olive oil. Top the polenta with a small mound (containing all the elements) of the pepper mix and serve immediately.

WINE MATCH – **Fino Sherry**

Fino sherry is nutty and almost salty in flavour – not a wine that most enjoy sipped on its own. But when it's paired with the right food, it becomes a refreshing, unique alternative to regular wines. This pairing works so well because the saltiness of the anchovies balances off the flavours in the sherry, which naturally complements fish and seafood. Plus, this style of sherry has quite a bit of acidity – perfect for the peppers and the capers. And if sherry's not your cup of tea, serve these up with something bubbly like Cava or Prosecco.

How is wine made?

"A fruit is a vegetable with looks and money. Plus, if you let fruit rot, it turns into wine, something Brussels sprouts never do."

—P. J. O'ROURKE

Wine is fermented grape juice. Pretty simple, right? You take some grape juice (which has natural sugars in it), add some yeast, and voila, the sugar turns into alcohol and you've got yourself some wine. So why is it that each and every wine tastes different from the next? And why grapes and not some other fruit?

Well there is something extra special about those juicy little grapes that makes them differ from any other fruit. First of all, a grape grown in France tastes different than a grape grown in Canada. In fact, a grape grown on the western slope of a hill tastes different from the same type of grape grown on the other side of the same hill! Why? Well, the French call it *terroir* and it basically means "the flavour of the land." And magically, mysteriously, grapes have a way of absorbing their terroir and releasing it in the form of aromas and flavours in wine. Not only that, grapes tend to thrive in conditions that make them struggle to survive – these hardy fruits grow in the sandiest, rockiest soil, in dirt that can't grow anything else.

The juice that is pressed from grapes is also special in that it has a naturally high sugar content which means that when it ferments you get a relatively high level of alcohol (at least in comparison to other fruits like apples) and it tends to last longer than most other fermented liquids. And finally, there are thousands of different varieties of grapes, each one with different aromas, flavours, and preferred growing conditions and climates. Tell me the last time you met a banana or an orange like that. So, with these special characteristics, it's no wonder that grapes ended up as our fruit of choice when it comes to making wine. But the grape is just the beginning.

Let's get back to the concept of "terroir." Although the French coined the term and Europeans in general place a lot of importance on terroir, it is applicable to wine from anywhere in the world. Beyond vine-growing and wine-making techniques, it is terroir that distinguishes for example, a Canadian Pinot Noir from a New Zealand Pinot Noir.

Most wine-producing regions in the world fall within two temperate bands: north of the Tropic of Cancer and south of the Tropic of Capricorn. These regions have widely varying climates and topography, but what they do have in common are summers that are long enough and offer enough sunshine to ripen grapes, and winters that are cool enough to allow the vines a break to rest and restore for the next growing season.

Grape vines can grow in all kinds of soil, as long as it isn't too fertile. High-nutrient soils give the vines an easy ride, which makes them weak and grow too many leaves (in sommelier-speak, that's called "vigour"). Vigour is bad for two reasons – first, lots of leaves on a vine dilutes the nutrients in the plant and in turn the flavours in the grapes, and second, leaves can block the sunshine from the grapes which makes it harder for them to ripen. The rocky, chalky, gravelly, or sandy soils you see in many wine regions are well-draining, meaning that water drains deep into the soil, forcing the roots of the vines to struggle and grow downward to seek moisture, making the vines stronger and more stable.

The weather in a certain year also plays a big part in how wine turns out, which is why vintage can be so important ("vintage" is simply the year listed on the label of the wine). Some important things that can happen due to weather:

Cold winter – an extremely cold winter can damage vines so that there are fewer buds, which leads to fewer grapes and low yield for the vintage

Late frost – a late frost in the spring when vines are already budding can affect the health of those buds

Amount of rain – too much moisture means a much bigger risk of rot and disease; it can also dilute the flavour in the grapes when this happens at harvest time; on the other hand, drought can be hard on the vines if there is no irrigation in place

Amount of sunshine – lots of sunshine and a long growing season results in grapes with high sugar content which makes wine with high alcohol level; if it's a cool growing season with little sunshine, the worry is reaching minimum alcohol levels in wine to meet regional standards

Once the grapes are grown and picked, their journey towards becoming wine continues. Now's the time that the juice needs to be extracted from the grapes and once upon a time, this was done with our feet. And not only was this a practical, simple way of crushing the grapes, it became a festivity – a harvest celebration that entire villages would take part in. Grapes were dumped into treading boxes that drained into containers set up below to catch the juice. While foot-treading still

occurs here and there (mostly in the name of tradition and tourism) most wine producers now use modern machines that crush and destem the grape bunches into what is called "must."

For white wine, the must is then pressed to separate the juice from the skins, and the juice is fermented in either steel tanks or oak barrels. The winemaker makes this decision based on the grape variety and the style of wine to be made. Oak barrels add a whole other layer of aromas and flavours that can make wines more complex and rich. Though other types of wood can be used, both the aroma/flavour that oak gives and its other characteristics (like how hard and porous it is) make it the favourite choice for winemakers. Steel tanks, on the other hand, let the pure fruit flavours of the grape shine through in the wine. Neither method is better than the other, it's just a matter of style and preference. The white wine is then either bottled or allowed to age before bottling, in either tank or barrel. Sometimes wine that has been fermented in steel is transferred to barrels for aging. It all depends on the end result the winemaker is looking for.

If it's red wine that's being made, the crushed grapes sit in large vats for anywhere from a couple of days to a couple of weeks so that the juice is in contact with the skins. This is a really important part of red wine-making because this is how the wine gets to be red. Let me explain . . . if you take a red grape and cut it in half, you'll notice that the flesh inside is actually white. The skin is the only part that has colour so this period of "maceration" lets the colour in the skin leach into the wine. If the skins are removed with little or no contact with the juice, then you can make white or rosé wine from red grapes. The thicker the skins and the longer the maceration period, the deeper the colour of the wine will be. At this point, the rest of the winemaking process for red wine is the same as for white wine. The wine can be fermented in either steel tanks or oak barrels; it can be bottled young or have longer aging before bottling (again in either tank or barrel). Once the wine is bottled, it's shipped to stores around the world, and if you're lucky, it might find its way into your wine glass tonight.

ACT 2

"Wine makes daily living easier, less hurried, with fewer tensions and more tolerance."

—BENJAMIN FRANKLIN

There's nothing like a cold glass of wine at the end of a hectic day, especially when the weather's hot and it's patio season. White wine refreshes like nothing else, and this section is totally devoted to whites – everything from crisp, refreshing, light ones to rich, tropical, oak-aged styles, each paired up with Angie's mouth-watering recipes.

Albariño/Alvarinho

Although not that well known around the world, this grape's nickname in the Mediterranean is the "wine of the sea" because of the coastal proximity of the regions that grow it, and for its affinity for seafood. I like to call it Chardonnay's Mediterranean cousin, with its creamy texture, fruity aromatics, and refreshingly dry style.

This grape is grown in Spain and Portugal (where it's known as Alvarinho), and it's the Spanish version that echoes some of the things I love about Chardonnay. It has medium to full body with intense citrus and orchard fruit aromas and that seafood-friendly tart acidity. These are balanced off by a creamy texture, subtle nutty notes like almonds, and a bit of herbaceousness. My mouth is watering just writing about it!

Albariño grapes can be difficult to grow because they are susceptible to disease, but with careful vine-growing, they develop thick skins which actually contribute to the intense aromas of the wine. One of the most important things to remember about Albariño is that it is meant to be drunk young. Although it has amazing acidity to start, it fades quickly, sometimes in a matter of months, so drink up!

A note on Vinho Verde

Vinho Verde is a region in Portugal that uses Alvarinho as one of the main grapes in its blend. Although it still has the racy acidity of Spanish Albariño, it is lighter in body, has a bit of refreshing spritziness to it, and sometimes just a touch of sweetness. Like the Spanish version, this wine is meant to be drunk young – in fact the wine's name "Vinho Verde" translates to "green wine," a reference to the fact that it should be consumed young or "green." Vinho Verde is a great choice for summertime al fresco dining, or to sip on its own on the patio, just make sure that you're drinking one with the most recent vintage on the label.

Aromas & Flavours

Fruit flavours like citrus and peach
Nutty and herbaceous notes
Creamy texture balanced by tart acidity

Food Ideas

Seafood and fish, especially grilled
Ceviche
Tapas, especially those with garlicky vegetables, beans, fish, and light meats
Caesar Salad

My recommended regions for Albariño are:

Ríax Baixas, a region in north-western Spain, for a creamier, more intense version
Vinho Verde from Portugal for a lighter, spritzier version

Chardonnay

Chardonnay is the best known white wine on the planet, and likely one of the most controversial as well. Many of us love it, others hate it so much that they follow the ABC rule – "Anything But Chardonnay." Personally I don't understand the ABCers at all, and being the wine lover that I am, I do adore my Chardonnay. And that's because in many ways it is a blank canvas, a grape that can be made into any number of styles depending on where it's grown and what the winemaker decides to do with it. Of course the same goes for most grapes, but Chardonnay shines in different lights in regions around the world and with a range of winemaking techniques like barrel fermenting and/or aging, malolactic fermentation, *sur lie* aging, and as a sparkling wine (check out the notes below that explain all this stuff). And because it can be so many things, it pairs with a huge variety of food flavours, yet another reason why I can't believe some people don't feel the same way about it that I do.

Unoaked Chardonnay

So let's start with the blank canvas, the grape untouched, with its pure fruit flavours allowed to shine through. Unoaked Chardonnay is the great compromise wine, and I love it for what it isn't – it's not too light, it's not too heavy, it's not too tart, and it's not too sweet . . . just a nice, happy medium.

Because Chardonnay is mostly known for its big, buttery, oaky version, this fruity style hides in the shadows. It's fermented in steel tanks without any contact with wood, which means that only the flavours of the grape come through in the wine. Sometimes called "unwooded," this style of Chardonnay has crisp fruit flavours of peach, apple, and pear. It is medium in body and has soft but refreshing acidity.

A note on Chablis

Chablis is an appellation in the northern part of Burgundy, France. The only grape grown there is Chardonnay and it's bottled with the name "Chablis" on the label.

Some say this is the purest expression of Chardonnay because it's made in an unoaked style, and the wine's fruit flavours are complemented by the region's unique terroir – chalky soil that gives the wine a flinty, steely, and almost briny quality. The soils in Chablis are actually littered with shellfish fossils, and legend has it that this is why this wine pairs so perfectly with the briny flavour of oysters and other shellfish.

Sur Lie Aging

Sometimes winemakers like to add a little extra oomph to their unoaked Chardonnay, finding it too simple on its own. An easy way to do this without over-powering the fruity flavours of the wine is *sur lie* aging, which is the French terminology for "on the lees." Lees are the dead yeast cells that are leftover at the end of the fermentation process. Instead of filtering the lees out right away, they are left in with the wine to add yeasty, nutty complexities but removed before bottling.

Aromas & Flavours
Fruit flavours like peach, green apple, and pear
Minerally and briny flavours (especially in Chablis)
Soft acidity and medium body

Food Ideas
Raw oysters and ceviche, especially with Chablis
Fried fish and seafood like calamari
Shrimp or other seafood in a citrus marinade
Smoked salmon

My recommended regions for unoaked Chardonnay are:
Chablis, France for a steely, minerally version
Australia, New Zealand, and Canada for a fruitier version

Oaked Chardonnay

Okay, this is what Chardonnay is famous for – big body and mouth-filling flavours with a creamy texture, and toasty, oaky notes. And here's how it's done – instead of fermenting and/or aging the wine in steel tanks, the winemaker uses oak barrels. Fermenting the wine in oak barrels gives a more subtle oaky flavour to the wine, and aging in oak barrels gives more concentrated aromas and flavours. The intensity of the oakiness also depends on several other factors – how long the wine is left to age in the barrel (the longer the oakier); whether the barrel is new or used (new will give more oak); where the oak is from (American gives more powerful, harsher oak flavours compared to French); and how charred the inside of the barrel is (more charred = smokier, heavier oak flavours, less charred = vanilla, toast, and softer oak flavours).

When this style of wine is done right, the natural fruit flavours and acidity of the wine are in balance with the aromas and flavours from the oak; that is, neither overpowers the other but instead they complement each other. I find this style of Chardonnay so delicious that I'd rather have a glass of it than dessert.

A note on white Burgundy

Burgundy, France is Chardonnay headquarters. This is the classic region for Chardonnay, and although Chablis (in northern Burgundy) offers up its trademark steely unoaked style, the rest of the region has perfected the art of balancing fruit and oak to create full bodied, complex, and satisfying Chardonnays. In comparison to oaked Chardonnay from California or Australia, the Burgundian style is more elegant, partially because they use French oak which imparts a more restrained oakiness to the wine than American oak does.

If you see a bottle of white wine that has "Bourgogne" on the label, you've got yourself a Chardonnay. Like all French wine regions, Burgundy is broken down into many different appellations, which are the names you'll see on wine labels. Burgundy's Côte de Beaune is the main appellation for this style of Chardonnay, and some of the best villages in this region are Meursault, Puligny-Montrachet, and Chassagne-Montrachet. They can be pricey, but if you are part of the ABC ("Anything But Chardonnay") band, splurge on a bottle and see what you've been missing.

Malolactic Fermentation

Malolactic fermentation . . . I know it sounds complicated but it's actually a simple little trick that adds the rich, creamy texture that we all know and love in Chardonnay (and if it seems like a mouthful to say, just call it MLF and you'll sound like a pro). And here's what it means. "Malo" = malic acid, which is naturally occurring in grapes. Think about the tartness of a green apple – that's malic acid. The process of MLF converts this tart, sometimes harsh acid into the softer lactic acid, which is the acid in milk. So the next time you have a glass of Chardonnay in your hand, give it a swirl, take a sniff and then a sip. If you smell a buttery, dairy aroma or feel a smooth, creamy texture in your mouth, you've just experienced the magic of MLF.

Aromas & Flavours
Ripe fruit flavours like peach, pineapple, and mango
Oaky flavours like vanilla, hazelnut, toast, and smoke
Creamy, buttery texture and full body

Food Ideas
Rich, creamy cheeses like Brie, Camembert, or Cambozola
Rich seafood like lobster and crab
Roasted poultry
Creamy, cheesy pasta dishes

My recommended regions for oaked Chardonnay are:
California or Australia for big, oaky, tropical fruit bombs
Burgundy, France for their classic, elegant style
Experiment with regions around the world to see what style you like best – think Canada, South Africa, Chile, Argentina, and Italy

Chenin Blanc

Chenin Blanc is a well kept secret, loved by those who know it, and a wonder to those who are just discovering it. It is the chameleon of the wine world, making wines ranging from light, simple and dry to richer and more complex, from refreshing bubbly to long-lived, unctuous nectar-like dessert wines, and even brandies.

Chenin Blanc is native to the Loire Valley in France where it is made into the whole range of wine styles. Although the Loire Valley is still one of the grape's main regions, it has spread to the New World because it's easy to grow in various climates and soil types and has good resistance to disease. And for a grape that isn't so well known, it's more common than you might think. Nearly a third of the grapevines in South Africa are Chenin Blanc, where it is also known as "Steen," and in California, it is the third most widely planted white wine grape. It's also planted across Central and South America in Chile, Argentina, Brazil and even Mexico.

Made in its light and simple style, Chenin Blanc is the perfect quaffing wine. It's aromatic with floral, grassy, peach, pear, and apple aromas. It has a clear, almost watery appearance, then surprises you on the palate with medium body and soft fruit flavours. This is the style that you'll often see from New World countries like South Africa and the Americas, and in the Loire Valley, this style is made in Saumur and Anjou appellations.

Vouvray is my favourite appellation from the Loire, and here they make a more complex version of Chenin Blanc, with grassy aromas that remind me of hay or straw, and with just a touch of sweetness to make it an off-dry style. Loire's sparkling wine is called Crémant de Loire and it shows off Chenin Blanc's zesty acidity and fresh floral aromas. And finally, the luscious Loire dessert wines Coteaux du Layon and Quarts de Chaume have a distinct honeyed, tropical flavour – dessert in a glass.

Aromas & Flavours

Fruity flavours like peach, pear, and apple

Floral, grassy, or hay-like aromas

Honeyed, tropical flavours (in dessert wines)

Food Ideas (for dry and off-dry styles)

Low-acid vegetables like cauliflower and squash

Pungent cheeses like Emmental or Gruyere

Poultry or light meats like pork

My recommended regions for Chenin Blanc are:

Loire Valley, France, especially Vouvray, Anjou, Saumur (for dry and off-dry), Cremant de Loire (for bubbly), and Coteaux du Layon and Quarts de Chaume (for dessert)

South Africa (where it's sometimes called "Steen")

California

Gewürtzraminer

This is the grape that's hard to say, but easy to drink . . . especially after you've had a couple of glasses. And if there were a wine that you could spray on like perfume, this would be it. The aromatic nature (what sommeliers call "the nose") of Gewürztraminer (pronounced Guh-VERTZ-trah-meen-er) makes it so distinct, that we sommeliers love it – so easy to pick out in a blind tasting! And since it's such a mouthful to say, most of us just call it Gewürz.

There are two classic descriptors for this grape – rose petals and lychee, which basically translates to floral and fruity. A lot of grapes have these characteristics, but in Gewürz they are very intense and very distinctive. The floral aromas have a very strong rose character to them and the fruit is very tropical. If you've never had a lychee, think mango and ripe apricot.

The other thing that's interesting about this grape is what its name means in German – *gewürtz* translates to spicy, and *traminer* means grape. And that leads me to the other distinctive feature of Gewürztraminer – it often has a spicy aroma, a sweet spice like ginger, nutmeg, or clove. All these exotic aromas and flavours, combined with a rich, almost oily mouthfeel, make it an ideal match for Chinese, Thai, and Indian food, especially when it's made in a slightly off-dry style.

There isn't a lot of Gewürz grown around the world, mostly because it's a challenging grape to grow. This grape ripens fast, but it also needs time to develop all those aromas and flavours, which means that it grows best in cooler climates that can extend the ripening period – the cool region of Alsace in northern France is where most Gewürz comes from. Cool climates also help maintain the acidity in this grape, which is the maker or breaker of the wine. With all the intense, perfumey qualities of this wine, it can be a bit over the top and almost seem cloying without enough acidity to balance everything out. But paired with the right food, Gewürztraminer is sure to please.

Aromas & Flavours

Sweet tropical fruit like lychee, mango, or apricot

Perfumey and spicy aromas of rose petal, ginger, nutmeg, or clove

Mouth-coating, almost oily texture

Food Ideas

German or Alsatian dishes like sauerkraut, smoked fish, bratwurst, pork chops, or Muenster cheese

Chinese, Thai or Indian dishes with spice and exotic flavours

My recommended regions for Gewürztraminer are:

Alsace, France

Pfalz, Germany

Niagara Peninsula and Okanagan Valley, Canada

Grüner Veltliner

Austria's signature grape Grüner Veltliner has just recently splashed onto the global wine scene. Coined the "Gru-V" wine, it really is groovy, especially for a wine gal like me who was ready for something new in a white. Grüner is medium in body, with orchard fruit flavours like peach, pear, and apricot. It can have some sweet, floral aromas as well but there are two things that really stand out to me – distinct nutty aromas and flavours, and a subtle spicy kick that reminds me of white pepper. If this all sounds strange to you, you've gotta try Grüner Veltliner for yourself.

What makes this grape especially groovy is its amazing food-friendliness. Since my infatuation with Grüner began, I've paired it with dish after dish, always happily surprised at how well it works with everything – rich seafood, spicy jerk chicken, the distinct flavours of Indian curry, simple salads, and the list goes on. There are a couple reasons that this wine works with so many foods. First, it has both acidity and quite a bit of body. Acidity is really important when it comes to food, because lots of food has its own dose of natural acidity, so a wine needs it too to balance that off. But having a nice medium body means that richer textures in food won't overpower the wine. Those nutty complexities add to Grüner's ability to stand up to bold flavours and textures. And finally, Grüner is often made in a slightly off-dry style, meaning there's a small bit of sweetness in the wine, which is perfect for cooling your taste buds after spicy food.

Though there are small plantings of Grüner Veltliner in Germany and in Canada, it's pretty much only made in Austria. And although it's rare on the wine store shelves, it's well worth seeking out, especially if you love white wine and want to taste something new. I promise you won't be disappointed.

Aromas & Flavours
Fruit flavours like peach, pear, and apricot
Distinctive nutty and spicy characters (think white pepper)
Crisp, tongue-tingling acidity balanced by medium body and a touch of sweetness

Food Ideas
Salads with flavourful ingredients like fish, eggs, or potatoes
Asian spices
Vegetable dishes, both raw and cooked
Fish, seafood, and chicken

My recommended regions for Grüner Veltliner are:
Austria (and let me know if you see it from someplace else!)

Malvasia

If you love Gewürztraminer, then Malvasia is something you've got to try. Malvasia is an aromatic white grape with intense floral, spice, and sweet fruit, and just like Gewürz, it can be made in styles ranging from dry and off-dry to powerful dessert wines.

Malvasia originates from Italy, where it's grown throughout the country, but especially through central and southern Italy, including the islands of Sicily and Sardinia. There's also quite a bit grown in California for both dry and sweet styles of wine, and in the Mediterranean, you'll see Malvasia blended in Spanish and Portuguese whites (as well as fortified White Port and Madeira – see pages 320 and 326).

Whether dry or sweet, Malvasia has aromas and flavours of honey, ripe pear, and sweet baking spice like nutmeg or cinnamon. The sweeter versions are intense and lingering on the palate, and the most common one you'll see is called Vin Santo (see page 331 for more on this wine). The dry and off-dry styles pair well with the same kinds of food that Riesling and Gewürztraminer do, like seafood and spicy cuisine.

Aromas & Flavours
Sweet aromas of honey, nutmeg, and cinnamon
Floral aromas like orange blossom and honeysuckle
Fruity flavours like ripe pear, peach, and apricot

Food Ideas
Grilled calamari or other seafood antipasti
Mild, white fish
Asian cuisine
Smoked duck or turkey

My recommended regions for Malvasia are:
Italy, especially Lazio and Frascati (where it is blended with other grapes)
California
Rioja, Spain and Portugal

Pinot Blanc

Pinot Blanc is the white sibling in the Pinot family (Pinot Gris and Pinot Noir being the pink-grey and red members respectively), and is the most overlooked of the three. This isn't surprising, considering that it originates from Alsace, France where luscious and aromatic Gewürztraminer and Pinot Gris abound.

But just because Pinot Blanc isn't strikingly aromatic, that's no reason to neglect this wine, which is a great alternative to unoaked Chardonnay. In fact, its leaves and vines are so similar to the Chardonnay vine that the two were often confused in vineyards across Europe. It's medium to full in body with aromas and flavours of apple, pear, and melon with a clean, crisp finish. It has enough body to stand up to lots of different foods, and satisfies a white wine hankering with its ripe fruity flavours. I can almost picture myself now, lounging in the garden on the hammock without a care, a glass of Pinot Blanc in hand.

Aromas & Flavours
Ripe, fruity aromas and flavours of apple, pear, and melon
Medium body and clean, crisp finish

Food Ideas
Crab cakes or other fried fish and seafood
Baked ham
Potato and leek soup
Quiche

My recommended regions for Pinot Blanc are:
Alsace, France
Niagara and Okanagan, Canada

Pinot Grigio/Pinot Gris

The first thing you've got to know when it comes to Pinot Grigio and Pinot Gris is that they are the same grape. The Italians call it the former, and the French the latter, and they are made into two completely different styles of wine. This grape is in the same family as Pinot Noir (which is red) and Pinot Blanc (which is white), and it's somewhere in between the two, with a pinkish-grey coloured skin.

Pinot Grigio

Pinot Grigio is the lighter, crisper version of this grape, traditionally made in the northern parts of Italy, but now being made around the world. This style is hugely popular for one simple reason – it's a crowd pleaser. In general, Pinot Grigio is super simple, easy drinking, and fruity – the perfect alternative to the other big white – Chardonnay – which is often made in a mouth-filling, oaky style.

Pinot Grigio has a soft, floral aroma like orange blossom, and is refreshing and light on the palate, with gentle fruit flavours of green apple, lemon, and orange, a subtle minerally note, and sometimes just a touch of citrusy sweetness.

Aromas & Flavours
Light, refreshing and simple green apple and citrus
Soft floral like orange blossom
A touch of stony, mineral notes

Food Ideas
Light seafood and fish
Grilled vegetables
Pasta and gnocchi with light sauces
Light meats and poultry with fruit sauces

My recommended regions for Pinot Grigio are:
Northern regions of Italy such as Veneto, Fruili, and Trentino-Alto Adige
California, U.S.A.

Pinot Gris

It's hard to believe it, but it is the same grape. Pinot Gris is the Alsatian version of this wine, and it is richer and fuller in style than Pinot Grigio. Instead of being light and refreshing, it is medium to full in body, and although it's usually made as a dry wine (you can find the odd dessert-style Pinot Gris though), it has luscious, ripe fruit flavours of orange peel, marmalade, pear, and melon, with spicy, honey, and sometimes floral notes. It has a smooth, creamy texture but still holds onto that clean, vibrant acidity that is also found in Pinot Grigio. You'll also often notice a slight rosy tinge to its golden colour, which comes from the pigment of the grape skins.

Alsace, France has the perfect climate for Pinot Gris, with cool but sunny summers which give the grapes time to develop ripe fruit flavours and intense aromatics. You'll also find outstanding Pinot Gris from Oregon, U.S.A., New Zealand, and some of the cooler regions of Australia. If you like your white wine to be mouth-filling and rich, then you'll love Pinot Gris.

Aromas & Flavours
Luscious, ripe pear and melon
Citrus notes like orange peel and marmalade
Spice, honey, and floral

Food Ideas
Steamed mussels in white wine or cream sauces
Quiche
Seafood or fish in rich sauces like Hollandaise
Creamy but pungent cheeses like Muenster

My recommended regions for Pinot Gris are:
Alsace, France
Oregon, U.S.A.

Riesling

Riesling is known in the wine world as the king of white wine, but when you bring up Riesling to the average Joe, most are unimpressed. Memories of sugary-sweet jug wine and horrible hangovers abound. Once you give it a chance, however, you'll realize that Riesling is misunderstood, and truly is the king.

There are three amazing things about Riesling. The first is the acidity that you'll find in just about every bottle of half-decent Riesling. This grape does well in cool climates, and when grown properly, it has bracing acidity that can balance off even the sweetest of wine styles. It is that acidity that makes Riesling in any style super food-friendly. Which brings me to the second thing that makes Riesling amazing – it works well in any style of wine, from bone dry to startlingly sweet and everything in between, including sparkling wines. And finally, it ages well. In general, white wines don't last past a few years after bottling, but even drier styles of Riesling can last and improve over decades. I recently had a 30-year-old bottle of German Riesling that was still mouth-wateringly tart.

So, what's the trick behind finding a Riesling that doesn't rekindle bad wine memories? The most important thing to keep in mind is that like other wines, all Riesling is not created equal. There's still bound to be a mass-produced hangover-in-a-bottle on your liquor store shelf with the name Riesling on its label. But once you know the level of sweetness you prefer and experiment with a few different regions, you'll find just the right Riesling for you.

Although most of us feel we prefer dry white wines to sweet ones, many of the popular whites out there do have a small amount of residual sugar (sugar left after fermentation is stopped) that leaves the wine a touch on the sweet side. New World Chardonnay, Viognier, and Chenin Blanc are but a few examples of the many whites that have a smidge of sweetness to enhance their fruit flavours. So even if you're sure you like 'em dry, you might want to take the plunge and try an "off-dry" Riesling. "Off-dry" simply means that the wine has a little bit of sweetness in it, but in well-made Rieslings, the acidity is so intense that bone dry styles can be a bit much. Trust me, a touch of sweetness in an off-dry Riesling can be the perfect balance. And if you love spicy food, off-dry wines are just the ticket to cool your taste buds after fiery hot food.

Decoding German Riesling

Old World wine labels can be confusing enough, but to make things worse, German wine labels are filled with fancy fonts and all sorts of lingo that doesn't mean much to the everyday consumer. But the wine inside the bottle is often world-class Riesling – stuff you don't want to miss out on. There are a number of quality categories that Germany uses to classify its wines, which break the country into specific wine regions. In quality German wines, you'll see the name of the region on the label. Some examples include Mosel-Saar-Ruwer, Rheingau, Rheinhessen, Pfalz, and Baden. These terms are just telling you where in Germany the grapes are from (like you might see Toscana in Italy or Bordeaux in France). You might also see terms like *trocken* which translates to "dry" and *halbtrocken* which means "off-dry." Some of the other lingo you'll see further categorize the wine into styles, listed here from driest to sweetest:

Kabinett – delicate Riesling perfect as an apéritif with crisp acidity and citrus/green apple flavours

Spätlese – translates to "late harvest," this style will have more concentrated flavours, a bit more body, and a touch more sweetness than Kabinett – perfect chilled down and paired with spicy ethnic food

Auslese – even sweeter that Spätlese, these wines are made from individually selected extra-ripe bunches of grapes

Beerenauslese (BA) – a rare, expensive wine made from individually selected bunches of grapes, ideally that have been suffering from noble rot (check out page 329 for more on this)

Eiswein – translates to "Icewine" and it's made the same way that the famous Canadian Icewine is, by leaving bunches of grapes on the vine until frozen before harvesting, resulting in a super-sweet, luscious dessert wine (more on Icewine on page 315)

Trockenbeerenauslese (TBA) – among the world's most expensive wines, these are produced in minute quantities, in only the finest vintages, from individual grapes that have undergone extensive noble rot.

Aromas & Flavours

Floral notes like honeysuckle and jasmine

Fruity flavours like apples, peaches, and sometimes citrus

Mineral notes that become more prominent with age like petrol and diesel

Food Ideas (for dry Riesling)

Vegetarian cuisine

Choucroute

Deep-fried food like tempura or zucchini sticks

Seafood of all kinds

Food Ideas (for off-dry Riesling)

Salads with candied nuts or fruits

Spicy Asian- or Indian-inspired cuisine

Pungent blue cheese

My recommended regions for Riesling are:

Germany

Alsace, France

Experiment with New World Riesling from Canada, New Zealand, Australia, Chile, and the United States

Sauvignon Blanc

I like to think of Sauvignon Blanc as the wine world's take on lemonade – it's light, tart, and refreshing – perfect to quench your thirst and so satisfying in warm weather. So with these cool, crisp, refreshing qualities, it's no surprise that Sauvignon Blanc is perfect with the same kinds of food. Leafy salads with vinaigrette, most vegetarian dishes, and tart goat cheese taste great with Sauvignon Blanc because the acidity in the wine is balanced by the acidity in the food.

Sauvignon Blanc is a grape originally grown in the Loire Valley in France. If you've ever seen a bottle of Sancerre or Pouilly-Fumé on a wine list, those are both Loire Valley Sauvignon Blancs, each named for the specific region (or "appellation") that they're made in. Apart from the Loire Valley, the Marlborough region of New Zealand has become known around the world for its very distinct version of Sauvignon Blanc – with ripe, tropical fruit flavours, strong vegetal notes (like green pea or bell pepper), and that same racy acidity that Sauvignon Blanc is known for.

So why does a Sauvignon Blanc taste the way it does? Well, the wine is made in steel tanks, without being aged in oak barrels, allowing the pure fruit flavours to shine through. That means the flavours in this wine come from the grape, not from the winemaker. This white grape thrives in cooler climate wine regions with lots of sunshine and cool nights that preserve the fresh flavours of the grape. And all those fruity, refreshing qualities are best enjoyed while they're still young, which means you should drink your Sauvignon Blanc within a couple years of its vintage; this wine generally doesn't get any better with age.

A note on Fumé Blanc

The term Fumé Blanc was coined by California-based wine mogul Robert Mondavi. Back in the 1960s when his Sauvignon Blanc sales were slow, he changed the labeling on his Sauvignon Blanc to Fumé Blanc (borrowing the *fumé* from Pouilly-Fumé of France) The word *fumé* actually means "smoked" in French, and not coincidentally, this style of wine is often fermented or aged in oak barrels, adding a toasty, smoky quality to the Sauvignon Blanc. Though this technique isn't the standard for making Sauvignon Blanc, it has become a classic flavour profile for Californian Fumé Blanc, appealing to American (and world-wide) consumers who prefer richer, more tropical fruit flavoured wines with softer acidity and creamy, vanilla-bean notes (like the American best-seller Chardonnay).

Aromas & Flavours

Tart citrus like lime, grapefruit, and lemon

Sweet, tart, ripe fruit like passion fruit, guava, green apple, and gooseberry

Herbaceous or vegetal like fresh cut grass, green bell pepper, and sometimes even asparagus or green pea

Food Ideas

Vegetarian cuisine

Salads

Goat cheese

Fish and seafood (especially oysters)

My recommended regions for Sauvignon Blanc are:

France, especially the Loire Valley (if you see Sancerre or Pouilly-Fumé on the label, you've got yourself a Sauvignon Blanc)

New Zealand, Chile, and South Africa

California (sometimes called Fumé Blanc)

Sémillon

When it comes to white wine, Sémillon is the laid-back, mellow fellow. This French grape is famous for the blends it shares with Sauvignon Blanc – white Bordeaux (a.k.a. Meritage) and the rich, sweet Sauternes dessert wine. But on its own, it produces a white wine that is medium in body with low acidity and soft, easy-drinking flavours of citrus, fig, melon, honey, and floral.

Sémillon is the main white grape planted in the Bordeaux region in France, but now more grows in Chile than anywhere else on earth. California also has lots planted, as does Australia, where it is sometimes blended with Chardonnay to create a full-bodied, fruity wine.

The really interesting thing about Sémillon is that unlike most white wines, this one can age well, sometimes for decades, slowly taking on a completely different set of aromas and flavours, becoming rich and deep with creamy, nutty, and honeyed qualities.

Aromas & Flavours
Soft, mellow flavours of citrus, fig, melon, honey, and floral
Medium body and low acidity

Food Ideas
Light, white fish
Creamy pasta salad
Simply prepared chicken or turkey

My recommended regions for Sémillon are:
South Africa, Chile, and California
Australia (also look for blends with Chardonnay)

Vidal Blanc

Vidal Blanc is most famous for its role in some of the best dessert wines in the world – late harvest and Icewines from the Niagara Peninsula in Ontario, Canada. And though this grape is perfect for these styles of wine due to its hardiness against cold weather and disease, it can also make a light, slightly off-dry style of white wine that's best described as Riesling's little brother.

Like Riesling, Vidal has floral aromas and fruity flavours of stone fruit like peach and apricot, a citrusy tangerine zing, and a touch of fruity sweetness. The aromas and flavours in Vidal are lighter and more subtle than big brother Riesling has, but they are pleasant nonetheless and it's the perfect patio-sipping wine – simple, satisfying, and refreshing.

The Vidal grape is what's known as a "French Hybrid" which means that it was created by crossing two "parent" grapes to create a new one. Just like the "cock-a-poo" was created by breeding a cocker spaniel and a poodle, the Vidal grape was created from Ugni Blanc (the French grape mostly used for brandy) and Seibel.

You'll very rarely see Vidal made as a regular table wine, but if you do be sure to grab a couple bottles if you're a fan of Riesling or if you like simple sippers like Italian Pinot Grigio and Soave. This hardy little grape is grown mostly in the cool climates of the Niagara Peninsula in Canada and in the eastern United States including the Finger Lakes region of New York State.

Aromas & Flavours
Stone fruit flavours like peach and apricot
Floral notes and soft, citrusy acidity
Usually off-dry with a touch of sweetness

Food Ideas
Mild, creamy cheeses
Fish or poultry with fruit sauce
Spicy Asian or Indian cuisine

My recommended regions for Vidal Blanc are:
Niagara Peninsula, Canada
Finger Lakes, New York State

Viognier

Okay right off the bat, I have to admit that I'm Viognier-obsessed. For a wine that only has a tiny percentage of the shelf space in wine stores around the world, you'll notice that in *this* book, it's paired up with quite a few of Angie's recipes. That's mostly because I love Viognier, but luckily for me Angie also uses a lot of Viognier-friendly ingredients.

Viognier has many characteristics that make it extremely food-friendly. It has a lush, full body that makes it delicious with rich seafood like scallops and lobster, without the sometimes overpowering oakiness of some Chardonnays. With all of its body, it still has a delicate quality to it. Think of it this way – if Chardonnay and Viognier were dating, Viognier would be the woman in the relationship.

It has the aromatics and exotic flavours of a Riesling or Gewürztraminer, without the intense perfume, making it a perfect pairing for the spice of Asian and Indian cuisine. And I'm not sure why, but there's nothing like the way the tropical fruit flavour and luscious texture of Viognier takes things like carrots, sweet potato, or squash up to a new level – just try some of the Viognier-matched recipes in this section and see for yourself!

So now I've sold you on the virtues of Viognier, let me tell you a bit about this wonderful wine. The Viognier grape originated from the Rhône Valley, where it still has the most plantings in the world. Most often, a small amount is blended in with Rhône Syrah to add an interesting complexity to the bold red wine's aromatics. It is also the grape of Condrieu, a tiny village in Northern Rhône that produces pricey yet delicious Viognier. You can now find budget-priced Viognier from all over the southern parts of France and wonderful versions in all price ranges from Australia, California, and even in Canada. This grape is happiest in warm climates with lots of sunshine, much like myself.

Aromas & Flavours

Juicy, ripe fruit like apricot, peach, pineapple, and mango

Sweet aromas and flavours like honey, honeysuckle, and orange blossom

Luscious, unctuous texture like crème brûlée

Food Ideas

Rich preparations of seafood, especially scallops

Thai or Indian flavours including curry and coconut milk

Sweet vegetables like squash, sweet potatoes, and carrots

Light meats like chicken, pork, and ham, especially in fruity or spicy preparations

My recommended regions for Viognier are:

Southern France, including Condrieu if you're looking for something extra-special

Australia

California

White Wine Blends

"In wine there is wisdom, in beer there is strength, in water there is bacteria."
—DAVID AUERBACH

I'm not sure why, but blends have a bad reputation. Lots of people think that blended wines are made to use up leftover grapes, or to try to cover up a bad harvest by mixing in some good with the bad. I suppose that may be the case sometimes, but some of the best wines in the world are blends. Think of the mighty red Bordeaux wines, or rich, intense Amarone. Both are blends. Ideally, a blend doesn't cover up negative qualities of a wine, but instead it enhances the best characteristics of each element. A synergy, if you will, with the sum being much greater than each of the parts. Read on for some of my favourite white wine blends.

Bordeaux
(Sauvignon Blanc/Sémillon or Meritage)

Although Bordeaux is famous for its big red wines, it's also home to a lively, fruity white wine made from a blend of two grapes – Sauvignon Blanc and Sémillon. Just as a good blend should be, this one truly does bring out the best in each of the grapes. The Sauvignon Blanc offers up crisp acidity, citrus flavours, and zesty, herbaceous notes while the Sémillon adds a smoother, rounder texture with flavours of honey, fig, and melon to create a pleasing balance. The wine is often aged in oak barrels to add toasty, vanilla qualities to the mix.

Bordeaux, France is the region where this wine was originally made, but other New World countries (mainly Australia and the U.S.A.) are trying out this combo too, and labeling it simply with the grape names Sauvignon Blanc/Sémillon. Another term you might see used for this blend is "Meritage" which was coined by a group of American vintners to describe the traditional Bordeaux blend.

So if you find that Sauvignon Blanc on its own is too mouth-puckeringly acidic, then try out a white Bordeaux blend – I'm sure you'll agree that there's synergy in the bottle.

Aromas & Flavours
Tart fruit flavours of citrus and green apple
Ripe, sweet flavours of honey, fig, and melon
Zesty acidity balanced by a smooth texture

Food Ideas
Rich seafood and fish
Bisques and other creamy soups
Creamy, herbaceous pasta dishes
Chèvre and other tangy, creamy cheeses

My recommended regions for Sauvignon Blanc/Sémillon blends are:
Graves or Pessac-Léognan appellations of Bordeaux, France
Australia, California, or Canada

Rhône
(Viognier/Marsanne/Rousanne/
Grenache Blanc/Clairette/Bourboulenc)

Dozens of different grape varieties grow in the Rhône Valley, and once again it is the red blends that are better known around the world – they account for as much as 95% of the wine production of this area. But the white wines produced in this region are vibrant, fruity, and well worth seeking out. I love these wines for their food-friendliness and the many variations there are. There are six main grapes that go into this complex blend: Viognier, Marsanne, Rousanne, Grenache Blanc, Clairette, and Bourboulenc – talk about variety in one bottle! And of course, depending on which grapes and in what quantities, the wines can vary widely in style and taste.

Viognier is by far the most popular and well-known white grape from the Rhône and is often bottled on its own with little or nothing else blended in (check out the section on Viognier on page 84). These wines are usually clearly labeled with the grape name because people recognize it and know what it tastes like. Lots of producers are now starting to add more and more Viognier to their blends to add the luscious body and aromatics that the grape is so famous for.

Next on the popularity and quality scale are Marsanne and Roussanne. These grapes are sometimes (but fairly rarely) bottled as single varietal wines but are mostly found as the main part of a blend. Marsanne does best in the northern parts of the Rhône Valley, whereas Roussanne is more common in the south, adding a honeyed, floral and nutty texture to many blends. The best expression of the Marsanne/Roussanne blend is from the Hermitage appellation ("Hermitage" is what you'll see on the wine label).

The remaining grapes (Grenache Blanc, Clairette, and Bourboulenc) are still among the dominant grapes planted in the region, though they are less fashionable and slowly being replanted with the more popular grapes. Like its red counterpart, Grenache Blanc shows up in most of the blends from this region, especially from the southern parts of the Rhône Valley, and gives the wines their body, high alcohol content, and spicy kick. Clairette is light in body but has intense stone fruit flavours (think peach and apricot), and finally, Bourboulenc adds both body and acidity to the blend. If your head is spinning, join the club . . . the main thing to remember is that all these grapes combined together equals yummy.

These wines, especially when they contain higher percentages of Viognier, Marsanne, and Roussanne, have an almost golden colour with high alcohol balanced by refreshing acidity. They have juicy, ripe fruit flavours of peach, with nutty, spicy, and floral notes. Because this is a very hot climate, some Rhône blends end up lacking in the acidity department, so be sure to try one of the specific appellations listed below.

Aromas & Flavours
Ripe stone fruit flavours like peach and apricot
Nutty, spicy, floral, and honey notes
High alcohol and refreshing acidity

Food Ideas
Rich seafood and fish, especially spiced or grilled preparations
Veal or chicken in rich sauces or flavourful preparations
Spicy dishes like paella or mild curries

My recommended regions for white Rhône blends are:
Côtes-du-Rhône – this general appellation is great for experimenting –
   you'll find amazing values as well as not-so-inspiring wines in this category
Côtes-du-Rhône-Villages – this is the next step up from Côtes-du-Rhône and though
   slightly more pricey, you'll find more and more tasty wines from this appellation
Some of the best, more specific appellations to look for – Hermitage, Crozes-Hermitage,
   Chateauneuf-du-Pape, and Condrieu

Orvieto

The town of Orvieto is located in central Italy in the region of Umbria at the base of a volcano. The volcanic soils are part of what creates the unique flavour of this wine – mineral, earthy, and nutty notes reminiscent of roasted almonds, all balanced by zesty fruitiness.

This blend of indigenous Italian grapes includes Trebbiano, Grechetto, Malvasia, Verdelho, Canaiolo Bianco, and Drupeggio. The result is a wine that falls in the middle of light, simple Pinot Grigio and toasty, rich Chardonnay – a wine of medium body that has a distinctive Italian earthiness that I absolutely love with pungent Italian cheeses and earthy mushrooms and truffles. It's also a perfect pairing for seafood, especially in creamy sauces on pasta.

Aromas & Flavours
Light fruity aromas and flavours including zesty lime
Nutty, earthy, and mineral notes
Medium in body with a smooth texture

Food Ideas
Seafood in cream sauce
Risotto with truffles
Earthy vegetables like parsnips, squash, and potatoes
Pungent Italian cheeses

My recommended regions for Orvieto are:
The Orvieto Classico appellation in Umbria, Italy

Soave

Soave is a simple starter-wine – you can sip it as an apéritif, pair with a light first course, and it's perfect as an introduction into the wine world. It's a light and straightforward white wine made in the Soave appellation in the Veneto region of north-eastern Italy, from a blend of two Italian grapes – Trebbiano and Garganega (sometimes a bit of Chardonnay is thrown in too). The more Garganega the better, for Trebbiano is an easy-growing, inexpensive, fairly bland grape with mild characteristics that don't add much in the way of flavour to the wine. Garganega, however, can be interesting and aromatic, with flavours of lemon, herbs, and subtle nutty and floral notes.

Legend has it that Dante, the famous Italian poet of the 13th century, named this wine Soave meaning "smooth," because of its mildness. And my favourite thing about Soave is just that – being so smooth and easy-drinking, it really is a great intro for non-wine drinkers. And with light, simple flavours in food, this wine can really come alive.

Aromas & Flavours
Light, refreshing, simple, and fruity – think lemon and other citrus
Mild nutty, herbal, and floral notes

Food Ideas
Simply prepared seafood, fish, or chicken
Light pasta dishes
Mild cheeses

My recommended regions for Soave are:
Soave (a small wine region in Veneto, Italy)

BAKED GARLIC AND ONION CREAM SOUP

This may be one of the easiest, sexiest soups around. All you have to do is throw some onions and garlic into a pan, cover it with delicious liquids and seasonings and pop it into your oven to do the rest of the work for you. While you read a book, (or just flip through this one) the garlic is going to slowly roast itself sweet, losing its aggressive garlic flavour, the onions are going to do the same and the liquids are going to transform into a savoury rich stock. In this case, I don't recommend switching the cream for milk, your soup will turn out to be thin and a bit flat. Call it moderation and enjoy, in this case it's worth it. **Serves 6 to 8**

6 large cooking onions, cut into 1/2-inch slices

2 heads garlic, cloves separated and peeled

4 cups (1 litre) chicken stock

1 cup (250ml) white wine

2 sprigs fresh thyme, stripped

1 teaspoon (5ml) coarsely ground black pepper

1 teaspoon (5ml) salt

4 tablespoons (60ml) unsalted butter

2 cups (500ml) 35% cream

*2 tablespoons (30ml) chopped fresh Italian
    flat leaf parsley*

- Preheat the oven to 350F (180C).

- Place the onions and garlic in a shallow roasting pan, and add the wine and 2 cups (500ml) of the chicken stock. Sprinkle with thyme, pepper and salt. Dot with butter.

- Cover the pan with aluminium foil and bake for 1 1/2 hours. Stir once or twice while baking. Your house will smell amazing.

- Remove the pan from the oven and puree the onions and garlic with the liquid, in batches, in a blender or food processor until smooth.

- With the motor on, gradually add the remaining 2 cups (500ml) stock and the cream. Pour the soup into a large saucepan.

- Adjust the seasoning and slowly heat through. Do not allow the soup to boil once the cream has been added or the cream will split.

- Sprinkle with the parsley and serve.

WINE MATCH – **Oaked Chardonnay**

The sweet flavours of roasted onion and garlic, as well as the creamy, rich texture of this soup both beg for a buttery, oaky Chardonnay. Mirroring the textures of both the soup and the wine are what make this match so amazing, but what's also important is not overwhelming the soup with a wine that's too tart. A new world Chardonnay from California is the perfect choice.

GREEN MEXICAN CORN CHOWDER

This soup is a beautiful bright green and the flavour will blow your mind. The sweetness comes from the corn, backed by the richness of the cream, combined with the fresh tartness of the tomatillo and the heat from the poblano – your tongue will think it's died and gone to heaven. Tomatillos are a Mexican cousin to the tomato, but green with a papery husk. They can ripen to yellow but for this recipe you need green firm fellas, and the paper around them should be pretty fitted, not too loose. Look for them in specialty grocers and of course Latin American grocers. Poblano peppers look like a big, darker green cousin of the jalapeno, usually about 2 inches wide and 5 inches long. They have a rich heat that can vary, but in the grand scheme of hot peppers they are mild to medium. They should be healthy looking, firm to touch and blemish free. If you can't find poblanos, sub in two jalapenos instead. Serves 6

2 tablespoons (30ml) vegetable oil

1 lb (454g) tomatillos, husked and rinsed

1 medium white onion, chopped medium dice

1 tablespoon (15ml) garlic, minced

1 large fresh poblano chili, stemmed,
*   seeded and roughly chopped*

2 cups (500ml) corn kernels, cooked and
*   cut from the frozen or defrosted cob*

3 1/2 cups (875ml) low sodium chicken stock

1/2 cup (125ml) 35% heavy cream

1/2 cup (125ml) fresh cilantro, washed, leaves
*   only, stalks removed, roughly chopped*

Salt and pepper to taste

- Preheat a large cast iron or heavy bottomed skillet over high heat. Add half of the vegetable oil.

- Cut the tomatillos in half from top to bottom and lay them cut-side down in the hot skillet. Cook until a deep golden brown colour, then flip and roast them on the other side for about 5 minutes. Take out of skillet and put them in a bowl to cool slightly.

- Set a large saucepan over medium heat, add rest of the oil and heat for about 30 seconds. Add onion, garlic and poblano pepper. Cook until tender but not browned, about 5 minutes. Pull them from the heat.

- In a food processor, purée the onion mixture, the tomatillos and 1 cup (250ml) of the corn until it's smooth. Slowly add 1/2 cup (125ml) of the chicken stock to the mixture to thin it out.

- Strain mixture through a fine mesh strainer into a large pot. With back of a spoon push down on solids to help move it through. Set pot over medium heat and stir in remaining chicken stock. Bring mixture to a simmer and add cream and chopped cilantro. Season to taste with salt and pepper and serve.

WINE MATCH – **Sauvignon Blanc**

When we were shooting *This Food That Wine*, this pairing became one of our favourites, because the Sauvignon Blanc complemented the dish in so many ways. The chowder is rich and creamy in texture and although the wine is just medium in body, it stands up to it nicely and more importantly, the crisp acidity of the wine cleanses the palate after the richness of the soup. The ripe, tropical flavours of a new world Sauvignon Blanc (go for New Zealand) cool the heat of the spice while complementing the sweet corn.

WILD MUSHROOM SOUP

Mushrooms are such an amazing ingredient, each type adds a different flavour. The result in this recipe is a really good earthy soup. If you wanted to make it a purely button mushroom soup, just don't skip the dried porcini – the broth from the soaking adds lots of personality. **Serves 6**

8 pieces of dried porcini mushrooms

5 tablespoons (75ml) olive oil

6 slices double smoked bacon (or regular
*   bacon), chopped finely*

1 medium cooking onion, finely chopped

3 lb (1.5kg) button mushrooms, sliced

1 large shallot, finely chopped

2 1/2 quart (2 1/2 litres) chicken stock

Salt and pepper

2 tablespoons (30ml) olive oil

2 lb (1 kg) wild mushrooms, (like portobello,
*   cremini, oyster, shitake or any other fun safe*
*   mushrooms you can find in your grocer)*
*   cleaned and sliced*

1/4 cup (60ml) chopped parsley

- In 1 1/2 cups (375ml) of warm water, soak the dried porcini until soft (about 20 minutes). Drain and reserve all the liquid except the last 2 tablespoons (30ml) (which will likely have some funky sediment in it); rinse the softened porcini and slice.

- Put a large saucepan over medium heat, add olive oil and heat through for 30 seconds. Add bacon and onion and cook until onion is translucent, about 5 minutes. Add the sliced button mushrooms and cook until are golden, 5 more minutes. Add the shallots and cook for about 2 minutes over a medium heat. Keep stirring to prevent any burning.

- Add stock, the sliced porcini and the soaking liquid. Bring to a boil, turn down heat to low and simmer for about 20 minutes.

- While soup is simmering, heat a large skillet over medium high heat, add olive oil and sauté wild mushrooms in batches. Cook until the juice has evaporated, about 6–8 minutes for each batch.

- Once soup has had 20 minutes to simmer, add the mushrooms to the soup and simmer for a further 30 minutes. Skim off any scum rising to the top.

- Add your chopped parsley just before serving.

WINE MATCH – **Chenin Blanc**

Soup can be tricky to match with wine and this is the perfect example – there are big flavours in this soup but a very delicate texture, so you need to find a wine that has the same characteristics. Though the main ingredients – earthy mushroom and smoky bacon – would usually work well with a red wine, the soup is brothy, so something red would probably take over. A white wine is the best choice here, and I love the flavour of a South African oak-aged Chenin Blanc paired up with this soup. It's light enough in body so it doesn't overpower, but the oaky flavours of the wine match the earthy, smoky flavours of the soup. An oaky Chardonnay would also do the trick, and if you want to be super-adventurous, get yourself an Amontillado Sherry, which is a fantastic pairing for brothy soups.

JERUSALEM ARTICHOKE SOUP

This silky rich soup makes an elegant first course or a really great lunch with a nice salad and some good crusty bread. Jerusalem artichokes are lumpy, brown-skinned tubers. They look a little like ginger root but have a sweet, nutty potato flavour. I can tell you from experience, don't even think about skipping the final step of putting the soup through a fine mesh strainer. This last bit of work will take your soup from a 7 to a 10 on the texture scale. **Serves 4**

1/2 cup (125ml) cold, unsalted butter

1/2 cup (125ml) sliced cooking onion

1/2 cup (125ml) celery root, cut in 1/2-inch dice

2 lb (1kg) Jerusalem artichokes, peeled and sliced

6 cups (1.5 litres) light chicken stock

Salt and pepper

- In a saucepan, melt half the butter. Add sliced onion and celery root. Cook, covered, on low heat until softened, but not browned.

- Add Jerusalem artichokes and 3 cups (750ml) of the stock. Add salt and pepper and bring to a simmer. Gently simmer about 20 minutes until the artichokes can be easily pierced with a knife.

- Pour soup in batches into blender and blend until smooth.

- Pour the soup into a fine mesh strainer placed over a clean saucepan. With back of a ladle push the thicker parts of the soup through the strainer until most of it has passed. If necessary, add some stock to adjust the consistency to your liking.

- To serve, gently heat the soup on low heat, being careful not to boil. Taste again for salt and pepper.

- While stirring, add remaining cold butter, bit by bit to the soup. When added cold, the butter adds a shine and richness that is incredible!

- Ladle into shallow warm soup bowls and serve immediately with some lovely crusted bread.

WINE MATCH – **Oaked Chardonnay**

This silky-smooth soup has a buttery flavour to it that meets its match in an oaked Chardonnay. Every time Angie and I serve this pairing up, it knocks people's socks off! Jerusalem artichokes are a somewhat unknown vegetable, but if you love Chardonnay you must find a grocer that sells them, because they are made to be served with the rich, toasty new world styles that are made in California and Australia. Choose a wine that has a nice balance between oak and fruit, then prepare to be impressed.

SPRING PEA SOUP

This little soup tastes and looks like spring in a cup. One thing to note is that when you make a soup to chill down and serve cold you will need to add a little more salt than you would to a warm soup. Chilling the soup mutes the flavours, and without the hot element of the soup there is a lot less aroma. So just make sure you give it a taste before you serve it to your guests. **Serves 4**

2 shallots, sliced

2 tablespoons (30ml) olive oil

1 lb (454g) fresh peas, shelled

2 tablespoons (30ml) dry white wine

4 cups (1 litre) light chicken stock

1/2 cup (125ml) 35% cream, plus a little
    extra for serving

Juice of 1/2 lemon, or to taste

Sea salt and freshly ground black pepper

Fresh pea sprouts for garnish (optional)

- Put a heavy bottomed soup pot over medium heat, add the oil and let it heat through for 30 seconds. Add chopped shallots. Gently sweat (your shallots will look like they are sweating rather than turning a caramel colour) over a low heat for about 5 minutes.

- Toss peas in with the shallots and cook for a further 2–3 minutes. Pour in the wine and cook until the wine has evaporated, about 1–2 minutes.

- Stir in stock and bring to a boil. Season with salt and pepper and turn the heat down to low. Simmer for 15 minutes.

- Blend in a food processor or blender until smooth, then pass through a fine mesh strainer into a bowl, rubbing soup through with the back of a ladle. Leave to cool and refrigerate.

- When the soup is well chilled, whisk in the cream.

- Taste to adjust the seasoning and squeeze in a little lemon juice to give the soup an added freshness.

- Serve in bowls with a little extra cream drizzled on top and the fresh pea sprouts if using.

WINE MATCH – **Grüner Veltliner**

Peas are tricky to match with wine because they have such a vegetal flavour, but that's why we have Grüner Veltliner. My favourite food-friendly go-to white wine brings this dish to a whole new level, and in this pairing it's all about flavour. The fruity, nutty notes in Grüner are the perfect contrast to peas, and the wine has just the right amount of acidity to balance the soup without being too tart. I practically lived on this wine and food match last summer, and I was a happy girl doing it.

LAO FISH SOUP

This soup has a ton of flavour, but where it really impresses is visually. Unlike a puréed soup where you can chop things a little more roughly to start, take an extra minute or two and try to cut the onion, tomato, and mushrooms with a little added care. Although kaffir lime leaves add a distinct flavour of their own, if you can't find them, you can substitute 1–2 tablespoons (15–30ml) of lime zest. Serves 6 to 8

4 cups (1 litre) Asian soup stock (see recipe)

2 tablespoons (30ml) vegetable oil

1 small onion, coarsely chopped

1 teaspoon (15ml) Thai roasted chili paste

3 stalks lemongrass

3 lime leaves

3 slices ginger, sliced 1/8"-inch thick

1/2 cup (125ml) thickly sliced button mushrooms

1 tomato, seeded and cut into wedges

4 fresh Thai chilis

3 tablespoons (45ml) lime juice

2 tablespoons (30ml) fish sauce

1/3 pound (6 oz) firm white fish such as
    grouper or halibut, cut into 1/2-inch pieces

1/2 cup (125ml) coriander leaves

- Put a medium sized heavy bottomed soup pot on medium heat. Add your oil and give it 30 seconds to heat through. Toss in your onion and cook until the onion is soft but not browned. Add the Asian stock to the pot and stir in the chili paste.

- Trim the root end and tough outer leaves from the lemongrass, and then flatten it with the side of a knife. Cut into 1/4-inch lengths and add to the simmering soup along with the lime leaves. Allow to cook for 6–8 minutes.

- Strain the stock through a fine mesh strainer.

- Just before serving, warm soup over medium-high heat until barely simmering. Turn down the heat to low, add the sliced mushrooms and tomatoes and cook for 3 minutes.

- Add the ginger, chilis, lime juice and fish sauce to the soup, cook for 2 minutes. Adjust the flavour with additional lime juice and fish sauce if needed. (fish sauce is the salt in this soup so add it a little cautiously, tasting each time).

- Add the fish pieces to the soup, remove from the heat and allow the fish to cook gently in the stock off the heat for two more minutes.

- Add the coriander leaves and serve.

Asian Vegetable Stock
Makes 16 cups (4 litres)

1 yellow onion

1 leek

4 celery stalks

4 carrots

1/2 bunch scallions

1 garlic bulb

2 stalks lemongrass

1 tablespoon coarse salt

2 tablespoons vegetable oil

1/2 bunch cilantro

1 1/2 oz (42g) dried shitake mushrooms

2 teaspoons black peppercorns

20 cups (5 litres) cold water

2-inch piece of ginger, peeled and sliced

- Don't be too fussy about how you cut all these vegetables since we'll be straining them out. Roughly chop the onion, leek, carrot and scallions. Separate garlic cloves but don't peel them.

- Cut the top half of the lemongrass stalk, make a slit down the side and pull off the outer layer. Throw that part out, but cut the rest of the stalk into 3-inch long pieces. With flat end of knife, give the lemongrass a bash – as well as the garlic.

- In a heavy bottomed stock pot, heat oil over medium heat. Add chopped vegetables and season with salt. Stir well and cook for about 5 minutes.

- Add the rest of the ingredients with the exception of ginger slices, and turn up heat to high. Bring broth to a boil, then turn it back down to a gentle simmer for 20 minutes. Then toss in ginger slices and allow to simmer for 20 minutes more.

- When happy with the intensity of flavour, strain off the vegetables into another large pot and either allow stock to cool and freeze it in smaller quantities for later, or keep it warm to add to your Lao soup. You can refrigerate the stock for up to 3 days or freeze for a couple of months.

WINE MATCH – **Riesling (off-dry)**

There's nothing like the flavour explosion of Asian cuisine, and I love how this dish does it while still being super-light. There's no better accompaniment than an off-dry Riesling for this soup, and here's why. Riesling has a way of being full of flavour while also being light as a feather, and that's just what this dish needs. By choosing a wine that's off-dry, you get a bit of sweetness which cools the heat of the chili paste, and the mouth-watering acidity in the wine balances off the tart flavours in the soup.

PANCETTA KALE BREAD SOUP

A good friend of mine made this soup for me one afternoon and I fell madly in love with it. This traditional peasant soup is hearty comfort food. If you love garlic like I do, the earthy flavour of the kale, combined with the smoky bacon and the soaked chewy garlic toasts in a delicate garlicky broth may draw one single tear from the corner of your eye. **Serves 6 to 8**

2 lb (1 kg) kale

2 1/2 oz (70g) pancetta

6 tablespoons (90ml) extra virgin olive oil

2 cups (500ml) minced onion

3 cloves garlic, finely sliced

Salt

12 thin slices of country style bread, grilled
    or toasted and rubbed with some fresh garlic

2 teaspoons (10ml) freshly ground black pepper

1 cup (250ml) freshly grated Parmesan cheese

- Stem, wash, and finely shred the kale. You will have about 10 cups (2.5 litres).

- Cut the pancetta into a fine dice.

- In a good sized soup pot, heat some olive oil over medium heat. Add minced onions, pancetta and your sliced garlic. Cook until the onion is soft and the garlic is a nice golden colour, but not browned.

- Add in your kale. It looks like way too much, but this stuff shrinks down a lot. Start adding in what you can and mix it in well with the onion mixture. Once you have fit it all in your pot give it about 2–3 minutes to cook down a little.

- Add 10 cups of water and bring the pot to a boil. Once it has started to boil turn down the heat to a simmer and cook on low for about 20 minutes. If you're prepping this soup for dinner this is about as far as you go until about 15 to 20 minutes before you are ready to eat.

Contd . . .

TIP

"Great garlic toast is simple. Brush the bread with some olive oil on both sides and either toast it on a grill or bake it at 350F (180C) in your oven. When it comes out of the oven and is still nice and warm, cut a garlic clove in half and rub it on the bread. This is not only a great toast for this soup, but is also a classic base for bruschetta, garlic bread or just a lovely thing to serve on the table along side soups and salads.

- About 20 minutes before you are going to serve, start to bring the soup back up to a gentle boil, and again, down to a simmer. Taste to see if it needs more salt.

- Put toasted bread in the bottom of each bowl and spoon your soup over top trying to get a good amount of the kale as well as the stock.

- Finish each soup with a drizzle of the best extra virgin olive oil you have, some freshly ground black pepper, and about 2 tablespoons (30ml) of grated Parmesan.

- Serve with some extra cheese and pepper on the table.

WINE MATCH – **Soave**

Though the ingredients in this dish are hearty and flavourful, the end result of this soup is actually quite mild so a light wine without too much acidity is perfect. Soave works well because it's got just a soft tartness to it that doesn't overpower the soup and herbaceous notes that play off the vegetal kale.

LYONNAISE SALAD

I love Lyonnaise salad at brunch, lunch and dinner. It has clean flavours of fresh, warm poached egg and crispy, smoky little pieces of bacon on bitter, hearty endive with curly visual flare. The vinaigrette is kept super simple so it lifts the flavours of all the ingredients. Don't freak out if your poached egg breaks as you place it on the salad. It will anyway as people start to eat, and the yolk, as it coats the endive, melts all the flavours in the salad together. **Serves 4**

1 small head curly endive, washed and torn
   into bite sized pieces
8 oz (225g) bacon, cut into 1/4-inch strips
2 tablespoons (30ml) olive oil
6 tablespoons (90ml) red wine vinegar
Fine sea salt and freshly ground pepper

For croutons
Sliced baguette or good quality bread,
   crusts removed and cut into cubes
Olive oil
Salt and pepper

For eggs
4 eggs
3 tablespoons (45ml) white vinegar

- First make the croutons. Preheat your oven to 350F (180C). In a good sized bowl, toss the bread cubes with the olive oil, salt and pepper. Spread into a single layer on a baking sheet and bake, turning once after about 10 minutes or when bread has turned golden brown. Once they are done pull them out of the oven to cool.

- In a medium saucepan bring 2 quarts (2 litres) of water to a boil and turn down to a gentle simmer. Add the white vinegar.

- Crack each egg, one at a time, into four small cups. With a large spoon give the water a swirl by stirring once or twice in a clockwise motion. While the water is still moving gently slide the eggs one at a time into the boiling water. Cook until the whites are just set which should take about 4 minutes.

- Lift the eggs out of the water with a slotted spoon and slip them into a bowl of warm water while you finish the salad.

Contd . . .

- Put your endive into a large bowl.

- In a sauté pan, fry the bacon until lightly browned. Discard all but 4 tablespoons (60ml) of bacon fat. Add the olive oil to the reserved bacon fat and warm it up slightly on the stove.

- To finish the salad, pour the oil over the endive and toss well. The heat should slightly wilt the leaves.

- Add the red wine vinegar to the hot pan and let cook until it has been reduced by half, about 1–2 minutes. Pour over the salad and toss again. Taste for seasoning and add more salt and pepper if you think it needs it.

- To serve, divide the endive between 4 plates. Sprinkle with the bacon and the croutons. Place a poached egg on top and serve immediately.

WINE MATCH – **Grüner Veltliner**

Eggs are tricky to match with wine because of their very distinct flavour, and so I am relying on good ol' Grüner for this salad. It's perfect here because not only does it work well with the eggs, it has enough acidity for both the greens and the vinaigrette, and has enough body to stand up to the bacon. If you're serving this for brunch, step it up a notch with a bubbly wine like Champagne or Cava.

CARROT AND CUMIN SOUP

Toasting your spices seems like one of those things you might want to skip but it truly makes a huge difference to the flavour in your dishes. If you think this might be something you'll do on a regular basis (once you're hooked you won't think twice) buy a coffee grinder to use only for spices. Your morning coffee will thank you. **Serves 6**

6 large carrots, peeled and roughly chopped

2 onions, peeled and roughly chopped

2 stalks celery, chopped

2 cloves garlic, chopped

2 teaspoons (10ml) whole cumin seeds
(quickly toasted in a skillet until fragrant,
then ground in a mortar and pestle or a
coffee grinder)

3 tablespoons (45ml) canola oil

Salt and a few drops of Tabasco

1 cup (250ml) white wine

4 cups (1 litre) chicken or vegetable broth
brought to a boil

Chopped fresh chives (optional garnish)

Sour cream or crème fraiche (optional garnish)

- In a heavy bottomed soup pot warm oil over medium heat. Add onions and celery and cook about 5 minutes until the onions are translucent.

- Add carrots, garlic and ground cumin seeds to the pot with salt and Tabasco. Cook gently for about 20 minutes, giving it a good stir now and then.

- Add wine and turn up the heat to bring to a boil.

- Pour in hot stock and simmer until the carrots are really tender, which should take around 10 minutes.

- In a blender or food processor, blend the soup until really smooth and creamy. I find it works best if you put the veggie chunks in first and add stock to blend.

- You can put your soup through a fine mesh strainer here or leave it a bit more rustic – totally up to you.

- Serve soup hot in warmed bowls with a swirl of sour cream and some chopped fresh chives.

WINE MATCH – **Pinot Gris**

I love this pairing because the floral aromas in Pinot Gris really highlight the fragrant cumin in the soup. The other important thing is choosing a wine that has enough body, and this wine works beautifully, with its smooth texture and fresh shot of acidity. Be sure to choose a Pinot GRIS, not a Grigio which would be too light. Viognier would be another great choice for this soup.

PEAR AND PECAN SALAD WITH PARMESAN

I use the candied pecans in this recipe on their own all the time. I add them to cheese plates, put them into bowls for snacks or bag 'em and hand them out as hostess gifts on holidays. This salad is sweet, salty, peppery, and tangy all at once. The flavour is complex and pleasing and the presentation generally gets people pretty revved up for the rest of the dinner. Serves 6

1 cup (250ml) pecans

1 cup (250ml) maple syrup, divided in half

2 pears, just ripe, unpeeled, cored and
 sliced vertically

2 bunches fresh baby arugula, washed
 and dried

Vinaigrette

1/2 cup (125ml) white wine vinegar

1 tablespoon (15ml) Dijon mustard

2 tablespoons (30ml) lemon juice

1 1/2 cups (375ml) grapeseed oil

Salt and pepper

Freshly grated Parmesan cheese to taste

- Preheat your oven to 350F (180C). Line a baking sheet with aluminium foil.

- In a small bowl combine the pecans and 1/2 of the maple syrup, stirring to make sure all the pecans are coated. Allow these to soak for about 20 minutes.

- In a second bowl combine the sliced pears with the other half of the maple syrup and marinate while you put together the rest of the salad.

- Drain your pecans and spread them out flat on the cookie sheet. Bake them for 20 minutes or until they are tender when poked with a fork. They will be screaming hot when they come out of the oven so just let them cool before you take them off the cookie sheet.

- Put arugula in a large bowl. If prepping this salad an hour or two ahead of serving, cover the arugula with some damp paper towels to keep it fresh.

- Whisk together the white wine vinegar, the lemon juice and the mustard. Gradually whisk in the oil to create an emulsion and thicken the dressing. Season with salt and pepper to taste. Set aside.

- Heat your grill pan or sauté pan over high heat.

Contd . . .

TIP

I do love salads but one of my pet peeves is over-dressed, soaking wet greens. A trick to avoid this is adding the amount of vinaigrette you think you'll need to just coat half. Add in the remainder of the greens and toss everything together. Adjust as needed. In my opinion the vinaigrette should be a subtle touch and shouldn't be running off the salad and onto the plate.

- Drain the pears and quickly grill so that there are grill marks on one side. If you are using a sauté pan, pull them from the pan and store on a plate once the pears start to get caramel in colour.

- Toss the arugula with the dressing and divide the greens between 6 plates.

- Arrange the grilled pear slices over the greens and the candied pecans on top of that. With a vegetable peeler shave 3–4 Parmesan curls on top of salad and serve.

WINE MATCH – **Malvasia**

One of the most important tips to remember when pairing wine and food is considering the sweetness of both. If you've got sweet elements in your dish, you have to balance that in the wine pairing, otherwise your wine ends up tasting bitter and nobody's happy. This dish has candied nuts and pears. That sweetness plus the acidity in the vinaigrette are the two key things to think about when choosing a wine. Malvasia is often made in off-dry styles, so it has enough sweetness to balance them. I also love the floral aroma and how it plays off the flavour of the pear. If Malvasia's tough to find, try an off-dry Riesling which also works perfectly.

COLD THAI SHRIMP SALAD

I recently sat on my folks' back deck and my mom served this salad for lunch. I've been thinking about it ever since. On a hot, sunny day I have a lot of love for cold potatoes, which in this salad soak up the spicy peanut dressing. The mixture of crisp and tender vegetables with marinated shrimp and the flavourful dressing are truly satisfying. The beautiful thing about making this for a party is that everything is cooked and prepped a head of time in order to chill it back down, giving you little to do once your guests arrive. You can cook the potatoes and the eggs the day before, just leave them whole until you are ready to serve so they don't dry out. Oh yes, with shrimp, 62–80 count means that you are looking for the size of shrimp for which you get 62 to 80 shrimp per pound. **Serves 6**

Dressing

6 tablespoons (90ml) smooth natural
    peanut butter

4 tablespoons (60ml) cider vinegar

1 tablespoon (15ml) brown sugar

1 1/2 teaspoon (7.5ml) salt

4 garlic cloves, minced

2 teaspoons (10ml) lime juice

Cayenne pepper to taste

1 cup (250ml) boiling water.

The Shrimp

3/4 lb (335g) Pacific white shrimp
    (62–80 count) peeled and deveined

2 tablespoons vegetable oil

Zest of 1 lime

2 cloves garlic, finely chopped

1 teaspoon (5ml) crushed red chili flakes

Vegetable oil for cooking

- In a small bowl add all the ingredients for the dressing and pour the boiling water over top. This will help to melt the peanut butter down. Give everything a good whisk and store in a container until you are ready for it. You can make this dressing up to a week in advance if you like.

- Toss the cleaned shrimp with the oil, lime zest, garlic and chilli flakes in a container with a lid and shake to make sure everything is well mixed together. Let the shrimp marinate for 30 minutes.

- Put your potatoes in a saucepan and cover with water. Add about 2 teaspoons of salt to the water and bring to a boil. Cook the potatoes until a knife inserted goes in easily. This should take about 20 minutes. Strain and cool before you pop them into the fridge.

- While the potatoes are cooking, cook your eggs to hard-boiled, 10 minutes. Immediately put them under cold water until they have completely cooled off. Peel and cut them into 6 wedges each.

Contd . . .

The Salad

1 large head Romaine lettuce

2 medium carrots

18 new potatoes

2 ripe tomatoes

1 cucumber

1 red bell pepper

6 hard-boiled eggs

Salt

2 limes, cut into wedges for garnish

- Cut the romaine into bite sized pieces, wash and dry the leaves. Thinly slice the carrots, and cut the cucumber and the red pepper into bite-sized pieces as well.

- Mix together all the veggies (except the tomato which you'll add at the last minute). You can cut the potatoes in half or quarters depending on the size. Add the eggs in at the last minute or you'll have your beautiful yolk pieces all over the place.

- On a grill or in a skillet on high heat, toss the shrimp with some of the oil and cook them for about 1–2 minutes on each side or until the shrimp has turned a nice bright pink. Allow the shrimp to cool and toss in with the vegetables.

- Cut the tomato into 6–8 wedges, add to the salad just before serving, drizzling the peanut sauce all over everything and garnishing with lime wedges if you like.

WINE MATCH – **Gewürztraminer**

This salad has A LOT going on in it, so you could always serve up some sparkling wine with this salad and have a sure hit. But why not try something a bit more daring? I'm thinking Gewürztraminer. With its exotic flavours, mouth-filling texture, and bright acidity, it can stand up to all the stuff happening in the salad and still hold its own.

ROASTED ASPARAGUS WITH CAPER MAYONNAISE

The flavour of roasted asparagus is so perfect on its own that you need to pair it with a sauce that simply enhances rather than takes the dish in another direction. Mayo and asparagus are classic partners as the mayo has a clean tanginess that lifts the flavours of the asparagus. The capers add a salty depth that harmonizes the ingredients and adds a subtle unexpected kick. Serves 6

About 36 or slightly more, medium-thick
   asparagus spears, the ends snapped off

2/3 cup (190ml) extra virgin olive oil

1 teaspoon (5ml) sea salt

12 capers, finely chopped

4 tablespoons (60ml) mayonnaise

4 tablespoons (60ml) heavy cream

- Preheat the oven to 400F (200C). Arrange your asparagus on a baking tray so that each spear is laying flat. Drizzle with olive oil and season with salt and pepper. Slide them into the oven and bake until a knife inserted into the stalk goes in easily, about 8–10 minutes.

- Stir the chopped capers into the mayonnaise. Whisk in the cream. Give your sauce a taste and season if necessary.

- When the asparagus is cooked, arrange on individual plates or on a platter. Drizzle your caper sauce over the asparagus like a belt and serve.

WINE MATCH – **Chablis**

Asparagus has an unusual taste that is tough to pair with wine. But after experimenting with lots of options, I found a match that I love with this dish – Chablis. This is steely, minerally, unoaked Chardonnay from the northernmost part of Burgundy, France. It has lots of acidity that is always important when pairing wine with vegetables (the capers need some tartness as well), but the best part about this pairing is how wine contrasts with the sauce. Rich, creamy mayo up against a super-crisp wine is the yin and yang of yummy.

BUTTER LETTUCE WITH ORANGES, GOAT'S CHEESE, TOASTED WALNUTS AND SHALLOT VINAIGRETTE

This salad is all about mixing textures and flavours. Salty, crunchy toasted walnuts with sweet, fresh oranges and tangy, creamy goat's cheese are a pretty seductive combination on a bed of tender butter lettuce. Because the lettuce is so delicate, it is important for the success of this salad that you dress it moments before you serve it, or the acidity of the vinaigrette will start to wilt the leaves and will make this bright and beautiful salad look flat. Serves 4

2 large navel oranges

1/4 of a small red onion, sliced as thinly
*   as you can*

1 medium head of butter lettuce, washed,
*   dried and torn*

1/2 cup (125ml) goat's cheese, crumbled

1/2 cup (125ml) walnuts

Olive oil

Salt and pepper

Vinaigrette

1/2 cup (125ml) of grapeseed or canola oil

2 tablespoons (30ml) of white wine vinegar

1 medium shallot, minced

Salt

Preheat oven to 350F (180C). Toss walnuts with a little olive oil and 1/2 teaspoon (2.5ml) of salt. Roast them on a baking tray until toasty-smelling and golden, about 10 minutes. Set aside to cool.

- Segment the orange (see tip). Give membranes a good squeeze over your orange pieces and discard.

- In a little bowl, mix your chopped shallot, grapeseed oil and white wine vinegar. Stir in some juice from the oranges to taste, and a pinch of salt.

- Dress the butter lettuce lightly with the vinaigrette.

- Divide the lettuce between the 4 plates. Artfully arrange the oranges on top of the lettuce. Scatter crumbled goat's cheese and thinly sliced red onion.

- Add your toasted walnuts to the plate and finally, drizzle a little more of the vinaigrette over the oranges and the cheese and serve.

WINE MATCH – **Fumé Blanc**

Fumé Blanc works in so many ways with this salad. First, it has lots of acidity, which is an important element for any wine paired with salad (salads have 2 levels of acidity – the veggies and the vinaigrette). A wine with low acid would just taste flat and bland next to a dish like this. Next, it has citrusy flavours that mirror the orange in the salad, and any wine made from the Sauvignon Blanc grape is best friends with goat's cheese, so we've got another amazing pairing right there. Finally, because this wine is aged in oak, it has a nuttiness and a richness that makes the pairing even more perfect with the toasted walnuts in the salad.

Cut a thick slice off both ends of the orange. Stand orange onto a cutting board and use a sharp knife to cut away the peel, trying not to remove too much of the fruit. Hold the orange over a bowl and carefully cut out the segments, dropping them into the bowl with the juice. Avoid the core and discard any seeds.

SPRING SALMON SALAD

This is a really pretty salad. The pink salmon against the green of the spring vegetables makes you want to put on your Sunday best and use your manners. The vinaigrette is the star of the show here. As the cucumber sits in the vinegar, it leaks out flavour and gives the vinaigrette an unexpected freshness. The range of textures in this salad, from the soft tender salmon to the crunchy spring peas will keep your senses awake the entire course. You can make this salad any time, but in the springtime, don't be afraid to add in any fresh in-season vegetables that inspire you. **Serves 4**

Salmon

12 oz (340g) salmon, cut into 3
*   4-oz (110g) fillets*
Lemon juice
Olive oil
Salt and pepper

Vinaigrette

1/2 cup (125ml) English cucumber,
*   cut into a 1/4-inch dice*
1 shallot, finely diced
1 tablespoon (15ml) white wine vinegar
Salt and pepper
2 tablespoons (30ml) extra virgin olive oil

Salad

2 handfuls young ruby red or butter leaf lettuce
1 bunch scallions
1/2 cup (125ml) shelled peas (you can use
*   good quality frozen peas if you like)*
2 to 3 stalks of asparagus, sliced on
*   the diagonal*

Lemon juice
Salt and pepper

- Preheat your oven to 400F (200C).

- Lay your salmon out on a parchment-lined tray. Squeeze a nice amount of lemon juice and drizzle a little olive oil over the fish, season with salt and pepper. Pop it in the oven. It will depend on the thickness of the fish as to how long it will take to cook, but it will likely be between 10–14 minutes. If you are in doubt just flake it open a bit and look to make sure it's cooked evenly all the way through.

- Once it's finished pull it out of the oven and let it cool. Break up the pieces in its natural flakes and set aside or pop into the refrigerator.

- In a small bowl, mix together your chopped cucumber and shallot. Pour the vinegar over top, add a pinch of both salt and pepper and stir in the oil. Give the vinegar some time to soften up the shallot a bit and mellow it out. Set this aside while you make the rest of the salad.

- Wash and dry your lettuce.

- Cut off the ends of your scallions and peel off the outer layer. Thinly slice the scallions on the bias, it looks nice. Put them into a medium bowl.

Contd . . .

- Bring a pot of really well-salted water up to a boil. If you are using freshly shucked peas parboil them until they are bright green and tender to bite, about 30 seconds. Pull them out of the water with a sieve or a slotted spoon. Rinse them immediately under cold running water and set aside in the same bowl as the scallions.

- All asparagus spears, like all people, have a natural breaking point. For the asparagus it's usually somewhere around the bottom third of the stock. Break it off and get rid of the ends. Before you boil the asparagus, get a big bowl of ice water ready. Pop the asparagus into the boiling salted water and boil until it's bright green and you can easily slide a knife through the thickest part of it, 1–2 minutes. Pull out the asparagus and chill down immediately by plunging it into the ice bath. Once it's cooled, maybe 30 seconds or so, pull it out and lay the asparagus flat on a paper towel. You don't want to leave it in the cold water or it will get soggy. Cut the asparagus into 1-inch pieces (cutting them on a bias looks nice here too). Add them to the bowl with the peas and scallions.

- To assemble the salad, dress half the lettuces with about half the vinaigrette. Give the lettuce a taste to make sure it doesn't need any extra salt or vinegar, etc. If you are happy with it then add the rest of the lettuce and dress it lightly.

- Divide the lettuce up onto the plates. Gently sprinkle the salmon onto the lettuces. Dress the scallions, peas, and asparagus with the remaining vinaigrette and scatter them over the salmon and lettuces and serve.

WINE MATCH – **Sauvignon Blanc**

Sauvignon Blanc, especially from Marlborough, New Zealand, has a distinct vegetal flavour to it, and sometimes even reminds me of asparagus or green pea. So since those ingredients are actually in this dish, Sauvignon Blanc is the perfect match here. The wine has lots of acidity which is needed to balance the vinaigrette.

MUSHROOMS ON TOAST

This recipe is one of my all-time favourite lunches. Feel free to switch the variety of mushrooms. I'm sure there are many people who would prefer wild mushrooms to spruce it up, but here, I prefer good ol' button mushrooms. Although the meaty mushrooms in their white wine cream sauce do soften the toast just a little, you don't want your toast to be too crisp or it will crumble too much when you are eating it. A good goal is to toast the bread until crispy around the edges and still somewhat tender in the middle. Use good quality country bread cut fairly thick. Serve with a crisp green salad and of course . . . a glass of wine. Guaranteed, the rest of your day will flow as it should. **Serves 2–4**

2–3 tablespoons (30–45ml) butter

1/2 lb (225g) button mushrooms, sliced

2 cloves garlic, finely chopped

2 tablespoons (30ml) finely chopped shallot

2 teaspoons (10ml) fresh thyme leaves

3 tablespoons (45ml) white wine

3 tablespoons (45ml) 35% cream

4 thick slices of sourdough bread

Olive oil

Salt and pepper

2 tablespoons chopped fresh parsley

- Preheat your oven to 350F (180C).

- Lightly brush bread with the olive oil and season just a little with some salt. Place bread slices on a baking tray and slide them into the oven until they are toasted around the edges and still a little chewy in the centre; you can tell this by giving the bread a poke with your finger or a spoon. Put the bread aside while you make the mushroom cream sauce.

- In a large sauté pan, heat 1 tablespoon (15ml) of the butter over medium-low heat. Once the butter begins to foam, add your shallots, garlic and thyme. Sauté until the shallots are translucent, 2 minutes.

- Turn temperature up to medium and add the other 1–2 tablespoons (30-45ml) of butter. Let it melt and get foamy again and add mushrooms. Season with salt and pepper and cook them until the mushrooms have released their moisture, about 3–4 minutes.

- Add your wine to the hot pan and cook until most of the wine has evaporated; a minute or so.

- Pour in cream and cook for another minute or two until the sauce has started to thicken. Taste again and season with salt and pepper if it needs it.

- Pull pan off the heat and stir in parsley. Spoon the mushrooms on to the toast and serve right away.

WINE MATCH – **Oaked Chardonnay**

Chardonnay that's been oak-aged has toasty, nutty aromas and flavours that complement the earthiness of mushrooms, making it one of my favourite choices for any dish that has them in it. I especially love it with this recipe because both the wine and the dish have rich, creamy textures that balance off each other. Is it lunchtime yet?

SAVOURY SQUASH, ONION AND FETA TART WITH CREAMY YOGURT SAUCE

Phyllo is perfect for those who prefer to avoid making pastry from scratch. Be forewarned though, you need to allow for time to defrost the phyllo properly. In this recipe the crunchy layers harbour some pecans which are ground to provide texture and increase the flakiness of this dish. The sweet squash paired up with the salty feta and the savoury spices is an intense and hearty dish to be enjoyed as a main course or an elegant and unexpected side dish. The yogurt sauce is the perfect accompaniment acting as a palate cleanser and freshening up the flavours with a bit of sour tang. Serves 8

The Filling

4 cups (1 litre) cubed squash (about 1 1/2 lb)

3 medium cooking onions, sliced

Olive oil

4 cloves garlic, coarsely chopped

1 1/2 teaspoons (7.5ml) cumin seeds

1 1/2 teaspoons (7.5ml) ground coriander seeds

1/2 teaspoon (2.5ml) red pepper flakes

1 1/2 cups (375ml) feta, cubed

3 eggs

1/2 cup (125 ml) 35% cream

The Pastry

1/2 cup (125ml) unsalted butter, melted

1 package phyllo pastry, thawed

3/4 cup (190ml) maple candied pecans
   (see Pear and Pecan Salad with Parmesan
   recipe, see page 108), ground

The Yogurt Sauce

1 medium cucumber

2 scallions

2 cloves garlic

2 tablespoons (30ml) chopped cilantro

1 tablespoon (30ml) chopped mint

2 cups (500ml) plain yogurt

Salt and cayenne pepper to taste

- Preheat your oven to 350F (180C).

- In a medium bowl, toss the squash with some olive oil and salt and pepper to lightly coat.

- Lay them out on a baking sheet and roast them in the oven until they are soft and lightly coloured. Let them cool a little and then move them into a nice big bowl. Leave oven on for baking tart.

- Slice the onions into wedges about 1/2 inch thick.

- In a sauté pan, warm the olive oil over medium heat. Add the onions and the garlic to the pan and cook slowly until the onion is very soft but not browned.

- Add the cumin and ground coriander seeds along with the red pepper flakes. Cook for another 5 minutes, you'll find that your spices will start to stick to the pan. Don't blame yourself, just add a tablespoon of water or white wine if you like and give the spices a stir. You are in charge, not them. Once everything has melded together stir this in with the roasted squash.

- Cube your feta to about the same size as the squash and fold it in gently to the rest of the mix.

- Butter a 10-inch springform pan with the melted butter, (springform pans are great for dishes like this because you can remove the sides – it looks and serves better than from a pie plate).

- Lay a sheet of phyllo pastry on a clean work surface. You want the long side of the pastry to be closest to you. Brush the phyllo with butter and cut it into three pieces from top to bottom. Scatter some of the ground candied pecans over each piece and fold it in half the long way.

- Gently lift one and place it into the springform pan, it doesn't matter which way. Line up the next strip just slightly overlapping the first. Repeat previous step and keep going until you have a fully lined pan. You will have to turn the pan to make sure you have sides for your tart the whole way around. Drape the sides of the phyllo over the pan for now.

- Gently add your filling to the shell and even it out with a spatula.

- In a small bowl beat together the eggs with the cream until they are blended. Pour over the vegetable cheese mixture.

- Gently fold the pastry that has been hanging out on the sides of the tart, over the ingredients in the tart so that you have a middle peep hole for the ingredients but a crust that covers most of the surface.

- Brush the tops of the phyllo with the melted butter and place the whole thing on a baking sheet. Pop it into the 350F (180C) oven and bake for about 45 minutes or until the pastry is golden brown and the middle of the tart has set.

- Pull tart from the oven and let it set up for about 10 to 15 minutes before you cut into it. If you have a serrated knife (a good bread knife is perfect) it will make cutting the phyllo a lot easier. If not, use what you have and serve with yogurt sauce on the side.

To make the Yogurt Sauce

- Slice the cucumber in half lengthwise and with a spoon scoop out all of the seeds. Grate cucumber over a clean kitchen towel. Squeeze the grated cucumber in the towel over the sink, to get out all the extra moisture. Set aside in a medium bowl.

- In the bowl of a food processor add the garlic, scallions and the herbs. Add 3 tablespoons (45ml) of yogurt and blend until you have a smooth paste.

- Add this paste and the remaining yogurt to the bowl of cucumber. Mix well and season to taste with salt and cayenne pepper.

WINE MATCH – **Viognier**

Viognier and orange vegetables go well together. There's something about the tropical fruit and spice flavours and the luscious texture of the wine that are perfect for the sweet richness of squash. The tart also has zesty flavours that come from the feta and yogurt sauce, and the Viognier has enough acidity to work with these elements. Try this match out and see for yourself how a simple ingredient like squash can sing with the right wine.

ROQUEFORT AND GREEN APPLE TART WITH WALNUT CRUST

Blue cheese and apples are such good friends, it's nice to see them together in this beautiful custard tart. The cheese will crumble much more easily for you if it's cold. It's also important to cut the apples just before you lay them out on the tart, otherwise they'll turn brown on you and you'll lose some of the visual appeal. I think the walnut crust adds a nutty sophistication but, feel free to use your own favourite pie pastry or your favourite pre-made pie shell. All recipes are made to be altered.
Serves 8

2 tablespoons (30ml) olive oil

1 cup (250ml) chopped leeks, white parts only

1/2 teaspoon (2.5ml) salt

1/4 teaspoon(1.25ml) cracked pepper

3 eggs

1 cup (250ml) 35% cream

1 cup (250ml) Roquefort cheese, crumbled

3 Granny Smith apples

1 egg white, beaten

1 pre-baked walnut crust (see Bittersweet
    Chocolate Tart, see page 332 but change
    almonds for walnuts)

- In a sauté pan heat olive oil over medium-high heat. Toss your leeks into the pan with a pinch of salt and sauté until the leeks are soft and sweet, if they start to get a little colour just turn down the heat a little. Once the leeks are cooked set them aside to cool.

- In a small bowl beat the eggs. Add the cream and a little salt and pepper and set aside.

- To assemble the tart, crumble the Roquefort evenly over the bottom of your pre-baked tart shell.

- Sprinkle your leeks over the cheese and follow with the egg mixture, pouring it overtop.

- Slice the apples into thin wedges. Arrange the apple slices over the tart, covering the entire surface.

- Beat egg white in a small bowl and brush on apples.

- Carefully transfer the tart to a baking tray and pop into your oven for about 20 minutes, or until the egg mixture has set.

- Like most tarts you want to let this one sit for 20 minutes for everything to set up before cutting.

- This is lovely at room temperature as well, so feel free to make it a few hours ahead. When you are ready, cut into wedges and serve.

WINE MATCH – **Riesling (off-dry)**

An off-dry Riesling will work the same way that the sweet-tart flavour of green apple plays off the salty-pungent blue cheese in the dish. Riesling is naturally high in acidity, and when made in an off-dry style, it contrasts with Roquefort brilliantly while mirroring the flavour of the apple.

CRISPY SCALLOP AND POTATO SANDWICHES

A chef tries never to favour recipes, but just between you and me, this is one of my (and Stacey's) all-time favourites. This dish is a most impressive first course – crispy potatoes wrapped over a tender scallop – but the buttery citrus sauce puts the whole dish over the top. **Serves 6**

Scallop Sandwiches

12 large scallops

Salt to taste

Freshly ground pepper

3 large baking potatoes, peeled and washed

2 tablespoons (30ml) flour

1/2 cup (125ml) vegetable oil

Citrus Butter Sauce

2 tablespoons (30ml) fresh lemon juice

2 tablespoons (30ml) fresh orange juice

1/4 cup (60ml) lime juice

1 tablespoon (15ml) sugar

2 tablespoons (30ml) unsalted butter, cold
*   and cut into 1/2-inch cubes*

2 tablespoons (30ml) fresh chervil or oregano

Salt and pepper to taste

- Preheat your oven to 250F (125C). (This is to keep the sandwiches warm as we make them.)

- Slice each scallop horizontally into two 1/2-inch disks. Pat them dry with paper towel, put them on a paper towel-lined tray and pop into the refrigerator until you are ready for them.

- Using a cheese grater, shred your potatoes over a clean kitchen towel. Pull up the corners of the towel and tightly squeeze over the sink until all the extra moisture has been pushed out of the potatoes. Put the potatoes into a bowl and fluff them lightly with a fork. Add your flour and toss. Season with salt.

- Using half the shredded potatoes, prepare 12 small flat mounds about 1 1/2 inches in diameter and lay them on a parchment-lined tray. On top of each mound put a scallop disc. Cover each scallop with the rest of the potato.

- Put a large non-stick skillet over medium-high heat. Add your oil and heat it through for about a minute. You want the oil to be nice and hot, almost smoking but not quite.

- Using a spatula, carefully place 4 of the sandwiches in the skillet. Lower the heat to medium and let the sandwiches cook for about 4 minutes or until the potatoes are golden brown and crispy. Flip the sandwiches over and cook the same way on the other side for 3–4 minutes. Pull the sandwiches from the skillet and put on a paper towel to drain. Season with a little salt.

- Once you've finished all the sandwiches put them (without paper towel) back onto the baking tray and slide them into the oven to keep warm while you make you sauce.

Citrus Butter Sauce

- In a small skillet add your citrus juices and sugar. Turn up the heat to medium and bring to a simmer for about 4 minutes to reduce the liquid by a third and concentrate the flavours.

- Slowly whisk the butter cubes in a little at a time. It's important that the butter be cold, it's one of those chefy tricks that gives your sauce a lot of body and a really nice shine. Keep whisking until the butter has incorporated and the sauce is smooth.

- Add your chervil or oregano and season to taste with salt and pepper.

- Spoon the sauce onto warm plates and top with two of the crispy scallop sandwiches.

WINE MATCH – **Viognier**

Okay, this pairing is sinfully delicious, with all the flavours and textures in picture-perfect balance. Because Viognier is full bodied, it can stand up to the richness of the butter sauce and the fried potato. The citrus sauce echoes the fruity flavours in the wine, and Viognier's luscious texture is the perfect balance for the delicate scallops.

GRILLED SQUID WITH CHILIS

I love this dish – it's fresh and light and something a little different. When it comes to cooking squid it's all about confidence. Do it once and you'll realize how damn easy a dish like this can be. You start by asking your fish monger to clean the squid for you. You want the eyes and mouth removed. The body and the tentacles are all you need. The squid even tells you when it's cooked by curling up. How nice is that? **Serves 4**

4 cleaned squid, each no bigger than your hand

1 fresh red chili pepper, seeded and very
*   finely chopped*

3 tablespoons (45ml) olive oil

Zest of one lemon

2 tablespoons (30ml) lemon juice

1/4 cup (60ml) grapeseed oil

1/4 tsp (1.25ml) kosher salt

Freshly ground pepper

1 ripe avocado

1/2 lb (225g) arugula leaves

1 lemon

- Turn on your grill or grill pan to medium high to heat it up while you get the other ingredients together.

- In a small bowl, whisk together the grapeseed oil and the lemon juice. Season with salt and taste.

- Wash and dry your arugula and put into a bowl with a damp paper towel overtop to keep it from wilting.

- Clean the squid by cutting the body open on one side to make a flat piece, it will be a rough triangle in shape. Keep the tentacles in bunches. Using a sharp paring knife, score the inner side of the flattened squid body with parallel lines 1 cm apart, and then equally apart the other way to make cross-hatching. Try your best not to cut all the way through the squid, you want it about half way.

- Chop the chili and mix it with the olive oil. Brush the chili/oil mixture lightly onto the squid and season with salt and pepper.

- Put the tentacles and the squid body , scored-side down, onto the hot grill for about 1 or 2 minutes. Turn your little squid pieces over. They will curl up as soon as you do, once they have curled they are ready.

- Add your vinaigrette to the arugula to lightly coat.

- Spread the arugula between the four plates in a nice little mound.

- Cut your avocado into quarters and top each plate with some nice slices of avocado. Pop your squid and tentacles on top and finish each plate with a little wedge of lemon.

WINE MATCH – **Albariño**

Albariño is a classic pairing for grilled seafood, and it's perfect for this dish. It has lots of body and lots of acidity, so it balances without overpowering. An Albariño from Spain is a great choice, but if you want something that will cool the spice of the chilis a bit better, look for Vinho Verde from Portugal. Made from the same grape, this style is a bit sweeter and has a refreshing spritz to it that keeps it light and fresh.

MUSSELS IN A DIJON AND SAFFRON SAUCE

"I cook with wine . . . sometimes I even put it in food."

—UNKNOWN

You are going to need some nice bread with this dish because you'll want to sop up every last bit of this insanely addictive, saffron-infused, white wine cream sauce. Saffron is the world's most expensive spice, but you only need a little of this aromatic to go a very long way. It's important that you use the threads rather than saffron powder, as the flavour is much more intense. When you are buying mussels, they should be tightly closed, or close when you tap on them. If they don't it means they're dead and you need to throw them out. If there are a couple of mussels that aren't open in the pan once you've cooked them, those also should be thrown out. **Serves 6**

1 cup (250ml) Pinot Gris

1 medium shallot, finely diced

2 teaspoons (10ml) finely chopped garlic,

5 saffron threads

2 teaspoons (10ml) fresh thyme leaves

3/4 cup (180ml) 35% cream (this is not the time to use milk instead)

1 tablespoon (15ml) Dijon mustard

Salt and pepper to taste

2 lb (1 kg) of mussels, scrubbed and de-bearded

- Set a large deep skillet over high heat. Add your wine, shallots, garlic, saffron, and thyme to the pan. Heat the ingredients through, but don't bring them to a boil.

- Using a whisk, blend in the cream and the Dijon to the mixture. Continue to whisk for about 30 seconds. Taste the broth and season it with salt and pepper.

- Add the mussels to the skillet and gently toss them with the sauce.

- Cover the skillet with a lid and continue to cook over high heat for about 3–4 minutes or until all the mussels have opened.

- Ladle the mussels into bowls with the sauce.

- Serve with crusty bread and of course . . . a glass of wine.

WINE MATCH – **Pinot Gris**

Choose an Alsatian Pinot Gris that will work because the texture of the wine is full enough to stand up to those sweet, buttery mussels, and the fruit flavours contrast with the saffron and the Dijon without being overpowered. It also has just enough acidity to refresh your palate after the cream in the sauce. It's all about balance.

GRAPEFRUIT AND LOBSTER COCKTAIL

This dish is all about class. It's fresh, it's elegant, and it's so freakin' delicious! If you have it in you, prepare your live lobster from home, but if you have a good fishmonger, often you can buy lobsters freshly steamed and therefore save yourself an extra step. **Serves 6**

1 cup (250ml) of cooked lobster meat, from
    all parts of the body except the claws

6 lobster claws, shells removed

3/4 cup (180ml) ruby red grapefruit segments
    (see pg 117 for tip on segmenting)

2 teaspoons (10ml) finely chopped or
    grated ginger

1/2 cup (125ml) red and yellow peppers,
    finely diced

1 tablespoon (15ml) roughly chopped
    fresh cilantro

1 tablespoon (15ml) finely chopped fresh mint

2 teaspoons (10ml) finely diced shallots

Juice of 1 lime or more to taste

1 teaspoon (5ml) of canola oil

Salt and pepper, to taste

3 sprigs chives cut into 1-inch pieces,
    optional garnish

- Roughly chop the lobster meat, but not the claws.

- Segment the grapefruit. Squeeze any juice left from the membrane of the grapefruit over the segments and toss.

- To the bowl of juicy grapefruit add and mix together the ginger, peppers, cilantro, mint, shallots, lime juice and oil until it looks like everything is everywhere in the bowl.

- Add the lobster meat, including the claws to the bowl of grapefruit salad and toss gently to coat. Give it a taste and add any salt and pepper if you think it needs it.

- Toss the bowl into the refrigerator for about 15 minutes to chill it down and to allow the flavours to infuse with one another.

- Spoon the lobster cocktail into 6 decorative glasses and garnish with the chives.

- Serve cold.

WINE MATCH – **Fumé Blanc**

When you're making a dish that has fruit in it, it's fun to pair a wine that has similar flavours. Fumé Blanc has a citrusy, pink grapefruit flavour which matches the grapefruit in the dish perfectly. It also has richer body than most wines made from Sauvignon Blanc grapes (from the oak-aging), which means it balances the richness of the lobster meat.

TIP

Why are there different shapes and sizes of wine glasses?

Just like we have mugs for coffee and martini glasses for cocktails, wine glasses come in different shapes and sizes to suit different styles of wine. Here are the basics that you need to know. White wines tend to have more delicate aromas and flavours, so serving them in a smaller glass (with a smaller opening) helps concentrate them so they are easier to smell and taste. On the other hand, red wines have bigger aromas and flavours so a bigger glass lets you swirl the wine around and let those aromas out. Sparkling wine is best enjoyed in flutes – tall, deep glasses that concentrate the bubbles to keep them lasting longer.

Different glass shapes have been developed to bring out the best flavours and characteristics of different styles of wine. Experiment with these shapes and see if you can notice a difference. The most important thing to look for when buying stemware though, is that the bowl of the glass tapers at the rim. A glass that is narrower at the rim makes it easier to swirl, and it concentrates the aromas in the glass, making the wine easier to smell. And here's a good tip – a standard glass of wine is about 5 ounces, so choose glasses that are at least 10 to 12 ounces in size so you can still sniff and swirl your wine without splashing over the edges.

Ever wonder about the stem on a wine glass and what it's there for? Not only does it make your wine glass look pretty and elegant, it actually has a purpose – for you to hang on to. Especially when it comes to white wine, if you go to all the trouble of chilling it, you want it to stay cool while you're drinking it. And if you've got your hands on the bowl of the glass, your body heat is going to warm up the wine fast.

TIP

What does "nose" mean?

No, wine doesn't have eyes or ears but it does have a nose! The "nose" of a wine is sommelier-speak for how a wine smells – its aroma or bouquet. And surprisingly, though we often talk about wine *tasting*, it should actually be called wine *smelling*, since a lot of what we taste is actually experienced through the nose. Remember the last time you had a head cold? Ever notice that when your nose is plugged up your food doesn't taste like anything? That's why your sense of smell is oh-so-important when tasting wine. And once you get good at smelling wine, it's amazing what you can tell about it without even knowing what it is. Like when it smells like vanilla, caramel, or butterscotch, right away you'll know that the wine was aged in oak. Or when it smells like musty, moldy, wet basement, you'll wonder whether the wine is corked. Picking out all these aromas can be tricky at first, but keep practicing with every glass of wine you drink, and soon you'll agree that your nose knows more than your taste buds.

PAN SEARED MAPLE TROUT WITH APPLE TURNIP COMPOTE

This is a lovely local Canadian dish with a lighter approach to a sauce. The sweet maple syrup on the trout screams Canadian so why not add some apples and turnip to the dish to round it out, eh? A compote is just a chefy term for fruit cooked slowly in a syrup (in this case maple) so the fruit can keep its shape for visual and textural appeal. Serves 6

Trout

2 teaspoons (10ml) vegetable oil

3 rainbow trout fillets, about 6 oz (165g) each,
    halved vertically

1 1/2 tablespoons (22.5ml) good quality
    maple syrup

2 teaspoons (10ml) lemon juice

Fresh watercress sprigs (if you like)

Apple Turnip Compote

1 cup (250ml) turnip, peeled and diced
    into 1/4-inch dice

1/2 cup (125ml) unsweetened apple juice

3/4 cup (180ml) Spy apple, peeled, cored and
    cut into a 1/4 inch dice

1/2 teaspoon (2.5ml) fresh thyme leaves

Zest of 1 lemon

Salt and pepper to taste

- Start by making the apple compote. Put a medium sized skillet over medium heat. Add the turnip and apple juice to the pan and allow to cook for about 3–4 minutes or until the turnip is just tender.

- Add the apples, thyme and lemon zest. Cook until the apples are also tender but not mushy, about 2 minutes. At this point most of the liquid will have been absorbed. Pull the pan from the heat, season with salt and pepper to taste and keep warm.

- With paper towel, pat fish dry and season with salt and pepper. Put a second skillet on high heat. Add oil to pan and allow 30 seconds to heat through.

- Put the trout skin-side down in the hot skillet. Don't move the fish, give it 1–2 minutes to let the skin get nice and crispy, when that has happened the pan will let you take the fish without a fight. Carefully flip the fish and add the maple syrup and fresh lemon juice to the pan. Cook for another minute.

- Remove fish from the pan. Save the juices, you're going to drizzle them over the fish in a minute.

- To plate, divide the apple turnip compote by spooning it on to six plates. Top the compote with a piece of fish. Drizzle reserved pan juices from the trout and garnish top with fresh watercress sprigs.

WINE MATCH – **Vidal**

Always try to either complement or contrast the main flavours of the dish you're serving with your wine pairing. Vidal works well here with the trout because its light sweetness matches the maple syrup, and the fruitiness of the wine is perfect with the apple in the compote. It also has enough body for the flavourful trout. If Vidal isn't available, go for an off-dry Riesling or Chenin Blanc.

WHOLE TROUT PAN FRIED WITH SAGE AND PECANS

I'm pretty sure if sage were a person we would be friends. There is something so comforting and easy going about this herb. With the rich trout and the nutty crunchy pecans, sage seems to bring all the ingredients together. If you happened to have caught your trout and cleaned it yourself, nice work. If you're picking one up from your fishmonger, you'll want to have it cleaned but with the head left on. I really enjoy the simplicity of this dish and would serve it with some sautéed spinach and a nice potato salad. Serves 4

1/4 cup (60ml) all-purpose flour

1/4 cup (60ml) pecans, toasted

2 tablespoons (30ml) dried sage leaves

1 teaspoon (5ml) salt

Freshly ground black pepper

4 trout, about 1 lb each (454g each), cleaned, heads and tails left on

6 tablespoons (90ml) olive oil

- In a food processor pulse together the flour, pecans, dried sage, salt and pepper until the crumb is fine. Lay the coating out in a casserole dish. Sprinkle a little salt and pepper into the inside cavity of the fish and coat the outside with the flour/nut mixture.

- In a large skillet, heat 3 tablespoons (45ml) of the oil over medium-high heat. Carefully slide your trout into the pan and cook for 5–6 minutes, turning the fish only once and pan frying the other side for the same amount of time. The fish should be golden and crisp. Repeat with the second fish and serve immediately.

WINE MATCH – **Riesling**

Riesling is so food friendly, and I love pairing it with meatier fish dishes because it has enough body, especially when made in an off-dry style, to stand up to a fish with so much flavour and weight to it. The bright fruit flavours in the wine refresh your palate after each delicious bite, and contrast with the hearty crust on the fish. The minerally, stony notes in Riesling are also a nice balance to the crust, picking up the nutty, earthy flavours of sage and pecan. You should avoid really light-bodied white wines with this dish – they'd be overpowered by the fish.

ARCTIC CHAR WITH VEGETABLE CONFETTI AND BROWN BUTTER SAUCE

The veggies in this dish are called confetti because you're going to cut them a lot smaller than you would normally. To cut things smaller requires some patience, but, the more you do it the better you get. I find cutting the vegetables into thin strips vertically, then cutting across them horizontally to give you little squares is the easiest way. If you have never tried preserved lemons I highly suggest you get your hands on some. Their intense flavour without the bitterness of fresh lemon adds a huge punch. You can find them in most Mediterranean food stores and gourmet food shops. Serves 4

The Fish

4 pieces Arctic char fillets, 5 oz each (140g),
   skin removed

2 tablespoons (30ml) unsalted butter

1 tablespoon (15ml) olive oil

Salt and pepper

Brown Butter Sauce

1/4 cup (60ml) salted butter (it needs to be
   salted or it won't turn brown for you)

1/2 tablespoon (7.5ml) lemon juice

1 tablespoon (15ml) chives

Vegetable Garnish

1 tablespoon (15ml) of extra-virgin olive oil

2 sweet red pepper, roasted, peeled and
   cut into 1/4-inch dice

2 teaspoons (10ml) thyme leaves

Pinch of saffron threads

2 small zucchini (about 3oz or 85g),
   cut into 1/4-inch dice

10 oz (280g) button mushrooms,
   cut into 1/4-inch dice

2 tablespoons (30ml) dry white wine

1 tablespoon (15ml) finely chopped preserved
   lemon (or finely grated lemon zest)

Salt and pepper

- Preheat your oven to 200F (125C) to keep your ingredients warm once you've cooked them.

- To prepare the confetti, put a large skillet over high heat. Pour in your olive oil and let it heat through, 30 seconds. Add your zucchini, thyme and saffron. Throw in a pinch of salt and pepper and cook for about 2 minutes.

- Add your mushrooms to the zucchini mixture and let them cook for about a minute more.

- Add your red pepper, the wine, and the preserved lemon. Toss to coat and heat everything all the way through. Put the pan with all the vegetables in it into your oven to keep warm.

- Next, season the fish with salt and pepper. In a sauté pan over medium heat, warm up the butter and the olive oil until the butter turns foamy. Slide the fish into the pan and let it cook without moving it for about 4 minutes. Carefully turn it over and cook it for 4 minutes on the other side. Pop this into the warm oven as well.

- The butter sauce needs to be made at the last minute for the best results. You want to be pouring it over your fish while it's still foamy. So, put a clean sauté pan over high heat to get the pan hot.

Contd . . .

> **TIP**
>
> Preserved lemons have been preserved in a salt and lemon juice mixture. The rind becomes soft and edible and is the part of the lemon that you use in cooking, throwing out the pith and the flesh. The flavour is intensely concentrated without the bitterness. They are worth picking up to add to various dishes, as they are becoming pretty popular in mainstream cooking.

- Add your salted butter and turn down the temperature to medium heat. Cook the butter until it gets all foamy and starts to turn to a light brown colour, this will give the butter a really sexy nutty flavour (this is one of those great back pocket sauces you can throw on all types of things, especially fish).

- Once it has turned colour add the lemon juice and the chopped chives. Give it a quick taste and make any adjustment to suit your taste.

- While the butter is turning colour start plating your dish. On four plates divide up the confetti into mounds. Place the char on top. When your sauce is complete drizzle over and around the fish and serve.

WINE MATCH – **Fumé Blanc**

I love the balance that Fumé Blanc brings with its super-tart fruit flavours and rich body from oak-aging. It's perfect for a dish that has elements of both acidity (the veg) and richness (the sauce). The tartness of the Fumé Blanc stands up to the vegetable confetti and the intense citrus flavour from the preserved lemon, and the nuttiness of the brown butter sauce is highlighted by the toasty, nutty notes in the wine. Perfect in so many ways, especially on a warm spring evening.

LINGUINI WITH PESTO AND CHERRY TOMATOES

Pesto is one of those foods that should be in your pantry. I always keep some on hand to use if a soup needs a boost of flavour, or to toss with a simple pasta, add to sauces, or smear on crostini. Collect the big bunches of basil when in season and whip up some of your own in your food processor. Freeze it in ice cube trays and empty the frozen cubes into a freezer bag. There are also a lot of really good store bought pestos around. This is such a simple dish, silly to have in a cookbook, but the thing is when entertaining we usually try so hard we forget about the beautiful little basic dishes. At the end of the summer, pesto and cherry tomatoes on pasta is elegant, flavourful and 100% seasonal. It's even better the next day so make a little extra and keep it for your lunch. **Serves 4**

2 cups (500ml) of basil leaves, washed
   and dried

4 garlic cloves, peeled and chopped

1 cup (250ml) pine nuts, toasted

1 cup (250ml) best quality olive oil

1 cup (250ml) freshly grated Parmesan cheese

1 lb (454g) linguini

1 pint (500ml) cherry tomatoes, halved or
   quartered

- Combine the basil, garlic and pinenuts in the bowl of a food processor. Leave the motor running and add the olive oil in a slow and steady stream. Once everything looks well blended, scrape the pesto into a bowl and stir in the Parmesan. This will be more pesto than you'll need for 4 people so save some in your refrigerator for a week or freeze it in small batches.

- Bring a large pot of salted water to a boil. Cook linguini, drain and toss lightly with a little olive oil. Toss with your pesto and place a little mound on each plate.

- Garnish with your cherry tomatoes and another grate or two of Parmesan cheese.

WINE MATCH – **Sauvignon Blanc**

Something amazing happens when you pair tart Sauvignon Blanc with sweet, ripe tomatoes – the flavours of both somehow jump up a notch. But that's not the only reason for this pairing. Sauvignon Blanc has herbaceous flavours that match the pesto sauce in this dish, and the acidity in the wine is a nice palate cleanser in-between bites.

SALMON WITH CURRY COCONUT SAUCE

I absolutely love coconut curry sauces and am constantly trying to find different ingredients to incorporate into them. Salmon is one of my most recent and favourite additions. I love the meaty salmon with the flavourful green curry, which is a paste generally made from green chilis, cilantro, garlic, lemongrass and Kaffir lime leaves. It comes in jars and you can usually find it in the Asian section of your grocery store or at any Asian food mart. Kaffir lime leaves are plastic-looking green leaves from a lime tree in Asia. When broken open they are super-aromatic, smelling like fresh limes. You'll find them in fresh and dried form and can use either, but like all things, fresh are always better. Fish sauce in Asian cuisine is used as the salt component so add it carefully to avoid over-seasoning your dish. **Serves 6**

The Sauce

2 tablespoons (30ml) chopped shallot

2 teaspoons (10ml) minced or grated ginger

6 scallions, washed and trimmed

1–2 tablespoons (15-30ml) green curry paste,
*   to taste*

1/4 cup (60ml) chicken stock

1/4 cup (60ml) coconut milk

2 good handfuls of fresh Thai basil on the
*   stem (regular basil works, too)*

3 good handfuls of cilantro on the stem

4 kaffir lime leaves, torn

Vegetable oil

Sugar and fish sauce to taste

The Fish

3 tablespoons (45ml) green curry paste

1/4 cup (60ml) vegetable oil

4 pieces salmon fillet, each 5–6 oz (140-165g)
*   and 1 inch thick*

Cilantro to garnish

To make the sauce

- Heat a sauté pan over medium heat and warm up the vegetable oil. Toss in the shallots and fry for 2 minutes until they have softened but not browned, giving them the odd stir.

- Add the ginger, scallions and curry paste and mix in with the shallots.

- Pour in the chicken stock and stir everything together.

- Add the coconut milk and simmer for 3–4 minutes.

- Add 3 handfuls of cilantro and 2 handfuls of basil.

- Pour your sauce into a blender and blend everything thoroughly until it's smooth.

- Wipe out your sauté pan and add the sauce back to pan. Turn your heat to low and warm the sauce through, making sure not to bring it to a boil.

- Tear up lime leaves and add it to the pan, the torn leaves will infuse the sauce within a minute or two.

- Give the sauce a taste and adjust the seasoning with fish sauce (which you're using instead of salt).

- If you find the sauce a little too hot, add a bit of the sugar – it will help balance the heat. Set aside.

Contd . . .

For the Salmon

- Whisk the curry paste with the oil; rub over salmon and marinate for 20 minutes.

- Preheat an oven to 450F (230C).

- Put a nonstick or cast iron pan over high heat. Add the oil and let heat through for 30 seconds or until almost smoking.

- Place 2 fillets in the pan and sear for 2–3 minutes or until golden. Turn and sear the second side for another 2–3 minutes for the same result. Transfer the salmon to a baking sheet and roast until only the very centre of the fillet remains dark pink and a knife inserted in fillet for 5 seconds comes out warm, about 6 minutes.

- Reheat the sauce gently over medium-low heat. Cut salmon on the diagonal into 1/2-inch thick slices.

- Fan slices in centre of 4 large heated dinner plates.

- Spoon the curry sauce around the fish. Sprinkle some chopped cilantro over sauce.

- Serve, with rice in separate bowls.

WINE MATCH – **Viognier**

The richness of coconut milk is hard to match, but Viognier couldn't be more perfect with its luscious texture and tropical and floral flavours. I'm crazy about the way that Viognier can stay in balance while also enhancing Asian seasonings, especially how its ripe, juicy fruit flavours cool the heat of curry. Gewürztraminer is a great alternative if you can't get your hands on a good Viognier.

POACHED HALIBUT WITH PROVENÇAL VEGETABLES AND BASIL

There are times to use store bought stocks, but this is not one of them. Even though it's an extra step, making your own is really pretty easy and freshens up this dish like no store bought stock can. Good news is, you can make it up ahead of time and keep it in your freezer for up to 2 months for such occasions. Aren't you smart! **Serves 4**

The Fish

1 medium zucchini, cut into a 1/2-inch dice
    about 1 cup (250ml)

1 fresh fennel bulb, cut into a 1/2-inch dice,
    about 1 cup (250ml)

1/4 preserved lemon (see tip on page 138)
    or 2 tablespoons (30ml) grated lemon zest

6 cups (1 1/2 litres) poaching liquid
    (recipe on following page)

5 saffron threads

4 8-oz (225g) halibut steaks

Fine sea salt, to taste

Freshly ground pepper to taste

12 ripe grape tomatoes, quartered

1 small shallot, peeled and finely diced

1 tablespoon (15ml) drained capers

2 tablespoons (30ml) extra virgin olive oil

4 fresh basil leaves

12 niçoise olives, roughly chopped

1/2 fresh lemon

- Put all of the poaching liquid ingredients into a big pot. Bring to a boil over high heat. Lower the heat and let simmer for 3 hours.

- Remove from the heat and let stand until cool. Strain through a fine-mesh strainer. Store, tightly covered, in the refrigerator for up to 3 days, or in the freezer for up to 2 months.

- In a small pot, bring some salted water to boil. Blanch zucchini cubes, about 3 minutes. Pull it out with a slotted spoon and into an ice bath to stop the cooking process. Once they have cooled, about 30 seconds, lay them on paper towel to drain.

- Blanch the fennel cubes for 2–3 minutes or until tender. Remove the fennel from the boiling water and into an ice bath as well. If you are wondering why you didn't do them together, it's because they cook at different speeds. You have total control this way. Once they are cooked and cooled you can store them in the same bowl.

- Scrape all the pulp and the pith from the preserved lemon. Cut the rind into a fine dice and add to the zucchini and the fennel.

- Grab 2 cups (500ml) of your poaching liquid and put it into a small saucepan. Bring it to a boil, throw in your saffron and boil for 2 minutes. Set aside.

- In a large pot, bring another 3 cups (750ml) of poaching liquid to a boil.

- Season your halibut with salt and pepper on both sides.

Contd . . .

> ### TIP
>
> I'm always finding myself about to strain the stock down the drain and keep the solids. Trust me, check that you are straining into another pot before you lose the fruits of your labour!
>
> Cutting basil into strips can be done using the chiffonade method. Stack 5 to 10 leaves and roll them lengthwise like a cigar, then slice across to create long, thin strips.

Poaching liquid

4 quarts (4 litres) water

1/2 cup (125ml) Champagne or white wine vinegar

2 cups (500ml) dry white wine

1 tablespoon (15ml) fine sea salt

1 tablespoon (15ml) peppercorns

1 bay leaf

1 tablespoon (15ml) fennel seeds

1 tablespoon (15ml) coriander seeds

4 cloves garlic, peeled

1 large cooking onion, peeled and halved lengthwise

1 tomato, cored

1 medium fennel bulb, root trimmed, halved lengthwise

2 celery stalks , halved

1 medium carrot, peeled and halved

- Once liquid is boiling, turn it down to a simmer, then slide in your halibut steaks. Poach for about 7 minutes, depending on their thickness – poach thinner pieces of fish for a shorter period of time, of course. Remove steaks from liquid when done.

- While you are poaching the fish, in a medium saucepan over medium-low heat, add a little olive oil and lightly sauté the shallots for 1 minute.

- Add the fennel-zucchini mixture, and tomatoes and warm for about 30 seconds.

- Add the capers and the remaining olive oil to the pan. Season it all with salt and pepper. You're not re-frying the vegetables, just warming them all through together.

- Once they are warmed, pull from the heat and stir in the olives and squeeze in juice from the 1/2 lemon.

- To serve, cut the basil leaves into thin strips. Pull the skin off the halibut if it's still attached. Reheat the saffron broth if it needs it. Put your halibut in the middle of the plate, scatter your vegetables over top and pour some of the saffron broth around the whole thing. Sprinkle with basil and serve.

WINE MATCH – **White Rhône Blend**

One of my favourite ways of pairing wine and food is keeping a regional theme, so with all the Provençal flavours in this dish, you can't go wrong with a wine from southern France as well. The Rhône Valley is home to a handful of different grapes that are blended to create ripe, peachy wines with spice and honey notes and refreshing acidity. This style of wine won't overpower the delicate fish, but will hold its own next to the flavourful vegetables. Want something lighter? Try an Italian Soave, which is mild and easy-drinking.

SEAFOOD PAD THAI IN A SPICY TAMARIND SAUCE

When I get a craving for for this dish, nothing else will do. It's the complexity of flavours and the huge variety of textures that makes a big bowl so satisfying. The trick to any stir fry is to have all your ingredients ready ahead of time and in little bowls beside where you fry – just like you have your own cooking show. Thai rice noodles come in a variety of widths, I like the wider ones for this dish. They are also called cellophane noodles and can be found in most grocery stores. Tamarind paste is the pulp from the tamarind fruit, grown in Asia. It's both sweet and sour, and lifts the flavour of all the ingredients it's combined with. You can find the paste in cans or jars in some grocery stores, Asian and East Indian food marts. **Serves 6**

8 oz (227g) Thai rice noodles

1/4 cup (60g) tamarind paste

1/4 cup (60g) warm water

2 tablespoons (30ml) lime juice

2 tablespoons (30ml) grated palm sugar
  (brown sugar will work)

2 tablespoons (30ml) fish sauce

4 oz (110g) firm tofu

1/4 cup (60ml) vegetable oil

2 teaspoons garlic (10ml), finely chopped

2 eggs

1/2 lb (225g) white Pacific shrimp,
  62–80 count, peeled and deveined

20 medium sized scallops (approximately
  the size of a quarter), cleaned

Chili sauce to taste

1 cup (250ml) bean sprouts, washed

3 green onions, stems only (white removed)
  cut into 1 inch pieces

5 tablespoons (75ml) unsalted peanuts, ground

Cilantro to your taste (optional garnish)

5 lime wedges (optional garnish)

Red and yellow bell peppers to taste,
  thinly sliced (optional garnish)

Vegetable oil

- Put a large pot of water on to boil. Once it starts to boil, remove from the heat. Add your noodles, cover and let them soak until tender, about 5 minutes. Drain in a colander, rinse with cold water. Toss with a little vegetable oil to lightly coat and set aside.

- Combine the tamarind paste with the lime juice, sugar and fish sauce. Set aside.

- Cut the tofu into 1/2-inch cubes and set aside.

- Heat oil in a wok over high heat until it's just about to smoke. Add the tofu and cook until golden brown.

- Add your garlic and stir fry for 20 seconds.

- Add the eggs and cook, without breaking the yolk, for 1 minute.

- Add the seafood and cook for 1 minute.

- Stirring constantly, add the noodles and sauce.

- Add the chili sauce, to your liking, for heat.

- Remove the wok from the heat and toss in the bean sprouts, yellow pepper, green onions, and ground peanuts.

- Divide the pad Thai onto 6 plates to serve. Garnish with cilantro and lime wedges if you feel so inclined.

WINE MATCH – **Gewürztraminer**

Thai food is often enjoyed with beer, but us wine lovers have found the perfect match for its complex flavours in Gewürztraminer, and it's becoming the new classic pairing for Thai cuisine. The wine is so aromatic and intense, it stands up to the big flavours in the dish. It doesn't mirror the flavours, but creates a whole new layer that brings the dish up to a new level without being overpowered.

BAKED TROUT EN PAPILLOTE

Baking fish in parchment paper seems a little daunting at first but it's such a flavourful and easy way to cook, once you get the hang of it. By sealing the fish in an envelope you make with parchment paper, it cooks by its own steam, which keeps the meat succulently moist. Throw some flavourful ingredients on top, and a sauce is made for you right inside the package. You can wrap up individual portions ahead of time and store it in the fridge an hour or two in advance. You can also mix it up and use tilapia, salmon or halibut instead of trout if you like – all the steps are the same, the only variation is the thicker the fish, the longer it takes to cook. A traditional way of serving this dish is in its parchment on the plate. Using a knife, you should release the steam from the package for your guests at the table, to avoid burned hands. Serves 4

4 6-oz (165g) filets of trout

4 tablespoons (60ml) crushed coriander seeds

4 tablespoons (60ml) unsalted butter,
  cut into small cubes

2 tablespoons (30ml) lemon juice

2 tablespoons (30ml) soy sauce

1/2 cup (125ml) cilantro, chopped

Salt and pepper

4 pieces of parchment paper,
  about 12–inch square

- Preheat oven to 450F (230C).

- Place one trout fillet on a piece of parchment. Position the fillet about a third of the way from the bottom of the sheet.

- Cover the top of the fillet with 1 tablespoon (15ml) of the crushed coriander seeds.

- Sprinkle 1/4 of the soy and lemon juice over the fish. Scatter the fish with 1/4 of the butter and chopped cilantro. Season with the salt and pepper.

- Fold the larger portion of the parchment over the fish. Fold the edges closed by making continual small folds along the edges. Repeat with the other fillets. Place the packages gently on a baking sheet.

- Bake in hot oven for about 10 minutes. When cooked, gently remove the package to a plate and carefully cut open top at the table. Note that escaping steam can cause burns. Serve in the package.

WINE MATCH – **Pinot Blanc**

You don't want to overwhelm this simple dish with a wine that's too complex, so the perfect choice is the full, fruity Pinot Blanc. This wine has ripe fruit flavours and offers a happy medium of tartness and smooth texture so it'll stand up to the fish. The acidity in the wine is just enough to cleanse your palate and get you ready for another bite. Unoaked Chardonnay is a great alternative that will create a pairing similar to the Pinot Blanc.

ANGEL HAIR WITH FIDDLEHEADS, SMOKED SALMON AND LEMON WHITE WINE CREAM SAUCE

I get excited just thinking about this dish. I love fiddleheads! (I should put that on a t-shirt.) If you can't find them, substitute asparagus. The difference between hot and cold smoked salmon is the time and temperature it is smoked at. The end result is that hot smoked salmon generally looks more cooked through and has a more flaky texture whereas cold smoked salmon tends to be a little more tender in texture and has a more opaque appearance. If you prefer one over the other you can easily switch it up. **Serves 4**

4 cups (1 litre) fiddleheads

12 oz (335g) angel hair pasta

2 tablespoons (30ml) unsalted butter

2 leeks, sliced – just the whites
(wild leeks if you can get them)

4 cloves garlic, minced

1/2 cup (125ml) dry white wine

1 1/2 cups (375ml) whipping cream

1 1/2 teaspoon (7.5ml) lemon zest

1 teaspoon (5ml) salt

1/2 teaspoon (2.5ml) cracked black pepper

1/4 lb (115g) cold smoked salmon, thinly sliced

2 tablespoons (30ml) capers

1 large bunch spinach, stemmed and
roughly chopped

2 tablespoons (30ml) minced dill

2 tablespoons (30ml) minced chives

- Put a large pot and a smaller pot of water on, add some salt to both and bring them to a boil. One is for your pasta, the other for your fiddleheads.

- To prepare the fiddleheads, rub the brown paper scales off and rinse them under cold running water. Trim off the ends and make sure to drain them well.

- Once your pot is boiling well, toss in the cleaned fiddleheads and boil them until they are bright green and crispy tender, about 1–2 minutes.

- Drain them and run them under cold tap water until they have chilled down. Set them aside.

- In a large skillet, melt your butter over medium-high heat. Add the chopped leeks and garlic and cook for 2 minutes, stirring often, until the leeks are soft.

- Pour in the wine and scrape up any brown bits stuck to pan. Bring the sauce to a boil and let it cook until the wine is reduced by half, 1–2 minutes.

Contd . . .

WINE MATCH – **Pinot Grigio**

Fiddleheads are one of my favourite vegetables but tricky to pair with wine. I like Pinot Grigio with this dish because its subtle fruit flavours aren't too pushy when it comes to the ingredients in the dish. But the wine has enough body to stand up to the food, and the acidity in the wine is the perfect contrast to the cream sauce and the richness of smoked salmon. If you want to try something a bit more unusual, get yourself some Grüner Veltliner – it'll wow you with how versatile it can be with different flavours and textures.

- Add the cream and gently simmer until the sauce has slightly thickened.

- Add the fiddleheads, salmon, capers, spinach and half of the chopped herbs. Cook until the spinach wilts and everything else is heated through. Season to taste and pull your pan off the heat.

- While the sauce simmers, cook the pasta, drain and toss lightly with olive oil.

- Serve immediately, topped or tossed with the sauce. Garnish with the other half of the herbs and some freshly cracked black pepper.

TIP

What does it mean when you say a wine has "turned"?

When a wine has "turned" it basically means it has gone bad. The term can be used across the board for any wine faults but there are a few specific problems that it is usually associated with:

Oxidized – much like a wine will smell after it's been opened and sitting on the counter for a week, a wine can have contact with the air before it's been opened if the closure doesn't have a good seal or if it hasn't been stored properly. While wines under screw cap will rarely if ever have this problem, a wine with a cork closure can be affected. The reason wine is usually stored on its side is to keep the wine in contact with the cork, which provides a good seal. If the wine is stored upright and the cork has dried out, air can get in and oxidize your wine.

Old – most wine can age a little bit and still taste good, and some wine can even improve as it sits in the bottle over time. But like most things, wine can reach, and then pass, its prime. Think of a piece of fruit – a mango, for example. When you buy it in the store, it's usually not quite ripe and a little bit hard. If you cut it open at this point, it's edible but not at its juicy, sweet, ripe best. If left to ripen too long though, it passes its prime and doesn't taste that great anymore – overly sweet and almost rotten. Same goes for wine – if you leave it too long, it'll still be okay but not as good as it could have been.

Vinegar – if you've ever heard the term "volatile" that's sommelier-speak for a wine that has turned to vinegar. The wine usually doesn't taste sour but if you get a sharp smell from the wine that reminds you of vinegar or nail polish remover, the wine is volatile and is no good.

GOOD OL' ROAST CHICKEN

There is nothing like a whole roasted chicken to make your guests feel loved. Everyone should have a good roasted chicken recipe that they stand by. Try this one and make it your own. Play with different herbs, butter or olive oil, amounts of garlic, different types of wine, whatever inspires you. When you are doing a whole roast chicken it is worth it to pick up a free range bird that has been grain fed. When the chicken has lived as a chicken naturally should, the reward is much better flavour. Serves 4

Marinade

2 cups (500ml) olive oil

7 cloves garlic, finely chopped

6 sprigs fresh thyme

6 sprigs fresh rosemary

Freshly cracked black pepper to taste

Chicken

1 free range chicken, 4 lb (2 kg)

1 lemon, cut in half

3–4 sprigs thyme

3–4 sprigs rosemary

Salt

Sauce *(optional)*

1/2 cup (125ml) dry white wine

1/2 cup (125ml) chicken stock

3 tablespoons (45ml) cold butter (cubed)

Salt and pepper

- In a bowl large enough to fit your chicken, mix all marinade ingredients. Put chicken into the bowl and turn it over a couple of times to coat. If you have the time, refrigerate your chicken overnight, turning it over a few times to re-coat. If you are planning on using the chicken this evening give it at least 2 hours to marinate in your fridge. Pull from the fridge and bring up to room temperature for 1 hour.

- Preheat your oven to 425F (220C).

- Stand the bird up on its neck holding the back end. Season the inside cavity with salt and pepper, push the herbs and the two lemon halves into the cavity and tie the legs closed.

- Season the outside of the chicken with salt and pepper and put into a heavy duty roasting pan. Roast the bird for about 45 minutes to an hour (or 18 minutes per pound), until a meat thermometer registers 160F when the thickest part of the thigh is pierced .

Contd . . .

- Pull the chicken from the pan and let it rest for 10 minutes. It's been busy.

- If you feel like making a sauce for the chicken you can pour out the chicken juices from the pan (which are mainly fat) into a container and discard or save for another use.

- Pour 1/2 cup (125ml) of white wine and a 1/2 cup (125ml) of chicken stock to the roasting pan and scrape off all the brown bits to add flavour to your sauce. Boil the sauce for about 5 minutes to reduce and add 3 tablespoons (45ml) of cold cubed butter in batches, whisking. Give the sauce a taste and adjust the seasonings.

- Carve and serve your chicken, and ladle each piece with a nice drizzle of your sauce.

WINE MATCH – **Oaked Chardonnay**

Going back to the basics inspires a wine equally as comforting, so a nice buttery oak-aged Chardonnay fits the bill. Go for a white Burgundy for its classic, elegant style of fruit-oak balance. The wine won't overpower the mild flavour of the chicken, and it'll enhance the crispy, golden skin and the herbs used to season the chicken. The subtle lemony flavour of the bird will also be highlighted by the fruit flavours in the wine. And if you're a die-hard red wine drinker, Pinot Noir will complement without overpowering.

CHICKEN AND LEMON POT PIE

I know, you can argue this isn't really a pie because I've left out the crust. You can add one if you like but I find the puff pastry to be rich enough to satisfy my cravings without my insides feeling super-heavy afterwards. You will be making what is called a roux in this recipe, which is a mixture of butter and flour cooked together for a minute or two to get rid of the flour taste. That mixture is then thinned out with a liquid, like stock or cream. The roux thickens the sauce and is used in cooking quite a bit; it comes in and out of fashion. Now that you know what it is, you'll recognize it in many other recipes. **Serves 4**

2 tablespoons (30ml) olive oil

2 tablespoons (30ml) lemon juice

1 1/2 lb (675g) boneless, skinless chicken
    breasts

Salt and freshly ground pepper

Filling

2 teaspoons (10ml) finely minced garlic

1 large cooking onion, chopped

3 tablespoons (45ml) unsalted butter

3 tablespoons (45ml) all purpose flour

2 cups (500ml) chicken stock

2 teaspoons (10ml) dried tarragon

3 carrots, halved and cut into 1-inch pieces
    (1 1/2 cups, [375ml])

1 cup (250ml) of russet potato, peeled
    and diced into 1/2-inch cubes

1/4 cup (60ml) chopped dill

2 tablespoons (30ml) lemon juice

1 teaspoon (5ml) grated lemon rind

1/4 cup (60ml) 35% cream

Salt and freshly ground pepper

3/4 cup (180ml) green peas, defrosted if frozen

1 sheet prepared puff pastry, look for pre-rolled
    if you can find it and thawed if frozen

1 egg, beaten with a pinch of salt

- In a large bowl mix together the lemon juice and the oil. With a paper towel, pat the chicken dry and season the breasts with salt and pepper and toss together with the lemon juice/oil combo. Preheat your oven to 375F (190C).

- Lay your chicken onto a baking tray and cook until slightly pink in the centre, about 7 or 8 minutes, then remove from oven and let it cool.

- When you can handle it without burning your fingers, cut it into a 1 1/2 inch dice and set it aside.

- Heat butter in a skillet on medium heat. Add your onions and garlic and sauté for about 3 minutes, stirring often.

- Sprinkle in the flour and the tarragon and cook, stirring constantly for 1–2 minutes more.

- Add the carrots, potatoes, lemon juice, lemon rind and chicken broth and bring everything to a boil. Reduce the heat to a simmer and cook gently for about 20 minutes or until the vegetables are tender.

- At this point add in the peas, dill, chicken pieces and whipping cream. Season with salt and pepper to taste and simmer for 3–5 minutes longer or until your stew is looking thick and glossy.

Contd . . .

What does it mean when you say a wine is "corked"?

A "corked" wine is the most common wine fault you'll come across. It basically means that the wine has been affected by "cork taint" which makes your wine smell and/or taste musty or moldy (think wet basement, wet cardboard, or wet newspaper) or sometimes just a little bit flat (not as fruity and delicious as it should be). A wine can be overwhelmingly corked or just a teeny bit corked so unless you're good at picking it out you might end up drinking one without knowing it. Luckily for us, it's not poisonous to drink corked wine, just not quite as tasty. Cork taint comes from a bacteria called TCA (trichloroanisole) which can grow in the cork – the higher the level of TCA the more corked the wine will smell or taste. And that's why screw caps are becoming more and more popular.

- Spoon this mixture into a 2 quart (2 litre) ovenproof casserole dish.

- If you need to, roll out the puff pastry on a lightly floured surface to form a shape 2 inches larger than your casserole dish. Lay the pastry over the top, trimming the overhang to 1 inch and crimping the edges to seal the puff to the dish.

- Make some incisions in the top of the pastry to let steam escape. Brush the pastry with beaten egg.

- Slide your little pot pie on the middle rack in your oven for 30–35 minutes or until the pastry is a golden colour and the mixture is bubbly.

WINE MATCH – **Unoaked Chardonnay**

Unoaked Chardonnay is a nice balance of medium body, crisp acidity, and ripe fruit flavours so it works with lots of different flavours. With this dish, it has enough body for the rich filling and the acidity in the wine cuts through to refresh your palate. And the tart, fruity flavours complement the lemon flavour in the dish. Simple dish + simple wine = happy cook and happy diners.

CHICKEN ROULADE WITH APRICOTS AND TARRAGON

You may be wondering what in Sam Hill a roulade is. Basically it's thin meat that has been rolled around a filling. It sounds better than "chicken roll," which doesn't make your mouth water quite the same way. This is such a lovely tasting dish but the show-stopper really is in the presentation. You have to slice it for your guests to really show off. Feel free to vent when you are pounding out the meat, just be careful not to tear the meat or the rest of your job will be tough. **Serves 6**

1 cup (250ml) good quality day old bread,
  crusts removed, cut into 1/4-inch cubes
2 teaspoons (10ml) olive oil
1/2 cup (125ml) chopped cooking onion
1/4 cup (60ml) chopped celery
1 teaspoon (5ml) chopped fresh tarragon
  leaves
1/4 cup (60ml) chopped dried apricots
1 1/4 (310ml) cups chicken broth
1/4 cup (60ml) canned apricot nectar
1 1/2 tablespoons (22.5ml) Dijon mustard
6 large boneless, skinless, chicken breasts
Butcher's twine or skewers for securing
  roulades
1 tablespoon (15ml) olive oil
1/4 cup (60ml) dry white wine

- Preheat oven to 350°F (180C).

- Toss bread cubes with salt and pepper and lay out flat on a baking tray. Toast the bread, giving it a stir or two for about 8–10 minutes until the cubes are golden and toasty. Leave oven on for the chicken.

- Warm a large skillet over medium heat, and add the olive oil. Toss in the onion and celery and cook for about 5 minutes, until the onion is soft and sweet, but not browned.

- Stir in the tarragon, apricots and 1/4 cup (60ml) of the broth. Cook until almost all of the liquid has evaporated, about 2–3 minutes.

- In a big bowl stir together the toasted bread cubes and the onion mixture from the pan. Give the stuffing a taste, season with salt and pepper to your liking and put the bowl aside to let everything cool down. Once cooled put the stuffing into the fridge, up to a day in advance.

- In a small bowl whisk together the apricot nectar, the mustard and the rest of the chicken broth. Set this aside as well for up to one day.

- This is the best part of the recipe. I find this so cathartic at the end of a day. With a paper towel, pat your chicken dry and slide into a heavy duty freezer bag. Gently pound the breasts until they are about 1/4 inch thick.

Contd . . .

- Season the breasts with salt and pepper. With a spoon, or your hands, lay a tablespoon (15ml) of the stuffing out on the breast leaving a bit of an empty frame around the border of the flattened breast. It's tempting at this point to jam as much stuffing as you can get in there but you need to roll these up and have them cook without popping open on you.

- Roll the breasts up tightly to enclose stuffing. At this point you can either secure the seams with skewers or toothpicks, or if you have butcher's twine, tie up the breast in 3 or 4 places so it looks like a little roast.

- Warm your skillet over medium high heat. Add some more olive oil to the pan and warm it through until it's pretty hot, but not quite smoking. Pop each roulade into the pan without crowding, the breasts should have about an inch of space between them. Let them sit for three minutes. When the chicken has a golden brown crust, the pan will tell you by letting go of the breast.

- Once you have a nice sear, turn the roulade over to get the same colouring all the way around. As you finish them pop into a casserole dish in one layer.

- When you have finished browning all the roulades, turn the heat down to medium and pour your wine into the pan. With a wooden spoon scrape up any of the brown chicken bits that are left in the pan, this is actually where the flavour is going to come from in your sauce.

- Add the apricot nectar mixture to the wine, give it all a good stir and pour the whole thing over your beautiful little roulades.

- Cover the casserole dish tightly with foil and braise in the middle of your oven for about 25–30 minutes, or until the chicken is just cooked through.

- Once these are cooked through, move them to a cutting board and lose either the skewers or the string. Cover with tinfoil.

- Pour the liquid in the baking dish into a small saucepan and bring it up to a boil until it's been reduced by half, about 5 minutes. This concentrates the flavours and thickens the sauce. When it has reduced, taste for seasoning. While your sauce is rapidly boiling, cut the roulades diagonally into 1/2-inch thick slices and spoon sauce over top.

WINE MATCH – **White Rhône Blend**

The weather in the southern Rhône Valley is hot and sunny, which means ripe, sweet grapes and full bodied, juicy wines. Just the thing to balance off the sweet apricot filling in this dish. Remember, any element of sweetness in your food needs a wine that has some sweetness to offset it, and if the wine's not actually sweet, it can still work if it has ripe, juicy flavours that mimic the same effect. See if you can find one that has lots of Marsanne and Roussanne in the mix for a super-ripe, fruity wine. A straight-up Viognier will also work nicely with this recipe.

WHITE CHICKEN STEW WITH GARLIC

This is a classic French stew, invented a gazillion years ago. It has stood the test of time because it's delicate, refined and soul-satisfying. It's also not too much work. When you cook the ingredients for this dish, make sure you don't get any colour on the onions, or the chicken. If you do it won't be the end of the world but the stew doesn't look as pretty. Caramel colour on foods also lends its own flavour which in many cases we love, but here you need to pay attention and be a little gentler for the clean flavours we want to achieve. Serves 4

4 lb (2kg) whole free range chicken,
    cut into 8 pieces by your butcher
1/4 cup (60ml) unsalted butter
1/2 cup (125ml) diced carrot, 1/4 inch cubes
1/2 cup (125ml) diced cooking onion
    1/4-inch cubes
8 small cloves garlic, peeled but left whole
3 tablespoons (45ml) chopped shallots
2 sprigs rosemary
1 bay leaf
1 clove
1/2 cup (125ml) dry white wine
1/2 cup (125ml) chicken stock
1 cup (250ml) 35% cream
Salt and pepper

- Preheat your oven to 425F (220C).

- With a paper towel, pat the chicken dry and season the pieces with salt and pepper.

- In a big wide oven-safe pot, melt the butter on a medium-low heat. Once the butter has melted, add your chicken pieces skin-side down. In this case we don't want to get any colour on the skin, we just want it to cook slightly, turn it white to warm up the chicken pieces and get the cooking started on the right foot. As one side becomes white flip the piece over and do the same to the other side. Pull the chicken pieces from the pot and set them aside.

- Add the carrot, onion, garlic, shallots, rosemary, bay leaf and clove to the pot; cook until vegetables are softened.

- Add leg meat to your pot. Throw a cover on it and put into the oven to bake for 20 minutes.

- Because breast meat takes less time to cook we add the breast meat after the initial 20 minutes and bake until everything is cooked through, about 10 minutes longer after you've added the breast. Check to make sure there is no pink in the center. Remove chicken and the garlic cloves and keep warm.

Contd . . .

TIP

To cut a whole chicken into 8 pieces for a stew like this, cut the legs from the body. If you are unsure how to do this just start to cut down where you think you should and pull the leg down at the same time. Eventually there are two joints that come apart naturally so just follow that down with your knife. Now cut those two pieces into thigh and drumstick. Same principal applies, cut where you think the two will come apart and wiggle the drumstick a little, it will help to show you where the two bones separate. To take off the breasts, look for the backbone. Use your knife to remove the backbone and cut away the two breasts with the bone still on. Cut the breast into two.

If you aren't comfortable taking the chicken apart, ask your butcher to do it, but take a good look at the pieces. It will give you a visual of what you want to accomplish yourself one day. It's quite empowering.

- To make the sauce, put the pot back on the stove over medium heat. Add the white wine and the chicken stock to the pot. Bring the sauce to a simmer and let it continue to simmer for 10 minutes. Strain it into a clean saucepan.

- Bring to a boil and reduce it for 5 minutes longer. When you are happy with the intensity of flavour whisk in the cream and on a gentle simmer thicken the sauce for about 3 more minutes. Adjust the seasoning and return chicken and garlic to the sauce; heat gently through.

- To serve, place a piece of white and dark meat on a warm plate. Ladle some sauce and garlic over chicken and serve.

WINE MATCH – **Pinot Blanc**

This recipe is all about the flavour of chicken. The sauce is mildly flavoured with garlic, but it's rich with the cream that's added, so while you want a full-bodied wine, you don't want anything with overpowering flavours. Pinot Blanc is an excellent choice, because it gives you nice full body, and soft, ripe fruit flavours. You could substitute an unoaked Chardonnay here as well if you like.

SPRING POACHED CHICKEN

I get so excited for new spring vegetables after a long winter than I can't think of anything else to do but throw as many as possible into a huge pot, add a chicken and let it cook for a light and healthy meal. If you've never added flavoured mayo to a dish before it may freak you out slightly. Be prepared to be seduced. From beginning to end, this is one dreamy dish. **Serves 4**

4 1/2 lb (2.25 kg) whole free range chicken

1/2 bunch fresh flat leafed parsley

1/2 bunch fresh thyme

4 bay leaves

1 tablespoon sea salt

14 whole black peppercorns

3 cups (750ml) new potatoes scrubbed or
*   fingerling potatoes if you can find them.*

1 to 2 bunches baby carrots

2 handfuls baby turnips

1 fennel bulb, quartered, herby tops
*   removed and reserved*

2 handfuls fresh shelled fava beans or
*   green beans, cleaned*

2 handfuls fresh peas

1 bunch spinach, cleaned really well
*   and roughly chopped*

Olive oil

2 cups (500ml) mayonnaise

1 large clove garlic, minced

3 tablespoons (45ml) lemon juice

1 tablespoon (45ml) each of chopped chervil
*   (or parsley), chives and tarragon*

- Into a large stock pot put your chicken, parsley, thyme, bay leaves, salt, potatoes and enough water to cover the chicken by about an inch. Turn heat on high and bring the whole kit and caboodle to a boil. Once it's boiling, turn down heat, pop a lid on top, and simmer for about 20 minutes.

- Now add your baby carrots, turnips and your fennel. Simmer gently for another 30 minutes.

- On another burner, bring a medium saucepan to a boil with salted water. Toss your green beans or fava beans in until they are just tender and bright green, about 1 minute. Once they are, pull them from the boiling water with a slotted spoon and run them under really cold tap water.

- Add your peas and cook the exact same way, running them under cold water once they are tender. Set aside.

- Now is a good time to mix together the mayonnaise with the garlic, lemon juice and chopped herbs. Cover and set aside.

Contd . . .

- You can tell the chicken is cooked when you gently tug on the leg (try not to pull it off) and it easily comes away from the chicken. When this happens, gently remove the chicken from the broth and put it onto a cutting board, cover loosely with tinfoil and let rest.

- Toss your peas, beans and spinach into the broth.

- Carve up your chicken, cutting off or pulling off the legs and carving off the breasts.

- Taste the broth and season with salt and pepper to taste.

- To serve, divide up a good mixture of vegetables from the broth between 4 bowls and lay a piece or two of the chicken on top.

- Ladle some of the broth over top and serve with a nice dollop of your herby mayonnaise.

WINE MATCH – **White Bordeaux**
(Sauvignon Blanc/Sémillon blend)

This dish is so flavourful yet so light, so why not pick a wine that's just the same? I love the baby vegetables in this dish but the tricky thing is to find a wine that is delicate enough to not overpower their sweet, tender flavours and textures. The Sauvignon Blanc/Sémillon blend is just the ticket. It has crisp acidity from the Sauvignon Blanc and soft, mellow flavours from the Sémillon. Look for one that hasn't seen too much aging in oak (if any) – there are some great ones from Australia, or look for a white wine labelled "Bordeaux" or "Meritage." Dry Riesling or an unoaked Chardonnay would also be nice pairings.

JERK CHICKEN SWEET POTATO SALAD WITH COCONUT

Stacey introduced this salad to me, knowing my affection for sweet potatoes. I'm always in for a hint of sweetness paired up with something spicy. That's what I love about the flavours of this hearty salad. There are plenty of really great jerk sauces which you can find at any grocery store. It saves a few extra steps, which I'm always in support of so long as the food doesn't suffer and there will be none of that with this dish, only glory. 6 to 8 main course servings

The Chicken

1/4 cup (60ml) vegetable oil

8 whole chicken legs (4 1/2 lb or 2.25 kg),
    thighs and drumsticks separated

3 to 4 skinless, boneless chicken breasts

Your favourite store bought jerk sauce

Dressing

3 limes

1/3 cup (90ml) grapeseed or vegetable oil

2 tablespoons (30ml) honey

2 tablespoons (30ml) jerk sauce

2 cloves garlic, finely minced

1 teaspoon (5ml) minced jalapeno pepper

1/4 teaspoon (1.25ml) ground cumin

1/4 teaspoon (1.25ml) salt

The Salad

3 lb (1.5 kg) sweet potatoes

1 avocado, peeled, pitted and sliced
    1/4 inch thick

1 small bunch arugula, washed and torn

1 to 2 tablespoons grapeseed or vegetable oil

1/4 cup (60ml) coarsely chopped cilantro

2 large scallions, thinly sliced

1/4 cup (60ml) roasted and salted peanuts

1/4 cup (60ml) unsweetened coconut
    flakes, toasted

- Spread 1/2 cup (125ml) of the jerk sauce over your chicken pieces. Cover and refrigerate for at least two hours and up to one day.

- Make your salad dressing by zesting your limes and squeezing the juice into a ridiculously large bowl (we're going to be adding the chicken and the sweet potato just after they've cooked) with the oil, chutney, jerk sauce, minced garlic, the jalapeno pepper, cumin and finally the salt. Give everything a good whisk and set it aside.

- When you are ready to make the salad, preheat your oven to 400F (200C).

- Cut your potatoes into quarters, rub with some oil, season with salt and pepper and lay out on a baking sheet. Roast your potatoes until tender, about 15–20 minutes.

- Lay your chicken pieces on a baking sheet and roast until cooked through, 10–15 minutes.

- Once the potatoes are done, allow them to cool until you can handle them without burning your fingers. Cut them into a 1/2-inch dice, it doesn't have to be a perfect dice. You can lose the potato skins at this point.

- Throw the potato pieces into the salad dressing and give it a good toss.

Contd . . .

- When you can handle the chicken, shred the meat off the bone and into the salad dressing with the potatoes.

- Gently toss it all until the chicken, potatoes and dressing are all mixed together. At this point you can store all this meaty potatoey goodness for up to a day in the refrigerator.

- When you are ready to serve this salad, toss in the arugula, avocado, chopped cilantro, scallions, peanuts and the lightly toasted coconut flakes.

WINE MATCH – **Viognier**

This dish has a lot going on with spicy jerk sauce, sweet potato, peanuts, and toasty coconut, and each and every flavour is brought out when you pair this salad with Viognier. The luscious tropical fruit flavour and texture is the perfect balance to all the elements of this dish. If you're out on the patio enjoying this, a crisp, chilled-down rosé would also work and there's always super food-friendly Grüner Veltliner – I've enjoyed this dish equally as much with all three of the these choices.

PORK TENDERLOIN WITH TOMATILLO PESTO

Who said pesto has to have basil? In this pesto we are combining tomatillos with toasted pumpkin seeds, cilantro and a few other choice ingredients to make a tart, über-fresh pesto. Tomatillos are sort of a Mexican green tomato. They are really firm, have a thin papery husk around them and taste a little like lemon and apples. They have incredibly fresh flavour and are going to lift this dish to a whole new level. Serves 4

2 pork tenderloins, about 8–12 oz

(224–335g) each

The marinade

1/2 cup (125ml) sugar

1 1/2 tablespoons (22.5ml) salt

1 tablespoon (15ml) dried thyme

1/2 tablespoon (7.5ml) ground cumin

2 crushed bay leaves

1 tablespoon (15ml) black peppercorns

1 teaspoon (5ml) dried oregano

3 tablespoons (45ml) chili powder

4 whole allspice berries

4 cloves

1 stick of cinnamon

6 cups (1.5 litres) water

Tomatillo Pesto

1/2 cup (125ml) of hulled pumpkin seeds

1/2 cup (125ml) good quality olive oil

12 tomatillos, husked, rinsed and cut in half

1 cup (250ml) (packed) fresh cilantro

1 tablespoon (15ml) of sugar

Juice of 1 or 2 limes

5 cloves of garlic, peeled

A little extra olive oil for the tomatillos

- In a container large enough to hold both of the tenderloins, mix together all of the marinade ingredients and give it a good whisk. Slide in the pork loins, cover and pop into your refrigerator for a minimum of 4 hours but overnight if you can.

- When you and the meat are ready, pull the pork out of the marinade and let it come to room temperature. Season the loins with salt and pepper.

- Preheat your oven to 400F (200C).

- Put a large skillet over high heat. Add your olive oil and once it looks like it's about to smoke turn down the heat to medium high. Add your pork and sear until golden brown on each side. This will take 1–2 minutes per side. The pan will let go of the meat once the sear has happened so don't fight with the pan. It always wins.

- Once you've browned the loins, put them on a baking sheet and throw them into your oven for about 20 minutes, or until a meat thermometer reads 140F (60C). It's okay for your pork to be a little rosy. Pull the meat out of the oven, loosely cover with foil, and let it rest for at least 10 minutes. When the meat is ready, slice the tenderloins on a diagonal.

Contd . . .

TIP

You really need to marinate pork tenderloin, otherwise it's pretty bland. If you take a look at the tenderloin you'll see that there is very little fat. No fat, no flavour, no problem, we just need to be prepared to marinate the meat for a minimum of 4 hours but ideally overnight.

- While you are roasting the meat, whip off your pesto. In a clean skillet, dry toast your pumpkin seeds until they are golden and starting to make some popping noises. Move them out of the pan and into your food processor or blender. Add olive oil to the seeds and give them a quick blitz to break them up.

- Put the same skillet back on the stove over medium high heat. Once it has warmed, add a little more olive oil and warm through, about 30 seconds. Put your tomatillos cut-side down in the pan and sear them until they get some golden brown colour. Flip them over and sear the other side as well. You aren't trying to cook the tomatillos the whole way through here. We're just giving them some colour and adding a little flavour to your pesto.

- While you are searing the tomatillos, toss the cilantro, sugar, lime juice and garlic into the food processor with the pumpkin seeds and purée until everything is pretty smooth.

- Add the tomatillos once they are seared and blitz it all together again.

- Give the pesto a taste and adjust any changes you think need to be made. If it's too bitter, add a little more sugar, or maybe it needs a little more lime juice. If it's perfect than leave it be.

- To plate, either lay out the pork slices on a platter or on individual plates and drizzle the pesto over the pork.

WINE MATCH – **Albariño**

I love using a regional theme with my wine pairings, and with the Latin-inspired tomatillo pesto, I wanted a wine that brought to mind the same theme – hot sun, crystal-clear water, and powder-white sand. Albariño was my first thought, with its Mediterranean origins and its food-friendly qualities. Not only does this wine balance the tartness of the tomatillo, it has a full, creamy texture that won't be overpowered by the dish as a whole, with the spices and the tender, yet flavourful meat. This is a wine that's definitely worth seeking out for this recipe, but if you'd rather something more mainstream, a dry Riesling is a good substitute.

PORK CHOPS WITH APPLES, GRAIN MUSTARD AND CREAM

Pork, apples and sage are like the rat pack of flavours. They have a similar style and complement each other perfectly with a sweet earthiness that just warms the soul. Seasoning the pork chops the night before adds a ton of flavour and tenderizes the meat. It also helps the meat to cook more evenly. Cooking meat with the bone in helps to distribute both flavour and heat as well.

4 pork chops, each 1 1/2-inch thick, bone in

Cracked black pepper

Kosher salt

2 tablespoons (30ml) grapeseed or
  vegetable oil

6 large sage leaves, sliced into small strips

5 cloves of garlic smashed

1 red onion, diced

2 Granny Smith apples, cored and cut
  into thick slices

1 3/4 cup (435ml) chicken stock

3/4 cup (190ml) dry white wine

2 tablespoons (30ml) cider vinegar

1/4 cup (60ml) of grainy Dijon mustard

1 cup (250ml) heavy cream

- Preheat the oven to 350F (180C).

- Season pork chops with salt and pepper, cover and pop into your fridge for a minimum of 4 hours but ideally overnight. Pull the chops from the refrigerator 1/2 hour before you are about to cook them and let them come to room temperature.

- Heat a heavy bottomed skillet, large enough to fit 4 chops, over medium-high heat until the skillet is starting to smoke. Add oil, scoot it around the pan and add pork chops. Brown them on both sides.

- Pull the pan from the heat and add the sage, garlic, onions and the apples.

- Pour chicken stock, wine and cider vinegar over everything in the pan. Cover with aluminium foil or a tight-fitting lid and bake in oven for 30 minutes.

- In a small bowl, combine the mustard and the cream. Once the 30 minutes is up, pull off the foil and pour the cream mixture over the chops. Bake uncovered for another 20 minutes.

- You can either serve these family style on a platter or on four plates making sure you get a little of everything and finishing with a couple of spoonfuls of the sauce.

WINE MATCH – **Sémillon**

Sémillon is an overlooked wine, but is the perfect choice for this dish. It has medium body, and soft, easy-drinking flavours that work well with pork. What I really like about this pairing is that there's just enough acidity in the wine for the mustard, but it has enough body for the cream so there's a nice balance. The apple flavour in the dish plays off the fruit flavours in the wine and actually brings them out of the shadows and makes them shine.

Shop for wine like a Pro

"What I like to drink most is wine that belongs to others."
—DIOGENES, 320 BC, GREEK PHILOSOPHER

Let's face it, wine is just fermented grape juice (well, very tasty grape juice for sure), so it shouldn't be hard to shop for, right? But lots of people get intimidated just walking into a store and seeing hundreds (even thousands) of bottles staring at them. Should you go white or red, Australian or American, still or sparkling . . . and what exactly is Pouilly-Fuissé? Well, ponder no longer! Here's your ultimate wine shopping guide. Read it, memorize it, and then hit the wine shop!

Ask for help – yes, even you guys who are too proud to ask for directions when you're lost can do it. If you're not sure what you're looking for, ask for help. A good store has staff trained to know about the products they sell and should be able to help you out, and if yours doesn't, find yourself a new wine store.

Learn to read the labels – wine labels can be tricky to understand, but if you are familiar with the basic terms, wine shopping will be a lot easier. See page 307 for more on decoding wine labels.

Know your budget – wine shopping can get very expensive if you don't have a budget (trust me on this). So have a dollar figure in mind before you set foot in the store. This applies whether you just want to pick up a bottle as a hostess gift on the way to a dinner party, or you're stocking up for the month.

Don't assume expensive = better – sometimes you just might find your new favourite wine in the bargain bin. Seriously. This tip ties back to **Ask for help** and **Know your budget**. If you ask for help, you might discover a hidden gem, something unknown that that costs $15 but tastes like $40. Wine pricing varies so widely that it's almost impossible to rate the quality of a wine solely on how much it costs. Having said that, try going a bit more expensive now and then. You'd be amazed at the difference between most wines priced at say $10 compared to those at $20.

Read up – there are all sorts of resources out there to help you figure out what you want before you get to the store. Search online for the perfect wine pairing for the meal you're cooking up. Check out reviews or subscribe to wine newsletters (www.groovygrapes.com is a groovy one). These are easy ways to find out about what others think of the quality and flavour of wines currently on the shelf. Then call ahead or check your local store's web site to make sure the wine you want is in stock.

Experiment – the best way to learn about wine is to taste. So if you're wine shopping and a bit confused, why not pick up a couple bottles and experiment? Whether you love it, hate it, or aren't sure, you're likely to remember something you've tasted already for the next time you're out wine shopping. But please oh please, if you are trying out this suggestion, use it in conjunction with **Know your budget**! Wine stores and restaurants also do tastings which can be a fun way of trying out new wines without having to invest in entire bottles.

How to store your wine

"Wine is a living liquid containing no preservatives. Its lifecycle comprises youth, maturity, old age, and death. When not treated with reasonable respect it will sicken and die."

—JULIA CHILD

When it comes to storing wine, there are two separate things to consider. First is **how to store wine that's already been opened**. Ever opened a bottle of wine, had a glass with dinner, popped the cork back in, and then left it sitting on the counter until your next meal at home, which ended up being three days later? Somehow the wine doesn't taste nearly as good after it's been open awhile. There are a few things you can do to keep your wine fresher once it's opened.

Re-cork right away – if you know you're not planning on drinking a whole bottle at one sitting, put the cork back in the bottle as soon as you've poured your glass. The reason wine loses its oomph after a couple days open is because it oxidizes. Re-corking immediately will slow the process down a bit and keep your wine fresher for longer.

Keep it cold – even if it's red wine. If you want to hang on to your open wine for a few days, keep it in the fridge. When you're ready for another glass, take it out and let it warm for half an hour before drinking. It'll be almost as good as new for two to three days.

Get some gadgets – some of the gadgets on the market can actually help you keep your wine fresher. Two that I like are the vacuum pump and preserving spray. The vacuum pump comes with reusable stoppers and it pumps out the air in the empty part of your bottle of wine. I have one and use it in conjunction with the two tips above to keep my open wine as fresh as possible. I find it extends the life of wine by maybe a day or so. Preserving spray is basically a can of inert gases that you spray into your partial bottle of wine. It creates a blanket over the wine, keeping the oxygen away and your wine fresher. Again, my experience is that it extends wine life by a day or two.

However you decide to store your opened bottles of wine, keep in mind that how long it will stay fresh will also depend on the wine itself. Sauvignon Blanc or Riesling with lots of acidity, for example, stay fresher for longer. Same goes for sweet wines and fortified wines like port and sherry.

Now moving on to the other type of storage – **how to store your unopened wine**. If you keep a few bottles of wine on hand to drink over the next few months, a small wine rack on a countertop or stashing bottles in a cupboard is just fine. If you are hanging on to wine for a while (let's say any longer than six months), there are a few things that you should keep in mind.

Temperature – wine will mature more slowly and will generally stay in better shape if it's stored at a steady, cool temperature. Let's say around 15C (or 58F). At warm temperatures, wine ages faster and starts to lose some of its fruitiness and flavour. Fluctuating temperatures can also be hard on wine, so if your basement goes from hot to cold through the seasons, a consistently cool closet might be a better spot for your wine, even if it's in the bedroom. If you want to make sure you've got a safe spot to store your wine, you could think about investing in a wine fridge, especially if you live in an apartment that doesn't have a nice, cool spot. They range from hundreds of dollars to thousands, and the best ones not only let you regulate temperature, but also humidity.

Light – try to store your wine in a dark place. Bright lights, especially ultraviolet rays, can destroy wine. Notice how lots of reds are bottled in green or brown bottles that filter out light better than clear glass? That's because a lot of red wines are kept around longer than whites before they are consumed (because they're more ageable).

Vibrations – keeping your wine still also helps it have a longer life. Over long periods of time, vibrations can prematurely oxidize your wine. So although your fridge is cool and dark, the vibrations from the motor can be harmful (the dry air in fridges can flatten out flavours and dry out corks as well).

Odours – pungent odours from food and household products can slowly infiltrate your wine through the cork, so don't store your wine next to the leftover paint cans in the basement.

Store it sideways – try to keep your wine stored horizontally, the way most wine racks are built. In order to keep a good seal, corks need to stay moist from contact with the wine. If you store your wine upright, the cork can dry out and shrink, letting the air in and oxidizing the wine. If you've got screw cap wine, you can store it upright without a problem.

Here's a sad little story I'd like to share with you. When my love of wine was just blossoming, I started to stock my cellar with wines I had tasted and loved. Being the shopaholic I am, I bought and bought and bought and soon I had racks full of lovely wines waiting to be drunk. But because there was so much (and because I kept buying) months and years passed before I got to drinking a lot of it. And by the time I did, most of it was not as tasty as I remembered. It was wine meant to be drunk young, and I was drinking it past its prime.

The moral of the story is that precious few wines actually improve with age, at least with lengthy aging. If you want to start a cellar, do your research beforehand to make sure you select wines that will still taste good or better years down the road. Don't lose track of what you're storing, and when the time is right, drink up!

ACT 3

Act 3 is all about the reds. Red wine has just recently jumped ahead of white wine around the world in terms of consumption, and that's not just because we love the taste of it. Recent studies have shown that moderate consumption of red wine (like a glass a day) is good for your heart – yay! Now we all have a great excuse to enjoy a satisfying glass at dinnertime, guilt-free.

Red wines come in styles from light and fruity to rich and tannic and everything in between. They pair up brilliantly with heartier food, and warm you up in the cold winter months. So read on for a crash course in red wine. Angie's recipes in this section will make you want to stock your cellar with reds, reds, and more reds!

Baco Noir

Baco Noir is a rustic, flannel-shirt-sitting-by-the-campfire type of wine. It's a red grape grown in the cool climates of Canada and the eastern regions of the United States, and the wine has a woodsy, wild flavour to it. The Baco Noir grape is what's known as a "French Hybrid" – grapes that were created by crossing (kind of like breeding) other grapes to create new ones with certain characteristics. Mr. Baco came up with this one, and it's a very hardy grape that can weather the elements well, so that's why you see it grown in cool climates.

I like Baco when I'm in the mood for something with some heft to it, but without heavy tannins, and that's exactly what this wine has to offer. Its flavours and aromas include blueberries, blackberries, plum, and that distinctive earthiness that I keep going on about.

The surprising thing about Baco is that its appearance doesn't quite match how it feels in your mouth. This grape is deeply pigmented with a blue-black colour that will stain your teeth (and your clothes) so watch out! But once it's in your mouth, although it's full of flavour, it's just medium in body, has medium tannins, and surprisingly crisp acidity. Definitely a wine worth exploring, especially when paired up with spicy barbequed meats or aged cheddar. Next time you head up to the lake, pack up some Baco, fire up the barbeque, then sit back and enjoy.

Aromas & Flavours
Dark fruit flavours of blueberry, blackberry, and plum
Distinctive rustic earthy note
Low tannin, medium body, and lots of acidity

Food Ideas
Spiced meat dishes
Burgers, sausages, and other barbecued meats
Sharp, aged cheeses like Cheddar

My recommended region for Baco Noir is:
Niagara Peninsula, Canada

Barbera

The region of Piedmont in northern Italy is known for its red wines. Barolo and Barbaresco steal the spotlight with powerful, intense wines made from the Nebbiolo grape. But two other bright and cheerful grapes wait in the shadows, happy to please tired palates with their bright acidity and light fruity flavours. One is Dolcetto, the mainstay for everyday dining in Piedmont, and the other is Barbera.

As light and charming as it is, Barbera often has plummier flavours and intriguing earthy and tar-like notes (this is a good thing). Some winemakers are now using a judicious amount of French oak to add additional complexity and weight to this wine, making it more popular on the international wine scene.

Barbera is one of my go-to wines for food pairing. The earthy, tarry aromas are interesting and they add a certain *je ne sais quoi* to an otherwise simple style of wine. Barbera works with meats from lighter chicken and veal to richer red meats and even smoked ham. Its acidity makes it the perfect partner for salads, especially when topped with grilled meats like duck or chicken, and I love a glass of Barbera with an Italian cheese plate. Versatile and delicious, Barbera may stand on the sidelines but she's a winner at my dinner table.

Aromas & Flavours
Juicy, tangy fruit flavours of cherry, cranberry, plum, and blackcurrant
Vibrant acidity with low tannin
Medium bodied with earthy notes

Food Ideas
Hearty polenta and risotto
Pasta with tomato-based sauces
Veal and poultry dishes with tomato or mushroom sauces
Cured meats, dry cheeses, and sun-dried tomatoes and olives

My recommended regions for Barbera are:
Piedmont, Italy (especially Barbera d'Alba and Barbera d'Asti)
California, U.S.A.

Cabernet Franc

I like to think of Cabernet Franc as Cabernet Sauvignon's little brother. Cab Franc is similar in many ways to Cab Sauv, with its intense berry aromas and flavours, but in a lighter, livelier package. Where Cab Sauv is dense with full body, big tannins, and mouth-filling flavours, Cab Franc has lighter body, higher acidity, and fresh, herbaceous characters like jalapeño or green bell pepper.

The interesting thing about Cab Franc is that though I've likened to it Cab Sauv's little brother, genetically speaking, it's actually a parent. DNA analysis has uncovered that Cabernet Franc (a lighter style of red) and Sauvignon Blanc (a light, crisp white) are the parent grapes of Cabernet Sauvignon (a big whopper of a red) – talk about recessive genes!

Cab Franc originates from the Loire Valley in France, where it is the main red grape that is grown. It is bottled as a single varietal wine (which just means it's the only grape used to make the wine – no blending) and is labeled under appellation names such as Bourgueil, Chinon, and Saumur-Champigny. Bordeaux is the other French region where Cab Franc is grown extensively. It's used in the traditional Bordeaux blend, along with Merlot and Cabernet Sauvignon.

Because of its use in the Bordeaux or Meritage blend (see page 205), Cab Franc is now planted around the world. As some regions recognize its strengths as a stand-alone wine, they are bottling it on its own more and more. You can find great examples of Cabernet Franc from Niagara, Canada and California, U.S.A. where the styles range from the lighter, fresher Loire styles (in Niagara) to richer, oakier versions (in California).

One thing that really stands out with Cab Franc is its affinity for food; some even feel this wine should only be enjoyed with food so as to tame its natural acidity. It does especially well with leafy vegetables like spinach and other greens and herby dishes that echo the herbaceous quality of the wine and complement its light body and tart flavours. I love this wine with cabbage rolls, vegetarian lasagna, grilled vegetables, or pizza with roasted red peppers –great examples of how sometimes a lighter wine is just right.

Aromas & Flavours

Intense raspberry and blackberry flavours

Herbaceous, peppery notes similar to jalapeño, bell pepper, or green olive

Light to medium body with lots of crisp acidity

Food Ideas

Vegetarian dishes, especially with bell peppers, tomatoes, and eggplant

Dishes with herb sauces

Meats like chicken, duck, veal, and pork

My recommended regions for Cabernet Franc are:

Loire Valley, France, especially Chinon, Bourgeuil, and Saumur-Champigny

Niagara, Canada

California, United States

Cabernet Sauvignon

Cabernet Sauvignon has big shoulders. This burly, masculine wine is not only one of the most universally popular reds going, it also makes some of the longest lasting wines around (perfect for putting away). It has big flavours, big tannins, big body, and pairs up with big, meaty dishes.

It's no wonder it's often called the "big daddy" of the wine world, considered by many to be the greatest red grape of them all. Cab put California on the wine map, and it often puts the "super" in Super Tuscan (see page 212). It's also the grape behind the remarkable age-ability of red Bordeaux (see page 205).

But what does it taste like, you ask? Cab has mouth-filling flavours of blackcurrant or cassis, plum, black cherry, and other dark fruits. It also has rich, chocolaty notes and an unmistakable minty/herbaceous quality (think "After Eight" chocolates). The flavours and body are so substantial that this wine can undergo extensive oak aging without overpowering the natural fruit flavours and acids, and this barrel-aging lends aromas and flavours of vanilla, smoke, cigar box, and cedar. Then there are the tannins. Some red wines have velvety tannins, but this ain't one of them. Cab has a mouth-puckering, tongue-drying texture that comes from its very thick skins. It's these tannins that allow Cabernet Sauvignon to age so gracefully, some reaching their peak after decades in the bottle, and many benefiting from at least 5 or so years of aging, giving the wine a chance to mellow and soften.

That's not to say that you can't go out today and buy a bottle of Cab to enjoy tonight. Because of its immense popularity, winemakers (mostly in New World countries) now make softer, more approachable styles *à la* Merlot that don't need aging to be enjoyable. While these styles of Cab might not be as complex as the others, that doesn't mean they're not delicious. Check the back label on the bottle – many wineries now add in notes about the wine including when it should be consumed.

One of my favourite wine and food moments while we were shooting *This Food That Wine* was with Cabernet Sauvignon. Angie and I had just taken our first taste of Cab with our "guest du jour," and after swallowing her sip, Angie exclaimed in shock that her mouth just got turned inside out, which is a great way to describe how astringent and drying the tannins in this wine can be. Later we tried it again with beef tenderloin and she went on to say that sipping the wine on its own, she had been overwhelmed with tannins, but that this time around the protein-rich meat tamed the tannins so she could actually enjoy the delicious flavours in the wine. The perfect example of how pairing the right wine and food together can totally change a wine.

Aromas & Flavours
Deep, dark flavours of blackcurrant, blackberry, plum, and black cherry
Chocolate and mint notes
Oak flavours like vanilla, smoke, cigar box, and cedar
Rich, full body, and big, puckery tannins

Food Ideas:
Grilled red meats like beef and lamb
Peppercorn or other rich sauces
Sharp, aged cheeses like Cheddar

My recommended regions for Cabernet Sauvignon are:
California, U.S.A.
Bordeaux, France (some blends are mostly Cab, especially from the Médoc and Graves)
Most wine regions in the world, so experiment with wines from Chile, South Africa, Australia, Washington State, U.S.A., and Tuscany, Italy

Dolcetto

Dolcetto is the baby of the wine family in Piedmont, the cheerful splash of sunshine in the shady shadows of wine giants Barolo and Barbaresco. While the famous big reds of this northern Italian region demand most of the attention, Dolcetto is happy to please the locals at dinner time, and is about as common at the Piedmontese table as salt and pepper.

This wine is light to medium in body with tart red cherry and cranberry flavours, subtle floral aromas, and lots of bright, mouth-watering acidity. While it definitely doesn't fit the bill for your standard crowd-pleasing wine, Dolcetto is a star when it comes to enhancing food. Its crisp acidity and dry but gentle tannins make it friendly with all sorts of food flavours, and though it's not my favourite wine to sip on its own, I love experimenting with different food pairings, because Dolcetto doesn't disappoint.

If you're a fan of lighter styles of red like Gamay Noir and Valpolicella, or the next time you're in the mood for a red wine with your antipasti platter try Dolcetto for a change.

Aromas & Flavours
Tart, red cherry and cranberry flavours
Light to medium body with mouth-watering acidity

Food Ideas
Antipasti
Tomato-based pasta or pizza
Beef carpaccio
Cured meats such as salami and bresaola

My recommended regions for Dolcetto are:
Dolcetto d'Alba and Dolcetto di Dogliani, from Piedmont, Italy

Gamay Noir

Gamay Noir is the red wine for white wine drinkers. It's light to medium in body, has friendly, simple fruit flavours, and little to no tannin so it's easy to drink and easy to pair with food. It's also the grape of Beaujolais, France so if you see a bottle of wine with Beaujolais on the label, it's Gamay Noir.

The Beaujolais region in France is in the southern part of Burgundy and grows only Gamay Noir grapes. Here, the wines range from light, tart, and fruity with strawberry/cranberry flavours to medium-bodied, earthier ones with riper fruit flavours and a peppery kick. Beaujolais wines are labeled simply by the region or by "Beaujolais-Villages" (these tend to be the lighter, fruitier wines), and can be further classified by smaller appellations or "crus" which are the names you'll see on the label. These crus are Brouilly, Côte de Brouilly, Chénas, Chiroubles, Fleurie, Juliénas, Morgon, Moulin-à-Vent, Régnié, and the romantically named Saint-Amour, and it's these wines that have fuller fruit flavours and earthy qualities.

Canada's Niagara Peninsula also makes Gamay Noir, and they make it well, with their cool climate and perfectly suited soils. Canada's Gamay is peppery and light, with strawberry fruit flavours and tart, refreshing acidity.

Gamay is one of my favourite summertime reds because you can chill it down to bring out its fresh fruit flavours, and it pairs well with picnic and barbecue fare. It's also a great partner for vegetable dishes, because there's lots of acidity in the wine to balance off the natural acidity in most veggies.

A note on Beaujolais Nouveau

Beaujolais Nouveau is the new wine of the vintage, released the same year the grapes were harvested on the third Thursday of every November with splashy colourful labels, and bubble gum, candy-apple flavours. These wines are simple, fresh, and seem almost sweet with their candy flavours and bright purple-pink colour. They're also a fun way to brighten up dreary November days, which is why this tradition is so famous and long-lasting – aren't we all in need of a party as chilly winter looms? If you've never tried Beaujolais Nouveau, keep an eye open for it in November, and host your own Nouveau party!

Aromas & Flavours
Tart fruit flavours of strawberry, cranberry, and raspberry
Spicy notes of cracked black or white peppercorns
Earthy, mineral notes (from cru Beaujolais and some Canadian Gamay)

Food Ideas
Antipasti
Tomato-based dishes
Casual fare, especially fried foods
Grilled fish and vegetable dishes

My recommended regions for Gamay Noir are:
Beaujolais, France
Niagara, Canada

Grenache

While the masses sing the praises of Shiraz, I'm ga-ga over Grenache. Both grapes originated in the Rhône Valley in France, and both have made their way around the globe, settling in warm climates of the New World and producing satisfying, full-bodied red wines that soothe the soul.

Grenache is the most widely planted red wine grape in the world, because of its huge acreage throughout France and Spain that's used for delicious Mediterranean red blends (see page 205 for more on that). But on its own, Grenache is full-bodied, full of flavour, and super-satisfying. It's one of my favourite grapes to introduce to people who already love big reds like Shiraz and Zinfandel, because it's just as pleasing yet relatively unknown.

Grenache has juicy, ripe, red fruit flavours like raspberry, plum, and strawberry, with chocolaty, smoky notes and a nice, smooth easy-drinking texture. And watch out – it's high in alcohol, but it's so tasty and smooth you might not even notice. But the really great thing about Grenache is that though it's a big red, it's also really versatile with food. Because it's low in tannin, you can pair it with light meats without over-powering them, and because of its juicy, ripe fruit flavours, it also does well with spice, especially barbecue, Cajun, and Asian flavours.

Aromas & Flavours
Juicy, ripe red fruit flavours like raspberry, plum, and strawberry
Chocolaty and smoky notes
High alcohol and low tannin

Food Ideas
Spicy grilled meats (both light and red)
Ham and other smoky pork dishes
Roasted or stewed chicken in hearty sauces
Asian or Cajun flavours

My recommended regions for Grenache are:
Australia
Southern France, Spain, and California (mostly in blends)

Malbec

Malbec is like Merlot's quiet but quirky pal. Like Merlot, Malbec is a red grape from Bordeaux, France and produces medium to full bodied wines with dark fruit flavours and velvety tannins. But compared to Merlot, people are just starting to get to know Malbec, and it distinguishes itself from its hometown friend with its dark, inky colour and distinctive anise and smoke characters.

Though Malbec hails from France (where it now plays a very minor role in Bordeaux) it really has come into its own in Argentina, where it has become the country's signature grape. Argentine Malbec is made in a softer, lusher New World style when compared to its French counterparts, and the warm climate there makes the grape stand out from the crowd. It has ripe blackberry, cherry, and licorice aromas and flavours, a touch of earthiness, and an approachable texture that is best described as velvety – there are some tannins but they're soft and pleasant, not harsh as they sometimes are in French Malbec. And it has dark, rich notes of black licorice, chocolate, and coffee.

Because of Argentina, Malbec's popularity has caused winemakers in other New World countries like Chile, Australia, and the United States to plant the grape as well, though you'll mostly only see it blended with other grapes.

Back in France, you can find intense and distinctive Malbec from Cahors, a town near Bordeaux where the wines are required by law to contain at least 70% Malbec (sometimes referred to there as "Cot"). These wines are deep and dark in colour, and tend to be harsh when they're young. If you let them mellow a few years in the bottle, however, these wines are intense and delicious, especially when paired with local cuisine such as cassoulet or duck confit.

Aromas & Flavours
Rich fruit flavours of blackberry, plum, and cherry
Spicy, chocolaty, and black licorice notes
Full bodied, and can range from low to very strong tannins

Food Ideas
Hearty red meats such as beef, lamb, and game
Braised beef short ribs
Burgers and other grilled meats
Mushrooms, beans, and other earthy flavours

My recommended regions for Malbec are:
Argentina
Cahors, France

Merlot

Merlot. It's easy to drink, it's easy to say, and it's no wonder that it's become the darling of the wine world. Merlot hails from the Bordeaux region in France and if Cabernet Sauvignon is the king of Bordeaux, then Merlot is its queen.

But Merlot is misunderstood. Just like a blonde bombshell movie star, Merlot appears simple on its surface. Sensual, sultry and seductive, most write her off as uncomplicated. Appropriate for a one night stand perhaps, but certainly nothing to bring home to your parents – an easy indulgence, with no strings attached. But sometimes, there's actually a bit more to Merlot. As we've come to learn, sometimes the "dumb blonde" persona is just an act. There's more than meets the eye (and the mouth), and many a Merlot are the perfect example.

Regardless of Merlot's reputation as a simple quaffing wine, it remains hugely popular around the world. It's the most planted grape in the Bordeaux region of France and actually makes up for at least 90% of the blend of one of Bordeaux's most famed (and most expensive) wines – Château Pétrus. It's grown in just about every wine-producing country I can think of, and that's no surprise to me – Merlot is people-friendly, and I love drinking it. In fact, I'm sipping on a glass of Merlot as I write these lines.

Wine stores abound with fruity, smooth and delicious Merlot, and these wines are the ideal choice for cocktail wines at parties and for everyday drinking. They offer velvety-smooth texture paired with ripe, juicy flavours of plum, cherry, blackcurrant, and sweet vanilla. If you venture into the $20+ category, there you can find luscious, full-bodied wines with more complex fruit flavours layered with spicy, chocolaty notes and velvety tannins. Some of these are even age-worthy, and some of these are definitely worth taking home to your parents.

A note on Carmenère

Carmenère is a red grape that was originally grown in Bordeaux, France but is now the signature grape of Chile. There, it was mistaken for Merlot for many years because of their similarities both physically (grape and vine) and in aroma and flavour. It is a medium to full bodied red wine with easy-drinking, juicy plum and blackberry flavours, soft tannins, and a dark, inky colour. If you love Merlot and you love a good bargain, keep an eye out for Chilean Carmenère.

Aromas & Flavours

Ripe, juicy aromas and flavours of plum, cherry, and blackcurrant
Sweet, oaky characters of vanilla and toast
Velvety-smooth texture and full body

Food Ideas

Duck and other game birds
Hearty casseroles
Roasted meats and/or poultry, especially turkey with cranberry sauce
Burgers, sausages, and other barbecue fare

My recommended regions for Merlot are:

All over the world – my favourite regions are California and Washington State, U.S.A., Australia, Chile, New Zealand, and British Columbia, Canada
Bordeaux, France (some blends are mostly Merlot, especially from St-Emilion and Pomerol)

Nebbiolo

Nebbiolo reminds me of tar and roses. I know that sounds like a bad glamour rock band from the '80s, but seriously, next time you have the opportunity, take a glass of Nebbiolo, give it a swirl, and tell me you don't smell that distinctive nose of sweet, perfumed rose petals, and pungent, earthy tar.

Now if the name Nebbiolo doesn't ring a bell, there are a few really good reasons for that. First of all, it's mostly grown in Italy where wines are labeled by region rather than by grape, so Nebbiolo is hiding under the names Barolo or Barbaresco. And second, Nebbiolo isn't exactly approachable. Besides the fact that the price per bottle starts at about $40, it usually needs quite a bit of aging (we're talking at least five or ten years) before these austere wines with high acid and aggressive tannins expose their softer side. So I wouldn't say that Nebbiolo is particularly people-friendly.

That being said, I love Nebbiolo (I know, I know, you're starting to think, geez, this girl really is a wino, how many times has she already said "I love this grape, I love that grape"). But anyway, this grape offers much to love, if you just give it a chance. Once it's had some time to mellow, Nebbiolo explodes with rich texture and intense, complex aromas and flavours of sweet black cherry, earthy truffle, chocolaty mocha, spicy cinnamon, and of course, tar and roses.

And here's a tip for those of you too impatient to wait – Nebbiolo is a great candidate for the decanter. Give it a couple hours to breathe before serving and its roughest edges will soften. Not the same as years in the bottle, but a step in the right direction. Then serve it up with a rich, meaty dish (like Angie's lamb shanks) and get ready to swoon.

Aromas & Flavours

Rich, intense flavours of black cherry, spicy cinnamon, chocolate, and aromatic floral
Earthy flavours of truffle and tar
High acid and aggressive tannins that need considerable aging to soften

Food Ideas

Rich red meats
Braised meat dishes such as osso bucco
Pungent cheeses
Dishes with truffles

My recommended regions for Nebbiolo are:

Piedmont, Italy, especially the Barolo and Barbaresco districts
Australia and California, U.S.A. (they are just starting to experiment)

Nero d'Avola

Nero d'Avola is the grape of Sicily, and although it's not a huge player in the worldwide wine scene, I like it a lot so it gets a spot in this book. The literal translation of Nero d'Avola is "black grape of Avola" after the city of the same name in the southeastern part of the island of Sicily.

Sicily has a long history of wine making and is such a wine-rich land that the locals have as many words relating to wines and grapes as the Inuit allegedly have for snow. For generations, the Nero d'Avola grape made neutral but strong wines that were quietly shipped throughout Europe's cooler climate regions to beef up lighter styles of wine, and French producers nicknamed it *le vin medicine*.

Several decades ago, Sicilian winemakers began to tear out the Nero d'Avola plantings in favour of international grapes like Merlot and Syrah, in hopes of faster and bigger wine sales. But it is now making a comeback as a proud Sicilian wine, bottled on its own and in blends, and exported around the world with slow but steady success. Because of its plummy, spicy flavours and its warm, sunny homeland, you could compare Nero d'Avola to Shiraz, but it has bright acidity and a distinct Italian essence to it which comes to life when paired with flavours like sun-dried tomatoes, Italian herbs, and olives.

Aromas & Flavours
Deep plummy and berry flavours, sometimes with raisiny notes
Spicy, smoky, leathery notes
Fresh acidity and smooth tannins

Food Ideas
Spicy beef chili
Puttanesca sauce
Burgers and other grilled meats
Dishes with sun-dried tomatoes and olives

My recommended region for Nero d'Avola is:
Sicily, Italy

Pinot Noir

Ah, Pinot Noir. The diva of the wine world, and also known by many as the "heartbreak grape." Why, you ask? Well, here's the thing about Pinot Noir – it can make some of the most complex, delicious, interesting, amazing wines on the planet, but it's a bugger to grow. So the heartbreak comes in when vine growers and winemakers work so hard to produce one of these wonderful wines, but because of vintage conditions, the stubborn little grapes just don't cooperate. Hearts break at the thought that a vintage may go by without producing a great Pinot Noir.

So that's why I call Pinot Noir the diva of the wine world. These fussy little grapes with thin skins demand that all the conditions be just right before they can be made into a great wine. Thin skins mean that if there's too much rainfall before harvest, the sugars and flavours in the grapes can get diluted. It also means that the grapes are susceptible to rots and other disease in the vineyard. And if there's not enough sunshine, the grapes won't ripen to their full potential, and the flavours won't develop into what they should.

Those troublesome thin skins of the Pinot Noir grape also have a lot to do with how the wine looks and how it feels in your mouth, both of which can seduce you just as effectively as the aromas and flavours of this wine. Skins are where both the colour and tannins in a wine come from. So thinner skins mean that Pinot Noir has a less concentrated colour, especially if you compare it to a wine like Shiraz or Cabernet Sauvignon, both of which are thick-skinned grapes. It also means that the tannins in the wine are fairly light, and when tannins are soft and velvety, red wines can be extremely food friendly. Pinot Noir can be paired well with lamb or the classic Beef Bourgignon, but it is also just as at home with a piece of grilled salmon or tuna, or a cheese plate.

So let's talk about when the diva is pleased, when all the conditions are just right, and the winemaker does just the right things. That's when these grapes can be made into remarkable wines, with complex aromas and flavours which vary widely depending on where the grapes are grown. From most versions, you can expect strawberry and cherry, a subtle perfumey note, and the characteristic "earthiness" that Pinot Noir is known for. Earthy can sometimes mean mushroomy, or aromas like forest floor or freshly turned soil. Sometimes that earthiness is more on the "barnyard" side, which sounds like it would be a bad thing, but trust me, it can be a great thing, especially when balanced with spicy notes of clove, refreshing acidity, and a silky texture that seduces. New World styles (especially from California) can be fuller in body, with sweeter, juicier fruit flavours but some from cooler climates like Oregon, U.S.A. or New Zealand stay on the lighter, fresher side. With all these complexities and variations, it's no wonder that Pinot Noir is considered a "feminine" wine – we women can be complex, we can break hearts, but we are so worth it.

A note on Red Burgundy

Just as Burgundy is Chardonnay headquarters, it is also the homeland for Pinot Noir. Any red wine with "Bourgogne" on the label has Pinot Noir in the bottle, and while these can be some of the best wines in the world, it is also possibly the most confusing wine region to understand. As with most French wine regions, the land is divided into separate *appellations* or "villages" which are the names you'll see on wine labels. In Burgundy, these divisions are very detailed, with some plots of land consisting of only a few rows of vines. This is the perfect region to which the concept of *terroir* can be applied. The flavour of the land varies so much in Burgundy that wines from the same village and the same vintage can vary from awe-inspiring to no better than everyday plonk. It is this inconsistency that makes Burgundy so confusing yet so worth it to go to the trouble of trying to figure it out. My advice? Read lots of reviews before spending your hard-earned money on Burgundy – let the experts do the work for you.

Aromas & Flavours

Berry aromas and flavours like strawberry, raspberry and cherry,
  ranging from light and tart to ripe and rich
Classic "earthy" aromas that can include mushroom, forest floor, freshly turned soil,
  or funky barnyard
Silky texture and translucent ruby hue

Food Ideas

Earthy mushroom dishes
Stewed meats like the classic Beef Bourguignon
Rich fish like salmon or tuna

My recommended regions for Pinot Noir are:

Burgundy, France (the main region for Pinot Noir in Burgundy is the Côte d'Or, but you'll also see more specific appellation names on the labels) – remember to read reviews or ask for some expert advice before plunging into these wines
California and Oregon, U.S.A.
New Zealand, especially the Central Otago region

Sangiovese

Sangiovese is *the* grape of Tuscany, and depending on where in Tuscany it's grown and vinified, it can be the food-friendly darling known as Chianti, or the big, brooding Brunello di Montalcino. Tuscany is in the central part of Italy, where the growing season is warm and sunny, and the rolling hills are covered with row after row of grapevines. The Sangiovese grape dominates these grapevines and is responsible for Tuscany's world-famous wines that range from light and fruity to rich and bold. Sangiovese also makes an appearance in most "Super Tuscans," wines that feature blends of international grapes like Merlot, Cabernet Sauvignon, and Syrah (see page 212 for more).

But let's start with the friendlier mainstay of Tuscany – Chianti. Chianti was made to be drunk with food. There is no other wine I can think of that comes alive the way Chianti does with the right food pairing. And it's no wonder, with all the delicious gastronomical options there are in Tuscany. Classic tomato-based dishes, pasta with pesto and other herbaceous flavours, minestrone soup, antipasti platters with vegetables and spiced charcuterie, dry cheeses, and other Mediterranean flavours – these all call out for the bright, crisp acidity of Chianti wines. The tart, red cherry flavours, medium body, and soft tannins are perfect for this kind of food, and for a wine that might seem too tart on its own, those acids are brilliantly tamed by the fresh Mediterranean flavours of Italian cuisine. And gone are the days when Chianti was your average picnic wine in the straw-clad bottle – modern Chianti is wine that will impress, especially when you put it with the right food. One last tip – go for the Chianti that has "Classico" on the label to ensure a higher quality wine.

It's hard to imagine that cheerful Chianti and brooding Brunello are made from the same grape, but it's true. The darker side of Tuscany is embodied in this ripper of a wine that hails from Montalcino, just south of the Chianti zone. This wine is big and tough with full body and super-aggressive tannins. Brunello is actually made from a slightly different strain of Sangiovese that produces richer, heftier wines compared to the simple charm of Chianti. And similar to Brunello's brother in the north, the prodigious Barolo, this wine is not what you'd call accessible – it's pricey (we're talking $50+ for a bottle), and it needs to age before you drink it, usually at least for a decade. But also like Barolo, it's worth the wait. After you leave Brunello to hibernate, it wakes up as a powerful and intriguing wine, rich with flavours of chocolate, ripe blackberry, and smoky leather. But it's still not soft and easy-drinking – the brawny tannins need rich, flavourful foods and it's a sin to sip on Brunello without a decadent meal of rich beef, earthy truffles, and sharp cheeses.

A note on Montepulciano

Okay, prepare to be perplexed. I'm going to try to explain Montepulciano.

Vino Nobile di Montepulciano – a red wine made in Tuscany, with Sangiovese as the main grape, and small amounts of other Italian grapes blended in. It's similar to Chianti, but sort of a step down, if you will. A bit lighter and simpler, but nice as a quaffing wine and very affordable

Montepulciano d'Abruzzo – a red wine made in Abruzzi from the Montepulciano grape. Also a very affordable, simple, light to medium bodied red.

So yes, there is a wine named Montepulciano made from Sangiovese and there's another wine named Montepulciano made from Montepulciano. Confused? Me too. No wonder the New World just starting naming their wines after grapes.

Aromas & Flavours
Tart red cherry and strawberry fruit flavours with notes of spice and earth, lots of acidity, medium body, and smooth tannins (in lighter styles like Chianti and Vino Nobile di Montepulciano where Sangiovese is the main grape in the blend)
Rich, thick flavours of blackberry, chocolate, and leather with fierce tannins and mouth-filling full body (in Brunello di Montalcino, 100% Sangiovese)

Food Ideas for Chianti and other lighter styles
Light meat dishes such as veal or pork
Tomato-based pasta and pizza
Hard Italian cheeses

Food Ideas for Brunello di Montalcino
Rich meat dishes including the classic Steak Florentine
Heavy pasta dishes and stews, especially with truffles
Gorgonzola and other blue-veined cheeses

My recommended regions for Sangiovese are:
Tuscany, Italy especially Chianti Classico and Brunello di Montalcino
Australia, to try a New World style of an Old World staple

Shiraz/Syrah

First things first, Shiraz = Syrah. The Australians call it Shiraz, the French call it Syrah, and each name for this grape signifies a different style of wine, no matter where it comes from.

So let's start with Shiraz, an instant crowd-pleaser that has become synonymous with Aussie wine over the past decade. This style is accessible, affordably-priced, and made with people-friendly jammy fruit flavours and smooth, easy-drinking texture. I love Shiraz as a cocktail wine – something to sip on at a party, delicious and satisfying on its own.

Sometimes called a "fruit bomb," Shiraz is full and rich with big, ripe fruit flavours like blackcurrant, blackberry, black cherry, and plum. It's got a peppery spice, sweet chocolaty notes, and toasty vanilla aromas from aging in American oak. The Aussies have perfected the art of appealing to the masses with this affordable, reliable wine. But that's not to say that they don't also make complex, higher-end versions – they do that as well, yet still conforming to their big, mouth-filling style.

Now getting back to Shiraz's roots – French Syrah. While perhaps not as immediately likeable, Syrah makes some of the most intense, powerful, and complex wines around. Its stomping ground is the northern part of the Rhône Valley where wines like Hermitage, Crozes-Hermitage, and Côte Rôtie are made using the Syrah grape. Some call this a more elegant style of wine, but I say it's still delicious, just different. It still has the deep, dark fruit flavours of blackcurrant and blackberry, though maybe not quite as ripe and jammy as Shiraz, the black pepper spice is more intense, with earthy, almost meaty notes, and the tannins are big and astringent. Syrah is also planted throughout California, where over the past three decades winemakers have continued France's tradition of spicy, satisfying red wines.

The best thing about Syrah is that it tends to be more food-friendly than over-the-top Aussie Shiraz. Paired with robust red meats or hearty stews, there's no better warm-up for cold wintry nights.

A note on Petite Sirah

Just to keep you sufficiently confused, Syrah is the same grape as Shiraz, but it is NOT the same grape as Petite Sirah (sometimes also spelled Petite Syrah). It is, however, similar in aroma, flavour, and body. Also known as "Durif," this wine is quite full in body, with intense aromas and flavours of blackberry, blackcurrant, licorice, and peppery spice. It can range from soft to strong tannins depending on the style in which it's made, and it has a deep purple-black colour. There isn't a lot of it around, but if you happen to come across a bottle, pick it up instead of a Zinfandel or Shiraz, it's sure to please. Look for it from regions like California, U.S.A. or from Australia (where it's often labeled as Durif).

Aromas & Flavours
Dark fruit flavours of blackcurrant, blackberry, cherry, and plum
Black pepper spice
Styles ranging from rich and elegant to fruit bomb

Food Ideas
Hearty meat stew
Game meats like boar or venison
Smoked or grilled meats, especially beef and lamb

My recommended regions for Shiraz / Syrah are:
Australia, especially Barossa Valley and Coonawarra (Shiraz)
California and France (Syrah)
South Africa, Chile, and New Zealand (labeled with either name)

Tempranillo

I'm a huge fan of Mediterranean flavours in both food and wine – crisp white wines paired with seafood, intensely fruity yet refreshing rosé wines paired with grilled calamari or a Niçoise salad, and ripe vanilla-scented, berry-flavoured reds with robust meats and cheeses. Mmmm-mmm . . . I can almost feel the ocean breeze and the hot sun!

The signature red grape from Spain is Tempranillo, and although a lot of Spanish reds are blends, Tempranillo is a big player in those as well. The key regions that produce Tempranillo-based wines are Rioja, Ribera del Duero, and Penedes. And here's a little tip – Tempranillo is also one of the main grapes used to make the fortified port wines of Portugal, except there they call it "Tinta Roriz."

Tempranillo has a ripe raspberry flavour, with leathery and smoky cigar notes, bright, tart acidity, and soft tannins. Though medium in body, this wine can be quite full depending on what it's blended with and how long it's been aged in oak barrels.

Rioja reds, made mainly with Tempranillo and Grenache grapes, are known for their extensive aging in American oak barrels. Three different classifications identify the wines based on how long they've aged before release (in both oak barrels and in bottle) – Crianza, Reserva, and Gran Reserva – from least to most aged. Crianza wines from Rioja tend to be fantastic values, with affordable prices for medium to full wines with bright berry fruit flavours and sweet vanilla notes. Reserva and Gran Reserva wines have bigger oak flavours, mouth-puckering tannins, and summon much higher prices.

Aromas & Flavours
Ripe berry flavours of raspberry and mulberry
Leathery and smoky/cigar box notes
American oak notes of vanilla and toast

Food Ideas
Duck, quail, and other game birds
Rich poultry, pork, and veal dishes
Spanish Manchego and other dry cheeses
Spicy paella with lots of chorizo sausage

My recommended regions for Tempranillo are:
Spanish regions of Rioja and Ribera del Duero
Australia and California, who are now experimenting with this grape

Zinfandel/Primitivo

Zinfandel has experienced the classic all-American rags to riches story. Starting off as a relatively unknown and sparsely planted grape in Croatia called Crljenak, Zin found itself in California with a catchier name and today is known as America's "patriot grape," with over 50,000 acres planted and a huge following of Zin-lovers, including me.

Now please don't get confused with White Zinfandel, the sugary-sweet rosé wine that most of us drank back in college. Yes, it's made from the same grape, but what I'm talking about here is a wine not for the faint at heart – jammy, mouth-filling berry flavours, rich texture, and over-the-top alcohol levels make this red wine a far cry from the sweet and simple White Zin.

Zinfandel is best described as "jammy," meaning that the fruit aromas and flavours are super-ripe. For this wine, think raspberry, black cherry, and blackberry. It also has spicy notes that can vary from sweet cinnamon and clove to savoury black pepper, and a classic "brambly" quality that reminds me of woodsy, leafy, floral aromas. Zin is full-bodied, and usually has fairly soft tannins, so it feels pretty smooth in the mouth. But beware of its room-spinning alcohol levels (sometimes hitting 16% and even higher), which can catch you by surprise after sipping away on this delicious wine. If you love Shiraz, give Zin a whirl – maybe you'll find a new favourite.

A note about "Old Vines"

Wineries use all sorts of lingo on their labels to make their wine sound more enticing. A lot of the terminology is not legally controlled so it might not mean much to the consumer. Terms like "reserve" or "proprietor's blend" don't really tell you whether it's the winery's best wine or their regular, everyday jug wine. "Old vines" is kind of the same thing – it's telling you that the grapes came from old vines, but there's no way to tell whether they're 20 years old or 80 years old. Basically, as vines get older, they start to produce less fruit, which means that the grapes that do grow are more concentrated in flavour. The wine from these vines usually has bigger, more intense flavour, sometimes higher alcohol, and usually a steeper price tag. The good news is that Zinfandel has been growing in California since the 1800s which means that if the label says "old vines" there's a good chance that the vines are indeed quite old.

Primitivo

The mighty Zinfandel also has an Italian twin brother named Primitivo. DNA testing has shown that both Zin and Primitivo have the same fingerprint, and both trace their origins back to Croatia. Primitivo is grown in the southern parts of Italy and is similar to California Zin with its ripe berry and cherry flavours and smooth, mouth-filling texture. But it goes a bit easier on the alcohol levels, hitting a more average 12–13%, and it's often not quite as big in body, with tarter acidity to boot. All these characteristics combined mean that Primitivo is a great choice for food pairing, working well with lighter meats as well as richer ones, pastas, charcuterie, and grilled fare. Plus, you can usually find it at a lower price point compared to Zinfandel, so keep an eye out for it.

Aromas & Flavours
Jammy berry flavours of raspberry, black cherry, and blackberry
Spicy aromas like cinnamon, clove, or black pepper
Full body and smooth texture

Food Ideas
Hearty preparations of light meats like pork or veal
Game meats (especially with Zin)
Sausage or pepperoni pizza
Grilled burgers, sausages, and other barbequed meats

My recommended regions for Zinfandel are:
California, U.S.A.
Puglia, Italy (you'll see the name "Primitivo" on the label)

Red Wine Blends

Some of the most famous (and expensive) red wines in the world are blends. Blending or *assemblage* as the French say, is a traditional Old World winemaking technique that mixes different grapes together to create a wine that brings out the best of each part. It's also a great way to create a similar style of wine from vintage to vintage, regardless of climate changes and other growing conditions, because you can adjust the amount of each grape you include in the mix to create a consistent flavour. Traditional Old World blends are now mimicked throughout the New World, and new blends are also being created to satisfy changing consumer tastes.

Bordeaux
(Cabernet/Merlot or Meritage)

The big reds of Bordeaux are among the most famous, age-worthy, and expensive wines of the world. There are five main grapes that make up the mix – Cabernet Sauvignon, Merlot, Cabernet Franc, Malbec, and Petite Verdot – and the name Bordeaux comes from the region in France where the grapes are grown. Like all good teamwork, each of these grapes has strengths that fill in the gaps of other grapes – they complement each other to create wines that truly exemplify the meaning of synergy. Cabernet Sauvignon's grippy tannins are softened by Merlot's soft, ripe plummy flavours, and the other grapes add complexity, spice, and colour.

Bordeaux became famous centuries ago when the British fell in love with the wine. It became the drink of royalty, even earning the pet name *claret*. The notion of royalty and aristocracy remains with the wine today, putting it at the dinner table of our most special occasions. It doesn't hurt that the best of Bordeaux has a royally high price tag as well.

Don't be surprised, however, that there is affordable Bordeaux out there. The fancy stuff only accounts for less than 5% of the total wine production in the region, where everyday wine flows like Bordeaux's famous Garonne River. A simple "Bordeaux" on the label and prices in the $15 range identify the regular table wine, which is easy-drinking, fruity, and meant to be drunk young. If a Bordeaux district is listed on the label (such as Médoc, Graves, St-Emilion, Pomerol, Margaux, or St-Julien) you've moved a step up. And if the specific "Château" is listed, you're getting into the good stuff. Of course how good depends on the specific Château.

The greatest form of flattery is imitation, and with the success of Bordeaux, it's no wonder that the rest of the world wanted to cash in on it too. The name "Bordeaux" can only be applied to wine made in that region, so other countries that make wine from the same grape blend often simply call it "Cabernet Merlot" – the "Cabernet" referring to both Cabernet Sauvignon and Cabernet Franc. The other term you might see to indicate this style of wine is "Meritage," a term coined by a group of American vintners. It's an American word, not a French one, so the correct pronunciation rhymes with "heritage."

One last little note on Petite Verdot, the only grape in the mix that hasn't been covered earlier in the book. It plays only a very minor supporting role in the Bordeaux blend, but it's also produced as a single grape wine in countries like Australia and the United States. When tasted on its own, you can see what it brings to the blend – lots of tannins, a deep purple-black colour, and a distinctive smoky, cigar box note.

Aromas & Flavours
Rich, intense dark fruit flavours of blackcurrant and plum
Oaky notes of vanilla, cedar, smoke, and cigar box
Full-bodied with astringent tannins that soften with age

Food Ideas
Hearty red meats such as beef, lamb, and game
Roasted root vegetables
Smoked duck
Classic French dishes like Beef Wellington

My recommended regions for Bordeaux (Cabernet/Merlot or Meritage) blends are:
Bordeaux, France (base wines list "Bordeaux" on the label, and quality increases
  with specific district names and Chateaux)
Australia, U.S.A., Canada, and New Zealand

Southern Rhône
(Grenache/Syrah/Mourvèdre)

"This is Old World wine with California cleavage."
—JAY McINERNEY, NOVELIST AND WINE WRITER

There's no better way to describe southern Rhône wines than "sexy" – full in body with ripe, luscious fruit flavours that are a little rough around the edges – it can seduce like no other wine. The southern part of the Rhône Valley is where France meets California, with rustic, stony terrain and blistering hot sun that grow super-ripe, juicy grapes. While the more prestigious wines come out of the northern part of the Rhône, the south produces 90% of the wines in this region as a whole.

In the north, the wines are made from Syrah, but in the south, they're more liberal, growing around twenty different red grapes. The main grape is Grenache which produces full, delicious wines with juicy fruit flavours and high alcohol. The next contenders are Syrah and Mourvèdre, which provide peppery spice, tannins and deep colour to the softer Grenache. Cinsault is often featured in the blend as well, providing complex aromatics, and a handful of other red grapes will appear now and then to round out the mix. And since there are no rules that regulate how much of each is allowed in the blend, it's no surprise that the wines can range in style from over-the-top fruit bombs, to spicy, earthy blends, to lighter, crisper versions.

At the basic, $15 to $20 level, look for Côtes-du-Rhône, Côtes du Ventoux, and Côtes-du-Rhône-Villages, all of which tend to be in medium in body with lots of Grenache in the mix to create soft, strawberry-scented wines that satisfy. But my favourite southern Rhône wines have to be from Châteauneuf-du-Pape, Gigondas, and Vacqueyras, all of which are irresistibly delicious and can get to be pricey depending on the bottle.

Châteauneuf-du-Pape is the southern Rhône's most famous region and probably its best bet at competing with the wines of the northern Rhône. Here there can be up to thirteen different grapes in the blend, although the main players are still Grenache, Syrah, and Mourvèdre. The hot sun gives this wine an almost roasted berry fruit flavour, jammy but toasty at the same time, with spicy pepper notes and earthy aromas of freshly turned soil. This wine lingers around on your taste buds for a long, seductive finish. Zinfandel lovers out there should definitely try this wine. But if Châteauneuf is not in your budget, go for Gigonadas or Vacqueyras. Both of these wines are intense with ripe fruit and intriguing spice flavours and prices are in the $20 range.

As with most French wine styles, the New World has followed suit and is creating Rhone-style blends with a modern, oak-kissed stamp on them. In California, a group of vintners nicknamed the "Rhône Rangers" mimic Rhône blends in similar climate and terrain. And the Aussies make "GSM", (which stands for the grapes in the mix, Grenache, Shiraz, and Mourvèdre) a full-bodied, spicy red with classic black pepper spice and jammy, ripe fruit flavours.

Aromas & Flavours
Ripe, jammy, and sometimes almost "roasted" fruit flavours of strawberry,
  raspberry, and plum
Notes of spicy black pepper, herbs, licorice, and earthiness
Medium to full in body with soft to more aggressive tannins depending on
  the region and the grape blend

Food Ideas
Light meat or poultry in richer preparations to rich stewed meats
Hearty vegetables like zucchini, eggplant, or onions
Robust dishes with Provençal herbs and seasonings

My recommended regions for red Southern Rhône blends are:
Côtes-du-Rhône, Côtes du Ventoux, and Côtes-du-Rhône-Villages for
  widely accessible, medium-bodied, spicy, fruity wines
Châteauneuf-du-Pape, Gigondas, and Vacqueyras for irresistibly delicious wines

The Wines of Valpolicella
Valpolicella, Ripasso, and Amarone

Valpolicella is the land of red wine. It's in the north-eastern region of Veneto, Italy, and here, three main types of grapes grow – Molinara, Rondinella, and Corvina. These same three grapes are used to make all the wines of the region, and each is made in a completely different style. This section covers the dry wine styles, but Recioto, the sweet wine of Valpolicella, is covered in our dessert wine section (page 328).

Valpolicella

If you were to look at Valpolicella's wines as building blocks, you would start with Valpolicella at the bottom, the first block that's simple, light and fruity. The next step up is Ripasso, and finally the top level is Amarone della Valpolicella, which has the richest flavours, the biggest body, and the highest alcohol of the three.

Let's start off with the basic wine of this region, called simply Valpolicella. The three grapes (Molinara, Rondinella, and Corvina) are blended together to make a light to medium bodied wine that's easy-drinking, food-friendly, and low in alcohol. It has lots of acidity and tart red cherry fruit flavours, which makes it work with a lot of the Italian food flavours, especially tomatoes. And if it has tannins at all, they are light and soft. Valpolicella Classico (from the centre of the region) and Superiore (which denotes higher alcohol content) are wines to look out for – they have a little bit more body and flavour.

As the first building block in this series of wines, Valpolicella is uncomplicated and straightforward to drink, and it's made without any bells and whistles – no oak-aging or other fancy winemaking techniques. Those are saved for the wines to come.

Aromas & Flavours
Light fruity aromas and flavours of tart red cherry
Herbaceous and spicy notes
Light in body with bright acidity

Food Ideas
Antipasti
Beef carpaccio or tartare
Spaghetti carbonara
Tomato bruschetta

Ripasso

The middle building block of Valpolicella is Ripasso – the wine that fills the gap between light and simple Valpolicella and rich, deep Amarone. "Ripasso" means "re-passed" which is exactly how this wine is made. When making Amarone (the next section goes into more detail), the grapes are dried before fermenting them. Once the skins of the dried grapes are removed from the wine, they're not just thrown away. They are the magic ingredient that makes "baby Amarone," the wine called Ripasso. The skins from the dried Amarone grapes are added to Valpolicella wine and re-fermented. This takes the simple and fruity base wine and adds some of the richness that Amarone is famous for. The result is a wine that is medium to full in body, with a smooth, rich texture. The flavours are ripe cherry and plum with soft vanilla notes and lots of the classic Italian acidity.

This style of wine is relatively unknown, but it could be Italy's best kept secret. If you love fruity, full styles of wine like Grenache, Merlot, or Zinfandel, you must try Ripasso. Satisfying to drink on its own, it's also the perfect partner to all sorts of Italian cuisine, including meats, pastas, and cheeses, and especially when compared to pricey Amarone (which usually starts at $30 a bottle), Ripasso is affordable, with most in the $15 to $20 range.

Aromas & Flavours
Ripe flavours of red cherry, plum, and vanilla
Medium to full in body with a smooth texture and crisp acidity

Food Ideas
Veal Parmigiana
Rich pasta dishes
Strong cheeses

Amarone Della Amarone

The name "Amarone" loosely translates to mean "bitter," referring to the rich, deep flavours that are often found in this wine. It's made using a method called *passito*, a little trick that helps winemakers concentrate flavours and up the alcohol in a wine. At harvest time, the best bunches of Molinara, Corvina, and Rondinella grapes are hand-picked and set aside for Amarone. They're laid out on mats or racks to dry, and over several months they shrivel to a raisin-like form, and this is the key – as the grapes are drying and shriveling, what's actually happening is that the water content in the grapes is evaporating, leaving very concentrated sugars and flavours. Think about how a raisin tastes compared to a regular grape – way sweeter and way more intense. The dried grapes are then fermented and the wine you get is Amarone. It's full-bodied and powerful, with strong flavours of raisin and other dried fruits, stewed cherry and plum, and spicy, leathery notes. Amarone is almost port-like, with its high alcohol and rich, full body. It's not sweet, but because the flavours are so concentrated and ripe, it almost seems like it is. This wine is quite tannic in its youth but it ages well and softens into an almost dessert-like indulgence. I love this wine with strong cheeses, rich red meat dishes, and even a piece of bittersweet chocolate.

Aromas & Flavours
Rich, intense fruit flavours of raisin and other dried fruits, cherry, and plum
Earthy, spicy, and leathery notes
High-alcohol with an almost port-like body

Food Ideas
Hard Italian cheeses like Parmigiano or Asiago
Pungent blue cheeses like Gorgonzola
Rich red meat or game dishes

The Super Tuscans

Old World wine regions in France and Italy are known for their complicated wine laws regulating everything from grape type, alcohol level and harvest dates to how the wine is labeled after bottling. It's these wine laws that make many French and Italian wines complicated and inaccessible for the everyday wine consumer. Most are named after their regions, districts, or appellations that don't tell you what grape is inside the bottle, which makes choosing those wines pretty tricky.

These regulations, though sometimes frustrating and old-fashioned, keep the traditional wine styles alive in a wine world that is sometimes now more focused on marketing than winemaking. But they don't really allow for creativity or innovation, so in the 1970s when renegade winemakers in Tuscany wanted to start experimenting with French grapes like Merlot, Cabernet Sauvignon, and Syrah, the powers that be tried to bring them down.

Because these grapes aren't allowed in the traditional regional blends with names like Chianti, they had to be labeled *vino da tavola* – basic table wine. What the laws didn't allow for was that these grapes, when blended with indigenous Sangiovese, or on their own, created explosively intense and delicious wines. The misrepresentative classification didn't stop the winemakers, and the lack of regulations for vino da tavola meant that they could come up with their own unique names for their wines, like Sassacaia, Ornellaia, and Tignanello, just to name a few.

These wines came to be known around the world as the "Super Tuscans," wines made with internationally known grapes, sometimes on their own and often blended with native Sangiovese. Today they've reached cult status, not just for their intrepid beginnings, but also because they're so damn good. If you like 'em big and bold, save your pennies for a Super Tuscan (not only are they super tasty, they're also super pricey). These wines combine the spice and acidity that Italian wines are known for with the flavours and intensity of big New World reds.

Aromas & Flavours
Rich fruit flavours of blackcurrant, blackberry, black cherry, and plum
Spicy, leathery notes and a nice balance of acidity
Full body, big tannins, and intense flavours

Food Ideas
Red meats in rich preparations
Hearty pastas and stews
Strong, aged, and blue-veined cheeses

PORK STEW WITH PRUNES AND ONIONS

The French really know how to make a stew. Sweet and sour depth is what's going on in this pot with the mild pork, luscious plums, flavourful broth and glazed onions. I find making stew deeply satisfying and relaxing. The big pay off is the way a good stew can make your house smell delicious all day. If pearl onions are new to you, they are a sweet mild onion, roughly the size of an olive. **Serves 4**

1 1/2 lb (675g) stewing pork shoulder,
    cut to 1-inch cubes

1/4 cup (60ml) extra virgin olive oil

A good pinch each ground cinnamon, black
    pepper, dried rosemary, and dried thyme

1 teaspoon (5ml) finely grated orange zest

1 cup (250ml) finely chopped cooking onion

1 tablespoon (15ml) balsamic vinegar

1 tablespoon (15ml) Dijon mustard

1 1/2 cups (375) dry white wine

4 garlic cloves, finely chopped

2 medium carrots, peeled and cut into
    1-inch chunks

1 bay leaf

Salt

1 3/4 (430ml) cups chicken stock

14 pearl onions, peeled

1 tablespoon (15ml) unsalted butter

2 tablespoons brown sugar

8 large pitted prunes soaked in hot water
    to soften

3 tablespoons (45ml) 35% cream

- In a small bowl, mix together the olive oil with the cinnamon, black pepper, rosemary, thyme and orange zest, coat the pork with it and pop into your fridge for a minimum of 4 hours or overnight. Pull the pork out of the fridge and let come to room temperature for 30 minutes.

- In a heavy bottomed soup pot or a large, heavy flameproof casserole, cook the pork, covered, over medium-high for 5 minutes. Don't add any extra oil to the pot, the meat has marinated in lots. After 5 minutes, pull off the lid and sauté the meat while stirring until the pork is browned on all sides, about 10 minutes.

- Pull the pork from the pan and into a bowl and set it aside. Add the onion to the pot and cook until soft and sweet. Add a little extra oil or water to the pan if the onions are starting to stick. Once cooked, add them to the pork.

- Pour vinegar and 1 cup (250ml) of the white wine into the pan and scrape up all the porky, oniony, brown bits stuck to the bottom. Stir in the mustard and bring liquids to a boil until wine has turned into a glaze, about 2 tablespoons (30ml) worth. It's a fine line between glaze and burning so keep your eye on the pan and have your other 1/2 cup (125ml) of white wine ready. Once the first batch of wine is looking glazy, add the second 1/2 cup (125ml) and reduce again to about 2 tablespoons.

Contd . . .

TIP

There is a trick to peeling pearl onions that will make your life so much easier. Bring a medium saucepan of water to a boil and season it with some salt. Cut a little X in the root end of each small onion. Toss the onions into the boiling water and boil them for 2 minutes. Drain the pot into a strainer and run them under cold tap water until they've cooled off. With a sharp pairing knife cut a little slit through the outer layer on one side of each onion to remove the outer layer. It's a little extra work for an onion. Believe me, they are definitely worth it.

- Toss in your carrots, garlic, and bay leaf to sauté for 1 minute, stirring. Add your pork and onion mixture along with any juices from them that have leaked into the bowl, that's a flavour goldmine.

- Pour the chicken stock over top and season with some salt to taste. Bring the whole thing to a boil but then turn it down to a very low, barely there simmer.

- Cook, very slowly, for about 45 minutes.

- In a medium skillet melt together the butter, the sugar and 1/2 cup (125ml) of water. Bring this mixture to a simmer and cook until the water has evaporated which should take 4 or 5 minutes.

- Toss in the peeled pearl onions and roll them around in the sugar butter until they are well coated. Cook them over low heat for about 8 minutes or until they are tender and browned all over. Pull them from the heat and set them aside

- Once the meat has cooked for a total of 45 minutes, add the prunes and browned pearl onions.

- Cover the stew with a lid and continue cooking until the pork is incredibly tender, about 15 minutes longer giving the pot a gentle stir to keep anything from getting stuck on the bottom of the pan.

- Stir in your cream, pull pot from the heat and give the broth a taste for any needed salt and pepper.

- Serve this stew in warm wide bowls with the best crusty bread you can find.

WINE MATCH – **Pinot Noir**

This dish has light meat and white wine in it so you might automatically think a white pairing would be the right thing. It could work, but it might be tricky to find a white big enough to deal with the distinct and intense flavour of prunes, the other key element of this dish. I think a lighter style of Pinot Noir with lots of acidity is the perfect choice – not only does it have the earthy and berry flavours to match the prunes, it's light enough to not overpower the mild pork and the sauce. Go for a cool climate Pinot Noir from regions like Burgundy, Oregon, or Niagara.

CUBED PORK WITH GARLIC SPINACH
AND SPICY CHICKPEAS

This is one of those strange rustic dishes that you'll make once and immediately add it your regular rotation of dinners. I have. It's easy, attractive and really tasty. The tender pork snuggles in perfectly with the earthy chickpeas and the fresh green spinach. The flavours are clean and honest and simple. What is nice about using dried rather than canned chickpeas is that you have the opportunity to perfume them with aromatics and make them a little garlicky. It's really not extra work, you're just throwing stuff in a pan and letting it do its thing while keeping an eye on it. The chickpeas do the work for you, and the pay-off, in this case, is definitely worth it. Serves 4

1 1/2 cups (375ml) dried chickpeas

4 tablespoons (60ml) extra virgin olive oil

4–5 sprigs each of parsley, thyme and rosemary

2 bay leaves

Salt to taste

1 lb (454g) fresh spinach, washed and
*   stemmed, but not dried*

1 lb (454g) pork loin, cut into 1-inch cubes

10 garlic cloves, cut into slivers, plus 3 cloves
*   left whole*

1/2 teaspoon (2.5ml) red pepper flakes

Freshly ground black pepper

Juice of 1/2 lemon

- Fill a kettle or saucepan and bring 3–4 cups (750ml to 1 litre) of water to a boil. In a colander, rinse the chickpeas and pick through them looking for any pebbles, or non-chickpea-looking material.

- Toss the chickpeas into a big bowl. Pour the boiling water over top of the chickpeas to cover. Put a plate overtop to seal the steam in and let the bowl sit for 1 hour undisturbed. Drain the chickpeas and give them a rinse.

- Turn the chickpeas into a medium saucepan. Add to the pot 2 tablespoons (30ml) of the olive oil, the herbs, 3 whole cloves of garlic and the bay leaves. Cover the chickpeas with cold water and bring to a simmer over medium heat. Once they start to simmer, turn the heat down to low, cover the pot and simmer for about an hour.

- Add the salt after an hour (if you add the salt too early with dried beans the damn things will never cook properly) and keep simmering until the chickpeas are tender, likely another hour. Check the water level and tenderness of the chickpeas every 1/2 hour just to be safe.

Contd . . .

- Once they're cooked, strain them and pull out all the non chickpea items (the garlic, bay leaves, etc.) and set them aside for now.

- In a wok or skillet add your damp spinach and cover with a lid. Steam until bright green and just wilted. Pull the spinach out of the pan and squeeze as much of the moisture as you can out of leaves. Lay the squeezed spinach onto a cutting board and give it a good chopping.

- Wipe out the skillet you used for the spinach and heat up 2 tablespoons (30ml) of the olive oil over medium heat.

- Toss the pork into the pan along with the garlic and the red pepper flakes. Season the pork lightly with salt and pepper and toss it around the pan really well to coat it with the oil. If the garlic starts to cook too quickly just turn down the heat a bit. Cook everything for about 5–7 minutes, until the pork cubes are cooked.

- Add the chickpeas and the spinach and stir until just warmed through, give a squeeze of lemon juice and salt and pepper to taste. You are ready to serve.

WINE MATCH – **Cabernet Franc**

I love pairing Cabernet Franc with dishes that feature greens in them, because the wine has this distinct vegetal flavour (think bell pepper) that matches up just right with vegetables. Cab Franc tends to be on the light to medium side of reds, so it's also a great choice for a mildly flavoured meat like pork, which you don't want to overpower with a big, whopping red wine. Look for Cab Franc from the Loire Valley, with "Bourgueil" or "Chinon" on the label.

BACON-WRAPPED MAPLE PORK LOIN

All good Canadians know that bacon and maple syrup are two lost lovers who often only find each other on the weekend at breakfast time. I've decided to do something about it. Brining the pork helps to add a lot of flavour and moisture that may otherwise be missing due to the very little fat found in the loins of pigs these days. Serves 6 to 8

The Brine

8 cups (2litres) water

1/3 cup kosher (90ml) or sea salt

2 tablespoons (30ml) maple syrup

1 teaspoon (5ml) black peppercorns

2 sprigs fresh rosemary

1 large garlic clove, smashed

1 bay leaf

1 boneless pork loin roast, about 4 lb (2kg), trimmed

For roasting pork

3 garlic cloves, finely chopped

2 tablespoons (30ml) finely chopped fresh rosemary

3 tablespoons (45ml) maple syrup

16 bacon slices (about 1 lb)

1 tablespoon (15ml) cider vinegar

1/2 teaspoon (2.5ml) cornstarch

1 teaspoon (5ml) water

- To make the brine, combine all of the brining ingredients in a large saucepan over high heat until the salt dissolves. Pour into a deep 4- to 5-quart/litre container and cool to room temperature, uncovered, for about 2 hours.

- Add your pork roast to the brine. Make sure that it is completely submerged. Marinate in your refrigerator overnight or for at least a minimum of 4 hours.

- Put your oven rack in middle of the oven and preheat oven to 400°F (200C).

- Pull your pork out of the brine, which you can now get rid of. Pat the little roast dry with a paper towel and cut off any strings.

- Pop it into a roasting pan. Stir together garlic, rosemary, and 1 tablespoon (15ml) of syrup in a small bowl and rub all over pork.

- Lay your bacon slices over the width (not length) of the loin. Overlap them just a little and tuck underneath the roast to secure them.

- Toss your lovely little roast into the oven and roast until a meat thermometer comes to 140F. This should take about 1– 1 1/2 hours.

- Stir together 1 tablespoon (15ml) syrup and vinegar until combined. Brush vinegar mixture over bacon slices and continue to roast pork until thermometer registers 150°F, about 10 minutes more.

- Remove from oven and let stand in pan 15 minutes. Transfer roast to a cutting board with a lip, reserving juices in pan, and let roast stand, uncovered, while making sauce.

- Skim fat from pan juices and discard, then transfer jus to a small saucepan and bring to a simmer. Stir together cornstarch and water and whisk into jus. Simmer, stirring, until slightly thickened, about 1 minute. Remove from heat and stir in the remaining tablespoon of syrup. Serve pork with sauce.

WINE MATCH – **Pinot Noir**

Pinot Noir is a fantastic red wine match for pork because it's made in styles from light and tart to more ripe and full. This is great for pork dishes because in many ways, pork is like a blank culinary canvas – a versatile but mild-flavoured meat whose wine pairing is based mainly on how it's prepared. In this case, a new world style of Pinot Noir is perfect. Ripe berry flavours pair up nicely with the sweetness of the maple syrup, and toasty, smoky notes from oak aging stand up to the smoky, salty bacon.

TIP

Why are there different shapes of wine bottles?

Just like wine glasses, you'll notice a bunch of different bottle shapes (and colours) on the shelf when you go to the wine store. So what's the deal? Like many things in the wine world, bottle shapes come from tradition.

The two most common wine bottles shapes are the Burgundy and Bordeaux styles. Burgundy bottles have a gradual, sloping curve to their shape and are traditionally used for wines made in the region of Burgundy (Chardonnay and Pinot Noir). Chardonnay and Pinot Noir made around the world are often bottled in the same bottle shape, and you'll also see other styles of wine too, including Rhône-style wines made from Syrah and/or Shiraz.

Bordeaux style bottles have more defined "shoulders" and a straight, cylindrical shape. The original reason for this bottle shape was ease of storage (the even shape was easy to store on its side in racks). The shape also made sense for the style of wine – when pouring a bottle, the shoulders helped catch sediment formed in aged wines. Other red wines meant to be aged are also bottled in this style – wines like Barolo and vintage port, and white wines from Bordeaux were also packaged in this bottle shape.

For white wines, there is one other style of bottle you'll see – a taller, slimmer version of the Burgundy bottle, which is used traditionally for white wines from Germany and Alsace, France. Wines made from the aromatic grapes Riesling, Gewürztraminer, and anything else made in a similar style is now usually bottled in this narrower shape.

Nowadays, old world wine producers tend to stick to traditional bottle shapes associated with their regions, whereas new world wineries can go either way – traditional shapes for certain wine styles or whatever suits their marketing team and branding.

When it comes to bottle colour, you'll most commonly see clear glass, or various shades of green and brown. Wines that can be aged are usually bottled in coloured glass because the tint in the glass protects the wine from light which over the long term can be damaging to the wine. You'll usually see wines that have little to no shelf life in clear, colourless glass. Again, it all comes from tradition and these days the packaging is often dictated by marketing.

What about the thickness of glass? Thicker glass can also protect the wine inside the bottle from light or other environmental damage. On the downside though, thicker glass is more expensive in both materials and shipping, so thinner glass is now more common. Sparkling wine bottles usually have heavier glass (to hold up against the pressure inside) and a punt – a dip in the bottom surface of your wine bottle. Most often punts are found in higher-quality bottles, which can help in serving the wine – you can put your thumb in the indentation and pour with one hand.

BRAISED PORK SHOULDER WITH TOMATOES, FENNEL AND OLIVE

I love braising. In fact I'm looking to have "I ♥ braising" t-shirts made. Here's the thing, you do a little prep, cover it up, throw it into your oven and ignore it for a good chunk of time, while you make other food, read, hang out with your guests, just stand in your kitchen and inhale deeply, whatever suits your fancy. The end results – tender, fall-off-the-bone meat, and a sauce pretty much made for you with all the juicy delicious ingredients you included. **Serves 8**

1 boneless pork shoulder butt roast
   (3 lb, 1.5 kg), fat trimmed to 1/8 inch thick

3 tablespoons (45ml) vegetable oil

1 large carrot, finely diced

1 medium celery stalk, finely diced

2 small yellow onions, finely diced

1 1/2 teaspoons (7.5ml) fennel seeds,
   crushed in a mortar

4 sprigs of thyme

3 sprigs of rosemary

1 can (796ml) best quality Italian plum
   tomatoes, diced and strained, but juice
   reserved

3 tablespoons vegetable oil

4 cloves garlic, sliced

2 1/2 cups (625ml) chicken stock

1/2 cup (125ml) pitted kalamata olives

2 tablespoons (30ml) finely chopped
   Italian parsley

Salt and pepper

- Tie up your roast with some butcher's twine so it's compact and slightly rectangular in shape. Preheat your oven to 350F (180C).

- Season the roast with salt and pepper and heat up a cast iron or heavy bottomed skillet over medium heat. Lay the roast into the pan fat-side down. Sear it off for about 12 minutes on the fatty side. There is going to be a lot of fat melting off the roast so every few minutes spoon it out and into a heatproof bowl. Once the fatty side of the roast has a nice golden colour, sear the other 3 sides for a couple of minutes each side.

- Transfer it to a plate. Wipe the skillet clean and warm up the vegetable oil, still cooking on medium heat. Toss in your onion, carrots and celery and cook for about 8–10 minutes, or until the veggies are soft and a little caramel in colour.

- Add fennel seed, and cook for another minute.

- Now add your thyme, rosemary, tomatoes and their juice.

- Season the pan lightly with salt and pepper and give everything a good stir. Pour the vegetables into the bottom of a roasting pan and add the chicken stock.

Contd . . .

- Make some small incisions with a paring knife every couple of inches or so around your roast. Slide a slice of garlic in each incision.

- Pop the roast on top of the vegetables. Cover the roasting pan and move it into your oven for 1 hour and 20 minutes.

- Once the roast is done, pull it from the broth and onto a cutting board. Cover loosely with tin foil.

- Pull 3 cups (750ml) of the sauce and vegetables from the pan and into your food processor. Blend them on high until smooth.

- Return your blended vegetables to the sauce and stir together. Skim any fat off the top. The sauce should be fairly thick. Stir in your parsley and olives.

- Slice your roast. Arrange the meat on a platter or on individual plates and spoon a generous amount of sauce over each piece. Serve immediately.

WINE MATCH – **Sangiovese**

I like putting together wine and food that come from the same place – the flavours traditionally complement each other so it's an easy way to create a great match. Italian Sangiovese has lots of tartness that balances the acidity in tomatoes, and its earthy, spicy flavours round out the fennel and olives in the dish. Plus Sangiovese is about medium in body with fairly light tannins so it's not too overpowering with the pork. Look for a Chianti Classico to pair with this dish.

TOURTIÈRE

People take their tourtière recipes very seriously. This is a great recipe to start with but each time you make it make notes of things you would change or add. That is how recipes become family secrets. Don't skip the refrigeration of the pie crust to just get on with making the pie, it's one of those make or break pastry rules that will break you. Trust me. If you're not into making pastry, you can easily pick up store bought pie crust and proceed with the rest of the recipe. **Serves 6–8**

Pastry

2 1/2 cups (625ml) all-purpose flour

1 cup (250ml) vegetable shortening

1/2 teaspoon (2.5ml) salt

Ice water

Filling

2 tablespoons (30ml) olive oil

1 1/2 lb (625g) lean ground pork

1 onion, finely chopped

1 celery stalk, finely chopped

1 small carrot, finely chopped

4 cloves garlic, minced

1/4 cup (60ml) chopped parsley

*3 sprigs fresh thyme, leaves removed
    and chopped*

2 teaspoon (10ml) chopped fresh sage

1/2 teaspoon (2.5ml) dried savoury

3/4 cup (175ml) chicken stock

Pinch each grated nutmeg and ground cloves

Salt and pepper

1/3 cup (80ml) good quality bread crumbs

- Start by making the pastry. In a large bowl, combine the flour with the salt. Using a pastry blender or a fork, work the vegetable shortening into the flour until you have yourself a crumbly texture.

- Add some ice water a tablespoon at a time until you can just form a ball with the dough.

- Form the dough into a disk, wrap it in plastic wrap and pop it into your fridge for a minimum of 30 minutes.

- In a large skillet, heat up the olive oil over medium-high heat. Add the onion, garlic, celery, and carrot. Sauté for about 10 minutes or until soft and starting to turn golden brown.

- Add the pork to the pan and cook until you can't find any more pink, 5–10 minutes.

- Stir in the chicken stock, thyme, sage, savoury, nutmeg and cloves. Simmer for about 10 minutes or until almost no liquid remains. You want the mixture to be moist but not soupy. Season with salt and pepper.

- Stir in your bread crumbs and parsley and mix everything together. Set aside and let cool.

- Preheat oven to 425F (220C).

Contd . . .

- Cut the chilled dough into two pieces. Keep one covered with the plastic wrap. Lightly flour a work surface and roll out your pastry to 1/8 inch thickness. You need the pastry to be large enough to line a 9-inch pie plate. Roll out the second piece to the same dimensions.

- Line your pie plate with 1 of the rounds and trim the edge. Fill the pastry with the filling.

- Top the pie with your other circle and crimp the edges around the pie to seal everything really well.

- Slice 3 vents into the top of your pastry to allow steam to escape while it's cooking.

- Slide the pie onto a baking tray and into the oven. Bake the tourtiere for 45–50 minutes or until the pie is golden and the filling is heated through.

- Serve with your favourite chutney or sweet pepper condiment on the side.

WINE MATCH – **Baco Noir**

Tourtière is a hearty dish with lots of spicy and meaty flavours and a rich pastry crust. Its wine match has to have a lot going on as well so it doesn't get overpowered. Try a Baco Noir, which works well with its big fruit flavours and medium body – it's especially good because the acidity in the wine cleans your taste buds after the rich crust. If you can't find it, look for another red that's full, fruity, and easy-drinking, like Merlot or Tempranillo.

CROWN ROAST OF PORK

When you want something fancy but you don't want turkey, this is it. It's big, it's pretty, it screams abundance! Have your butcher prepare and tie the crown roast for you in advance, that way you don't have to fuss. I love it on holidays like Thanksgiving when you've got a crowd and you're looking for the wow factor as you place your dish on the table. Sometimes, it's all showbiz. **Serves 12–16**

One 8–9 lb (4 to 4.5kg) crown roast of pork
(up to 18 ribs)

Stuffing

16 pitted prunes, diced

16 dried apricots

1 cup (250ml) walnuts, toasted and finely
chopped

1 cup (250ml) orange juice

2 tablespoon (30ml) unsalted butter

1 cooking onion finely diced

2 celery stalks, thinly sliced

2 tablespoons (30ml) finely chopped fresh sage

1 tablespoon (15ml) finely chopped fresh thyme

4 garlic cloves, minced

1 1/2 lb (675g) mild Italian sausages

1 cup (250ml) good quality bread crumbs

2 teaspoons (10ml) salt

Freshly ground black pepper

Sauce

1 cup (250ml) orange juice

1 cup (250ml) chicken stock

1 tablespoon (15ml) honey

1 tablespoon (15ml) cornstarch dissolved
in 1 tbsp water

Salt and freshly ground black pepper

- To make the stuffing, bring the orange juice to a simmer. In a medium bowl, pour the juice over the prunes and apricots then cover with a plate for 30 minutes.

- In a large sauté pan, heat the butter until foamy. Add your onion and celery and cook for 5 minutes or until the onion is sweet and tender.

- Toss in the garlic, sage and thyme and cook for 2 more minutes. Scrape everything from the pan into a nice big bowl to cool.

- Slice down one side of the sausages and empty the meat filling into the onion mixture. Discard the casings.

- Add the walnuts, breads crumbs, soaked fruit, juice, salt and pepper. Mix it all together really well.

- To adjust seasonings, fry off about a tablespoon-sized piece of the stuffing in a small frying pan. Give the cooked stuffing a taste to see if it needs any salt or pepper. Adjust the seasoning if necessary.

- Preheat your oven to 400F (200C).

- Season your crown roast with salt and pepper. Rip off a good sized piece of aluminium foil and put it underneath the crown roast. Put the roast (with the foil bottom) onto a rack in a roasting pan.

- Loosely pack the stuffing into middle of the roast.

Contd . . .

- Pour 1 1/2 cups (375ml) of water into the pan. Slide the roast into the oven and roast it for 10 minutes. Turn down the temperature of the oven to 350F (180C). Cook for 25 minutes per pound or until a thermometer reads 160F. It's important to check the pan every half hour or so to be sure that there is still water in there. If you're getting low just throw in another cup.

- Once your crown is cooked, you can make your sauce. Carefully pull out the rack, cover loosely with foil and let the roast rest for at least 15 minutes.

- Whisk your cornstarch into the orange juice and chicken stock. While your pan is still hot, pour in the orange juice and the chicken stock. Over a burner on medium-high heat, bring the liquid to a boil, scrape up the brown bits off the bottom of the pan. Allow 2 minutes for the sauce to thicken, giving it a good whisk now and then. Season with salt and pepper and pour into a bowl or gravy boat for serving.

- Cut the string off of your roast. Carve into individual chops. Serve with the stuffing and the sauce.

WINE MATCH – **Tempranillo**

This crown roast has a super-flavourful filling – sweet apricot, prune, and orange juice (which is also tart); spice from the Italian sausage; earthy sage and thyme; and toasty walnuts. My wine of choice is Tempranillo – look for a Crianza Rioja which will have all the elements you're looking for. Earthy and spicy notes, a good dose of acidity, ripe berry flavours, and toasty oak notes create a wine that complements all the different parts of the dish. An Italian Sangiovese would be a nice alternative, or if you'd like a white wine, try Pinot Gris.

GOAT CHEESE STUFFED PORK TENDERLOIN WITH RED WINE BALSAMIC CHERRY SAUCE

Cherries and goat cheese and pork, oh my! Flavour, texture and colour all pop in this dish. Sweet, dark cherries against the rosy pork, contrasting with the bright white goat's cheese. It's lovely to look at, sweet, sour and savoury to taste. If fresh cherries aren't available you can use frozen. Just thaw them out and drain them ahead of time. **Serves 6**

2 pork tenderloins, centre cut, approximately
   6 inches (152 mm) each in length with
   silver skin removed

Salt and pepper to taste

3/4 cup (180ml) goat's cheese, crumbled

Zest of 2 lemons

1 1/2 tablespoons (22.5ml) chopped fresh basil

3 tablespoons olive oil (45ml)

1 teaspoon (5ml) cracked pepper

Butcher's twine

Salt and pepper to taste

1/2 cup (125ml) red wine

1/2 cup (125ml) fresh cherries, pits removed
   and chopped

1/2 tablespoon (7.5ml) balsamic vinegar

Salt and pepper to taste

- Preheat oven to 400F (200C).

- Use a sharp knife to "butterfly" the pork tenderloin. This is done by making an incision mid way through the length of the tenderloin (so it opens like a butterfly). Be sure to leave the loin with at least 1/2 inch (12 mm) uncut at the base. Do the same with the other loin.

- Season with salt and pepper. Cover with plastic wrap and using a rolling pin (or a meat tenderizer), gently pound on the meat until the surface is flat.

- In a medium bowl mix together the goat cheese, lemon zest and basil with 1 tablespoon (15 ml) of olive oil and the pepper.

- Pull the plastic wrap off the meat and spoon the goat cheese mixture evenly over the centre leaving a 3/4 inch border. Roll up to make a nice compact, even loin. Do the same with the other tenderloin.

- Use butcher string to make even ties on every inch of the loin, to keep the roll intact.

- Rub 1 tablespoon (15ml) of olive oil all over the pork loins. Season with salt and pepper.

- Set a large ovenproof skillet over medium-high heat, add the remaining olive oil and allow to it to heat up for about 30 seconds. The pan should be hot but not smoking.

Contd . . .

- Put the pork loins in the skillet and cook until a deep golden brown caramelized crust forms. Place the skillet in the preheated oven and allow them to cook for another 12 minutes or until a meat thermometer reads 145F.

- Pull the pork out of the oven, place the loins on a plate and cover loosely with foil.

- Put empty skillet back on the heat and turn up the stovetop to medium high. Add the red wine and with a wooden spoon, scrape up all the porky caramel bits from the bottom of the pan.

- Add half the cherries and the balsamic vinegar and continue to cook for 5 minutes.

- Add the rest of the cherries and cook for another minute. Once the sauce is slightly reduced and the cherries are warmed up, season with salt and pepper.

- To serve, slice the tenderloin with a sharp knife. Divide the pork onto six plates and drizzle with the cherry sauce. Serve immediately.

WINE MATCH – **Primitivo**

This is one of those pairings that really can't get any better. First off, use the same wine you're serving in the recipe itself – it's a great way to seal the deal on a perfect pairing because the flavours of the wine are right on the plate. Primitivo is not so full-bodied that it overpowers the delicate meat, but it's got enough body and flavour to balance the rich goat's cheese filling. The cherry flavour of the wine mirrors the cherry sauce, and the wine cleanses your palate after each bite with its refreshing acidity. If you can't find Primitivo, try Merlot or Sangiovese instead.

PRIME RIB OF BEEF WITH SHIRAZ PEPPERCORN GRAVY

The term "prime" rib in the chefy world is referring to the highest grade of meat which has a beautiful marbling of fat throughout, adding moisture and a ton of well-distributed flavour to your roast. If you've only ever known the black peppercorn, it's time to introduce you to a new world. Black, green and pink peppercorns have very individual personalities. You can often find them combined or you can buy them separately in most gourmet food stores. Together, they turbo-boost the flavour of the meat and add a little something different without stealing the show. When you have a cut of beef this good, you don't want to do anything but enhance its loveliness. **Serves 4**

4–5 lb (about 2-2.5 kg) prime rib roast

1/4 cup (125ml) unsalted butter, softened

3 tablespoons (45ml) all-purpose flour

3 tablespoons (45ml) mixed pink, green and black peppercorns, crushed lightly

2 tablespoons (30ml) Dijon mustard

4 cloves of garlic, minced

1 tablespoon (15ml) packed brown sugar

1 teaspoon (5ml) salt

1 tablespoon olive oil

1 onion, finely chopped

3 tablespoons (45ml) all-purpose flour

3/4 cup (180ml) Shiraz or other full bodied red wine

2 cups (500ml) beef stock

Salt and freshly ground black pepper

- Preheat your oven to 350F (180C).

- Pull the roast out of the fridge 30 minutes before you start cooking to let it come to room temperature. Put your roast, rib-side down in a roasting pan.

- In a small bowl mix together the butter, flour, cracked peppercorns, mustard, garlic sugar and salt. Rub over the top and sides of the roast and slide it into the oven.

- Cook uncovered for 1 1/2 hours. With a meat thermometer check the internal temperature, for medium rare you want 125F.

- When the roast is cooked, pull it out of the pan and move it to a cutting board placed in a baking tray with sides (this will catch any juices that escape while you are carving). Tent the meat with foil and let it rest for a minimum of 10–15 minutes.

- To make your gravy, pour the pan juices into a glass measuring cup and pop into your freezer for 10 minutes. This will make the fat rise to the top and a lot easier to scoop off.

Contd . . .

- Don't clean your pan yet though, we're going to make the sauce in there with all the flavour left from the roast. While you are waiting for the juices to cool and separate, add 1 tablespoon (15ml) of olive oil to the pan and warm up over medium-high heat. Add your onion and sauté until it's soft and sweet, about 2 minutes.

- Whisk in the wine and the beef stock and bring it up to a boil, while scraping off the caramel bits from the bottom of the pan. Scrape the fat from your pan juices while the wine and stock are reducing.

- Add the pan juices to the sauce and reduce until slightly thickened and flavourful, about 10 minutes.

- Season with salt and pepper and pour into a dish or gravy boat.

- Slice your prime rib and serve it with your rich gravy.

WINE MATCH – **Shiraz**

There are three good reasons to drink Shiraz with this dish. First off – you're cooking with Shiraz so the pairing is bound to be good. Second reason, the peppery crust on the prime rib will really bring out the pepperiness of the wine. And lastly, this dish needs a big, full bodied wine, and Shiraz delivers with its ripe, mouth-filling flavours and texture. And here's a tip – if you're planning to serve an extra-special bottle with this meal, don't feel obliged to use the same wine for the cooking, but do choose a good quality Shiraz at a lower price so you still get the same range of flavours.

MEATBALLS WITH ARTICHOKES, GREEN OLIVES AND SAGE

I love this dish for a couple of reasons. It's always a big hit and it's super easy to feed a crowd without being stuck in the kitchen all night. I like the combination of light, mild veal with deeper-flavoured beef. You can also easily double up the meatball portion of this dish and freeze some of them on a cookie sheet, then toss into a freezer bag or container, ready for the next time you need them. I usually serve this dish over a big bowl of buttered broad noodles and a wedge of Parmesan with a grater on the table for everyone to help themselves. **Serves 8**

7 tablespoons (105ml) olive oil

3 medium cooking onions, finely diced

Salt

Freshly ground black pepper

1 lb (454g) ground beef

1 lb (454g) ground veal

2 1/2 tablespoons (37ml) finely chopped
fresh parsley

5 tablespoons (75ml) freshly grated Parmesan

3 large eggs

1/2 cup (125ml) panko (Japanese bread crumbs)
or regular bread crumbs

1 jar (680ml) marinated artichokes, drained

2 large ripe tomatoes, peeled, seeded and diced

4 cloves of garlic, finely chopped

2/3 cup (150ml) green olives, coarsely chopped

3 tablespoons (45ml) coarsely chopped fresh
sage leaves

2 1/2 tablespoons (37ml) fresh lemon juice

3/4 cup (180ml) chicken broth

- Warm 4 tablespoons (60ml) of your olive oil in a sauté pan over medium heat. Add your onions, 1/2 a teaspoon (2.5ml) of salt and a pinch or two of pepper. Cook these over a moderate heat for about 8 minutes, until they are nice and soft. Just be sure not to let them brown.

- Meanwhile, toss your ground beef and veal in a mixing bowl and add the parsley, Parmesan, eggs, and panko crumbs.

- Remove 1/3 of the onions from the pan and add to the bowl with the beef mixture.

- Season the mixture with 2 teaspoons (10ml) salt and 1/4 teaspoon (1.25ml) ground pepper and mix thoroughly.

- Make a small meatball and fry it off until it is cooked through. This way you can tell if it needs any thing, maybe a touch more salt, or a little more cheese. Make the meatball something you love, it is after all the star of the show here. Once you are happy with it form the meat into 16 meatballs, each weighing about 2 oz, and set them aside on a plate.

- Put the rest of your onions into a large casserole dish (16 x 8 1/2 x 2 inches)

Contd . . .

- Preheat the oven to 350F (180C). The next step is to brown the meatballs. Warm the last 3 tablespoons (45ml) of olive oil in a large sauté pan. When the oil has heated up add your lovely little meatballs and brown them all over allowing about 1–2 minutes per side. It's going to be tempting here to jam your pan full, but to make sure these fellas don't dry out give each one some space, about an inch (1–2 cm) between each ball and cook them in batches if you need to. As you finish browning them just pop them right on top of your onion bed in the casserole dish.

- Drain the artichokes. Combine the artichokes with the tomatoes, garlic, olives, sage, and lemon juice. Season with 1/2 tsp (2.5ml) of the salt and a grinding of pepper. Mix well and distribute the vegetable mixture around the meatballs. Pour the broth over the dish, cover tightly with foil, and bake in an oven for 1 hour.

- Transfer the meatballs and vegetables to a large heated platter, pour some of the juices over them and serve.

WINE MATCH – **Barbera**

Barbera isn't a very well-known grape, but it makes wine that is extremely food-friendly – I really can't say enough about how well it works with different flavours, and especially with dishes that have tart or hard-to-match flavours. This one has artichokes and green olives, both of which have sour, briny flavours from being marinated, and after trying lots of different wines, I found Barbera to be the one that best balanced them. It also has enough body to not be overpowered by the meatballs, and the earthy note in the wine is a nice complement to the sage.

GRILLED BEEF SALAD WITH CASHEWS

A plate of grilled vegetables in the summer time, topped with some salty, crunchy cashews and tender slices of beef makes me one happy girl! The colourful plate wakes up your senses before you taste, and it has a variety of clean flavours – especially when the vegetables you use are in season. You can switch up the beef for nearly any other meat that you're craving. The whole kit and caboodle makes for a satisfying light lunch or a colourful first course for dinner. Serves 6

2 medium zucchini

1 large Spanish onion

1 medium eggplant, unpeeled

2 large sweet red peppers

2 heads Belgian endive

1/3 cup (90ml) olive oil

Salt and pepper

1/2 cup (125ml) extra virgin olive oil

2 tablespoons (30ml) red wine vinegar

2 tablespoons (30ml) balsamic vinegar

1 tablespoon (15ml) capers, coarsely chopped

Salt and pepper

1/4 cup (60ml) basil leaves, washed, dried and thinly shredded

2 strip-loin steaks, about 1 inch thick

Salt and pepper

1 1/2 cups (375ml) roasted, salted cashew pieces

- To make the vinaigrette, whisk together in a small bowl the olive oil, red wine vinegar, balsamic vinegar, and capers. Season with salt and pepper and set aside.

- To prepare the vegetables, start by slicing off the ends of the zucchini. Cut the zucchini lengthwise into 1/4-inch thick strips. Peel the outer layer of the onion and cut into 1/4-inch thick rings. Cut the eggplant the same way as the zucchini. You'll be grilling the peppers whole. Depending on your comfort level, you can cook up these vegetables all at once, or take your time. Completely up to you.

- Turn your grill or grill pan to medium high. If you are cooking your peppers on the grill, leave in one spot until the skin is charred. Once the pepper is blackened turn it to do the same to the other side. Continue charring the pepper until the whole thing is blackened and blistery. If you are making the salad indoors, preheat your oven to 400F (200C). Cut your peppers in half lengthwise and put cut-side down onto a baking sheet. Brush with olive oil and roast until charred and blistery. Toss your charred peppers into a bowl and cover with plastic wrap as they cool. The steam that the peppers let off will start the peeling off the skin for you.

- When the peppers are cool enough to handle, pull them from the bowl, remove the stem and rub off and discard the skin and seeds. Slice into coarse strips and set aside in a big bowl.

Contd . . .

- Brush your eggplant with some of the olive oil and season lightly with salt and pepper. Place on the grill or pan and let sit without moving for 1–2 minutes or until you get some nice little grill marks. Turn over and do the same on the other side. Pull off the eggplant when juicy and tender. Add to the bowl with the peppers.

- Brush the onion slices with the olive oil on both sides and season with salt and pepper. If you like you can use a metal skewer through the onion to keep them in their rings and make for easier flipping. If you don't have a metal skewer don't worry about it. Throw on the grill until the onion has nice grill marks on it. Flip it over to achieve the same on the other side. Once the onion is grilled, pull it off and add it to the bowl with the other vegetables.

- For the zucchini, you need to watch it a little more carefully, it tends to cook a bit faster. Brush with olive oil, salt and pepper both sides, put it on the grill to get grill marks . . . you know what you're doing by now. You are also going to grill the individual endive leaves, brushing with olive oil and seasoning first. Cook until they're lightly charred. Add to bowl of vegetables.

- Once you have finished grilling the vegetables, add the shredded basil to the bowl and toss with the vinaigrette to just coat (you might not need all the vinaigrette so add a bit at a time). Check the seasoning and set aside while you grill your beef.

- Turn the grill or grill pan up to high. Brush the steak with olive oil and season with salt and pepper. Throw the steak on the heat and cook 3–4 minutes per side until done to your liking. Cover loosely with tinfoil and let it rest for 5 minutes at least, while you arrange your vegetables on plates or a platter.

- Scatter cashews over the vegetables, thinly slice your steaks and arrange on the platter or plates and serve.

WINE MATCH – **Nero d'Avola**

The best thing about grilling vegetables is that it brings out their sweetness and adds a smoky flavour to them – both of which make them way more wine-friendly. I chose Nero d'Avola as the wine pairing for this dish because it has a bright, fresh acidity that you find in most Italian reds, which is perfect to balance the tart vinaigrette. It also has ripe berry flavours and toastiness from oak-aging that makes the wine big enough to stand up to the grilled beef. If you can't find Nero d'Avola, a Gamay Noir will do the trick nicely.

BEEF TENDERLOIN WRAPPED IN PROSCIUTTO

There is something so liberating about studding meat with bacon – in this day and age of fat avoidance, it generally goes against everything we're taught, but I'm tellin' you! The smoky pork flavour, pungent garlic and earthy rosemary that infuse into the tenderloin, are worth any extra effort, and yes, a little added fat. The prosciutto, which is wrapped over everything, melts in the pan and leaves behind great pan juices to make a simple red wine sauce. If you can get your hands on a venison or caribou loin, try switching it up. Amazing. **Serves 8**

3 lb (1kg 360g) beef tenderloin

3 cloves garlic, thinly sliced

1 bunch fresh rosemary

2 oz (56g) bacon fat, diced

Salt and freshly ground black pepper

1 lb (454g) thinly sliced prosciutto

1/4 cup (60ml) olive oil

2 cups (500ml) red wine

- Preheat your oven to 450F (230C).

- Along the grain of the beef, with a sharp little knife make a bunch of evenly spaced little incisions.

- Push into each slit some garlic, sage and a little piece of bacon fat. Decorate your loin like this all the way around. Season lightly with salt (the prosciutto is pretty salty) and a good cracking of black pepper.

- On a piece of parchment paper, lay out the prosciutto slices, slightly overlapping them and making a big rectangle which will be able to wrap around the whole tenderloin.

- Lay the studded loin on one end of the prosciutto rectangle and roll the loin up until it's completely surrounded with the prosciutto. To hold the prosciutto in place, use some butcher's twine and tie in 4 or 5 evenly spaced places.

- In a heavy bottomed skillet, heat the olive oil until just before it's about to smoke. Slide the beef into the pan and sear until golden brown on all sides.

Contd . . .

- Pour 1/2 the wine into the pan and pop the whole thing into the oven for about 10 minutes. Turn the loin over and cook for another 10–15 minutes or until a thermometer reads 125F (52C) for medium rare. Once it's done, pull the meat from the skillet and cover it loosely with foil to let it rest for 10 minutes.

- Put pan back on the heat and turn your burner to medium. Pour in the rest of the wine and scrape up all the caramel bits from the bottom of the pan. Bring the whole thing to a boil and reduce for about 5 minutes.

- For a fancier crowd, strain the sauce through a fine mesh strainer or a cheese cloth. Otherwise slice your meat and drizzle the sauce over top.

WINE MATCH – **Grenache**

This dish is the perfect vehicle to introduce Grenache into your life (if you haven't already). Grenache is one of my favourite red wines because of the way it works with food – it is full-bodied so it stands up to red meats like beef, but it's low in tannin so you can pair it up with salty prosciutto and its ripe fruit flavours come through to cleanse your palate. Look for Grenache from Australia, and if you can't find it straight up, go for a Grenache-based blend. Most red wines from the southern part of the Rhône Valley in France have lots of Grenache in them, and other countries like Australia and the United States are producing delicious blends as well.

PORCINI CRUSTED BEEF TENDERLOIN

This dish is a classic. Steak and mushrooms are a summer standby on barbecues all over the country. Why not bring the marriage indoors and switch it up with tenderloin steaks rolled in dried porcinis, giving the beef an earthy boost of flavour. Porcinis are pretty expensive, but for what you get back in flavour it's definitely worth keeping some dried in your pantry. For the sauce we use Cabernet Sauvignon, that's just a suggestion. If you have a really special bottle of wine to serve with the meal, for the love of food and wine, don't pour it in the pan! Use the same grape, just a cheaper version and the match will work out beautifully. **Serves 6**

6 beef tenderloin steaks cut to 1 1/4-inch
  (32mm) thickness
2 tablespoons (30ml) dried porcini mushrooms
1 tablespoons (15ml) olive oil
Salt and pepper to taste
1 cup (250ml) Cabernet Sauvignon,
  or any other full bodied red wine
2 tablespoons (30ml) unsalted cold butter,
  cut into 1/4-inch (6mm) cubes
Salt and pepper to taste

- Preheat oven to 425 F (220C)

- Place the beef on a clean baking tray. Using a coffee grinder (or mortar and pestle) grind porcini mushrooms to a fine powder. Pat the beef tenderloin dry with a paper towel. Season both sides of the beef with salt and pepper. Sprinkle each side of the tenderloin with the porcini dust.

- Place a large oven-proof skillet over high heat. Add your oil and heat through until it's hot but not smoking, about 30 seconds. Place the tenderloin into the skillet and cook for approximately 3 minutes on one side or until a deep, dark caramelized crust is achieved. Flip and repeat on the other side.

- Place the skillet into the preheated oven for approximately 3 minutes to cook meat to medium rare. Remove the skillet from the oven and transfer the beef to a plate. Save the skillet to make the sauce. Loosely cover the tenderloin with foil and allow it to rest for 5 minutes.

Contd . . .

TIP

If you think you might get into toasting and grinding some of your own spices, or in this case, mushrooms, it's a really good idea to pick up an extra coffee grinder dedicated such pursuits. You can, however, clean out the flavour in your grinder by running some rice through it and wiping it out with a dry towel. Your morning coffee and those you make it for, will thank you.

- Add the wine to the skillet used to sear the beef and place over medium heat. As the wine starts to bubble, scrape the caramelized bits off the bottom of the pan using a wooden spoon. Allow the red wine to reduce to 1/2 cup (125ml) (half of the original amount) then reduce the heat to low.

- Whisk the cubes of cold butter into the skillet a bit at a time. Whisk quickly to allow the butter to blend smoothly with the reduced wine. Season to taste with salt and pepper. Pull the sauce from heat.

- Remove the foil from the meat once rested and plate. Top the beef tenderloin with sauce and serve immediately.

WINE MATCH – **Cabernet Sauvignon**

Beef and Cabernet Sauvignon are a classic pairing for the one very important combination they create – protein and tannins. Cab is high in tannins, which dry out your mouth with their astringent texture. Pairing a high-tannin wine with a red meat smoothes them out because the protein in the meat coats your tongue, which makes the wine feel softer and smoother in your mouth, allowing you to taste its flavours better. Try it for yourself and you'll see that the best way to enjoy a tannic wine is with a big ol' hunk of red meat.

GRILLED RIB EYE STEAK WITH SHALLOT PARSLEY BUTTER AND GRILLED OYSTER MUSHROOMS

What we have here is the classic steak and mushrooms, fancied up using oyster mushrooms and topping the perfectly cooked steak with what chefs call a "compound butter," which translates into: butter that has been whipped with some added flavourings. In this case, the flavours are cooked shallots and parsley. One of the great things about compound butter is if you don't use all of it, you can freeze it for up to 3 months and cut off pieces as you need it. Serves 4

Steaks

4 rib-eye steaks, each 10 oz (280g),
*   about 1 inch thick*
1 tablespoon (15ml) oil for brushing steak
Kosher salt and freshly ground pepper

Compound Butter

3 tablespoons (45ml) finely minced shallot
1 teaspoon (5ml) lemon zest
1 teaspoon (5ml) kosher salt
1 tablespoon (15ml) finely chopped parsley
1/2 cup (125ml) unsalted butter, at room
*   temperature + 1/2 tablespoon (7.5ml)*

Mushrooms

20 oyster mushrooms
3–4 tablespoons (45-60ml) olive oil
Salt and freshly ground black pepper
1 tablespoon (15ml) balsamic vinegar
2 teaspoons (10ml) grated lemon rind

- To make the compound butter, start with a small skillet over medium heat. Melt 1/2 tablespoon (7.5ml) of butter. Add the shallots and cook for 1–2 minutes or until they are soft. Stir in the salt and pull the pan from the heat to allow the butter/shallot mixture to cool completely.

- In a food processor, whip the 1/2 cup (125ml) butter until soft.

- Add in the shallot mixture and the lemon zest and blend until everything is well combined. Transfer the butter to a medium bowl and with the back of a wooden spoon squish the parsley into the butter mixture until it looks evenly distributed.

- Lay the butter out on a piece of plastic wrap, and wrap to create a log shape, about an inch thick. Roll the log, moving it back and forth gently with the palms of your hands to tighten the butter slightly. Twist up the ends so you have a butter sausage and pop into your fridge until firmed up and you are ready to use it.

- To cook your steaks, bring the meat to room temperature for about 30 minutes. Brush them with some oil and cracked pepper.

Contd . . .

- Heat barbecue to high or your grill pan to medium high. Season steaks with salt just before they are ready to be cooked. Throw your steaks on the grill or grill pan, and cook the first side for 4 minutes. Flip over the steak and grill the other side for 3–4 minutes or to your preferred doneness.

- Loosely tent your meat for 5 minutes minimum to rest before slicing into it.

- To prepare the mushrooms, trim and brush off any dirt with a clean kitchen towel. Brush with olive oil and season with salt and pepper. Place your mushrooms on the grill or grill pan, and cook over high heat for 2–3 minutes or until the mushrooms are tender and juicy. As they cook up, pull them from the heat and into a large bowl. Once you have finished cooking them all, toss with the balsamic vinegar and the lemon rind. Serve alongside, or underneath your perfectly done steaks and top with a pat of your parsley shallot butter.

WINE MATCH – **Bordeaux (Meritage/Cabernet-Merlot)**

The beauty of blended wines is that when well made, they bring together the best features of the different grapes in the bottle. And the beauty of pairing blends with a dish like this is that the various elements of the dish can all be complemented by the complexities of the wine. Bordeaux or Meritage has Merlot as one of its main grapes – its ripe, fruit flavours contrast with the earthy grilled mushrooms. And the Cabernet Sauvignon in the wine has lots of tannins that are softened by the meaty beef. Both the French and new world versions of this blend would work equally well here.

BEEF STEW

There is something beautifully rustic about stew that screams for a heavy glass of wine and a tear of bread. The sweet winter vegetables and the tender, fall-apart beef cook themselves slowly and fill your house with a wonderful smell. If your favourite root vegetables are missing in these ingredients, then switch 'em up, using about the same volume as is in the recipe. Wine adds so much flavour to any recipe, but especially braised dishes. It just creeps in, makes itself at home, and adds a depth to the meat and vegetables that no other ingredient can. **Serves 4**

Olive oil

2 tablespoons (30ml) unsalted butter

1 cooking onion, peeled and chopped

4 thick slices bacon, cut into 1 inch pieces

1 bunch fresh sage leaves

1 3/4 lb (800g) stewing beef cut into
   2 inch pieces

Salt and freshly ground pepper

Flour

2 parsnips, peeled and cut in 1 1/2 inch chunks

3 carrots, peeled and cut in 1 1/2 inch chunks

1/2 butternut squash, halved, peeled,
   deseeded and cut into 1 1/2 inch chunks

1 lb small red potatoes

2 tablespoons (30ml) tomato purée

1/2 bottle red wine (375ml)

1 1/4 cups (310ml) beef stock

Fresh parsley, chopped for garnish

- Warm up your pot to medium heat. Add the bacon, and cook until fat is rendered, 4–5 minutes. Using a slotted spoon, transfer the bacon to a plate and reserve.

- Still on medium heat, add butter to the pan. When the butter has melted add your onions and sage. Fry until onions have softened, but not browned.

- Season your meat with salt and pepper and toss into flour, shaking off the excess.

- Add the meat to the onions and sage, along with the reserved bacon, vegetables, tomato purée, wine and stock. Add a little salt and a generous amount of pepper. Turn the heat up to high, pop on a lid and bring the pot to a boil.

- Once the stew has started to boil, turn the temperature down to low. Partially cover and allow your stew to slowly simmer for 2–3 hours.

- The stew is done when the meat is ultra-tender. Serve immediately or pop into your fridge for the next couple of days.

WINE MATCH – **Merlot**

Stewed meat is the ideal mate for a full-bodied, velvety-textured glass of red. My wine of choice is Merlot. Its rich, deep fruit flavours are big enough for hearty beef, but they also play off the sweetness of the mellow root veggies. Beef stew is the classic comfort food, and I love it with what I call "comfort wine" – something smooth but satisfying, fruity yet full, and just all around delicious. Go for new world Merlot, or instead you could also try Tempranillo, Pinot Noir, Zinfandel, or Ripasso.

BEEF RAGU WITH FARFALLE

I don't know about you but the Ragu I grew up on came out of a jar and didn't look anything like this. Turns out the original has all these lovely ingredients in it and the actual word comes from the French verb *ragouter* which means "to stimulate the appetite." And while it cooks, the smells from this earthy aromatic dish will get your appetite going! Farfalle is simply a pasta suggestion, it's the one that looks like bowties or butterflies. It's a nice wide pasta and the little folds hold sauce really well, but use your favourite. **Serves 4**

1/2 oz dried porcini mushrooms

1 sprig fresh rosemary

1 sprig fresh thyme

2 teaspoons (10ml) dried juniper berries

3 tablespoons (45ml) extra-virgin olive oil

1/4 cup (60ml) finely diced onion

1/3 cup (90ml) peeled and finely diced carrot

1/3 cup (90ml) finely diced celery

12 oz (336g) lean ground beef

1/4 teaspoons (1.25ml) salt

1/3 cup (90ml) Ripasso or other red wine

*1 1/2 cups (375ml) canned tomatoes with juice,
    coarsely chopped*

1 cup (250ml) beef broth

Freshly ground black pepper

1 lb (450g) farfalle

1 tablespoon (15ml) unsalted butter

Freshly grated Parmesan cheese

- In a small bowl, pour 1 cup (250ml) of warm water over the dried porcini and let them soak for 30 minutes. Pull them out and squeeze any porcini juice back into the soaking liquid. Rinse the mushrooms under the tap, and roughly chop them. Pour the porcini liquid through a clean paper towel and into another bowl (this will get rid of any dirty sediment), set aside.

- Tie up the rosemary, thyme, and juniper berries in a cheesecloth bag secured with butcher's twine.

- In a medium saucepan, warm up the olive over a medium-low heat. Add the onions to the pot and sauté until they are a nice golden colour, about 5 minutes. Add the celery and carrot and continue to sauté until they are slightly browned and tender, 5 minutes.

- Turn up the heat to medium high. Add the beef and cook, stirring all the vegetables up from the bottom, until there is no pink left in the meat, about 10 minutes. Season with some salt and pepper.

- Pour in the wine and cook for 5 minutes until it has reduced by half.

- Toss in the tomatoes, beef broth and porcini liquid. Bring to a boil. Toss in your cheesecloth bag and turn down to a simmer. Let the sauce cook gently for about an hour giving it the occasional stir (it will be hard not to). You'll know the sauce is cooked when a lot of the liquid has evaporated and the sauce has thickened up. Pull pot from the heat and keep it warm.

- Bring a large pot of salted water to a boil. Slide in your farfalle and cook the pasta to al dente. Drain the pasta and toss with the butter.

- Serve the pasta topped with your ragu and a generous helping of freshly grated Parmesan cheese.

WINE MATCH – **Ripasso**

Okay, I've mentioned this over and over, but it's really important to balance your wine and food when you're trying to create a great pairing, and one of the key elements that needs to be in balance is acidity. Tomatoes are full of acidity, and if you pair a wine that doesn't have lots of its own, it'll end up tasting flat and boring next to your meal. I recommend Ripasso for this dish because it's got full body and rich flavours to stand up to the beef, mushrooms, and herbs, but as an Italian, it can't help but have that classic acidity that is just perfect for tomatoes.

BRAISED BEEF SHORT RIBS WITH GREMOLATA

This is such a great dish. Slowly braised beef ribs just falling off the bone after slowly cooking in wine and rich stock. The really nice twist is the gremolata, which is simply a mixture of parsley, lemon zest and garlic. Its job is to add a splash of freshness to the flavours. The trick to great gremolata is making it just moments before you're ready to serve. **Serves 6**

6–7 lb beef short ribs, cut 2 inches thick,
*   between the bones*

1 cup (250ml) coarsely chopped cooking onion

3 tablespoons (45ml) olive oil

1/2 cup (125ml) coarsely chopped peeled carrot

2 plum tomatoes, coarsely chopped

7 cloves garlic, smashed

6 sprigs thyme

8 sprigs parsley

3 bay leaves

4 1/2 cups (1125ml) beef stock

2 cups (500ml) red wine

Salt and pepper

1/3 cup (90ml) parsley leaves

1 clove garlic, finely chopped

Zest of half a lemon, finely chopped

Salt and pepper

- Season both sides of the rib pieces with salt and pepper and refrigerate for a minimum or 4 hours or overnight. Bring the meat to room temperature for 30 minutes before you start cooking everything.

- Preheat the oven to 450F (230C). Lay the ribs, bone side down in a roasting pan and roast them in the oven until they are lightly browned. This should take about 20 minutes. Pull from the oven.

- Meanwhile, in a large skillet over medium heat, warm up your olive oil. Add your onion and sauté until the onion is soft and translucent. Toss in your carrot and cook until tender. Throw in your tomatoes, garlic, thyme, bay leaves and parsley. Sauté for a couple of minutes and season lightly with salt and pepper.

- Turn down oven temperature to 400F (200F).

- In a small saucepan, heat up your beef stock to simmering.

- Lay the vegetables out in a roasting pan big enough to hold the ribs. Lay out the ribs on top of the vegetables with the bones sticking up. Add your wine to the pan and top everything with your hot stock. Cover the pan with a tight fitting lid or with aluminum foil. Slide into your oven and bring your liquids to a simmer, check after about 10 minutes.

- Turn the oven down to 350F (180C). Let the meat simmer away for about 1 1/2 hours.

- When the meat is fall-off-the-bone cooked, pull the pan from the oven. Remove the meat and set aside, cover with foil to keep it all warm while you play with the braising liquid.

- Strain the braising liquid into a saucepan and bring to a simmer over low heat. You are reducing the liquid at this point to intensify the flavour but without boiling so the fat will rise to the top where you can skim it off. Once you are happy with the flavor of the braising liquid, keep it warm and make your gremolata.

- Chop the parsley, finely grate the lemon zest and mince the garlic. Stir it all together in a small bowl.

- Put some of the ribs into a warm wide bowl. Ladle your braising liquid over the top, sprinkle the gremolata over that, and serve.

WINE MATCH – **Southern Rhône blend (Grenache/Shiraz/Mourvèdre)**

Braised beef pairs up nicely with all sorts of red wines as long as they're full-bodied and full-flavoured. I love southern Rhône blends in particular because they have a spicy, earthy richness to them that shines next to tender, juicy beef. The best part about these wines is the Grenache content, which softens the tannins and ups the acid, making a wine that is velvety in texture with refreshing fruit flavours. This becomes important with the gremolata in the dish – the vegetal parsley and the zesty lemon peel could wreak havoc with tannic wines but a smooth but tart red does just fine.

BRAISED DUCK LEGS WITH ONIONS AND CABBAGE

If you're going to cook duck you need to know about rendering fat. It's one of those cooking tips that will forever change your relationship with this bird. Rendering is just melting fat off of meat over a low heat. Duck is fatty, so you cook it slowly, spooning the fat out of the pan as it melts, and that my friend is how you achieve crispy skin. The beauty is, duck fat is so flavourful, it's incredible to cook with. Cut up some potatoes, drizzle some of the fat over (if it's still liquid), season with salt and pepper and roast. From then on, I guarantee you'll rarely make your potatoes any other way. Serves 4

4 duck legs (drumsticks and thighs, attached)

Salt and pepper

1 tablespoon (15ml) fresh thyme leaves

3 large red onions, cut into 1/2-inch thick slices

1/4 of a Savoy cabbage, roughly chopped

1 bay leaf

3 tablespoons (45ml) sherry vinegar

3 garlic cloves, sliced

1/2 cup (125ml) good quality dry red wine (Grenache/Shiraz-based blend from the southern Rhône Valley)

1 1/2 cups (375ml) chicken stock

3 good quality canned plum tomatoes, roughly diced

- Trim any extra fat from the duck legs and season on both sides with salt and pepper. If you have time, cover and refrigerate for a minimum of 4 hours or overnight. If not, let the duck legs stand at room temperature for 1 1/2 hours.

- In a medium saucepan, warm your chicken stock, wine, thyme and bay leaf.

- Preheat the oven to 350F (180C).

- Grab a large skillet and warm it up (without any oil) over medium heat. Without crowding, lay your duck legs skin side down into the hot pan. Let them sit until they are a beautiful golden brown, which will take about 15–20 minutes. A lot of fat is going to come off the duck so as it starts to collect, carefully spoon into a bowl. When the legs are golden brown on the skin side you can pull them from the pan and onto a tray. Repeat until all of your duck legs have been browned.

- Rinse out your pan and dry it back on the stovetop. Pour about 3 tablespoons (45ml) of the duck fat back into the pan and warm it through over medium heat. Add your onions and garlic. Cook until your onions are soft but not browned, about 6 or 7 minutes.

- Add your cabbage, sherry vinegar, salt and pepper and sauté just until your cabbage wilts, about 3 or 4 minutes.

- Lay the cabbage mixture out in a large casserole dish. Arrange your duck legs over the bed of cabbage in one layer, skin side up. Scatter your tomatoes around the dish and pour the hot stock mixture over the duck and lightly season the dish with salt and pepper.

- Cover the dish with a tight fitting lid, or aluminium foil. Slide into the oven and let it all cook for 1 1/2 hours. You'll know the duck is done when the meat is falling off the bone.

- Gently pull the duck from the broth. Strain the stock into a pan and arrange your vegetables on a serving platter, setting the legs on top.

- Put the pan with the stock onto a burner and bring it to a boil. Boil the stock until it has thickened and there is about 1 cup (250ml) of liquid left. Taste the sauce and adjust the seasoning if necessary.

- Serve the duck and the vegetables with the sauce spooned over each serving.

WINE MATCH – **Southern Rhône blend (Grenache/Shiraz/Mourvèdre)**

These duck legs are falling-off-the-bone tender, but they are big on flavour so I choose a wine match that is much the same – smooth, soul-satisfying, spicy and fruity all come together in red wines from the southern Rhône in France. Though new world regions also make this blend, I recommend sticking with the classic here and specifically, Châteauneuf-du-Pape, an appellation in the Rhône Valley that makes rich, seductive wines that balance the flavourful duck and sweet, braised veggies. Don't forget our cooking with wine tip – use the same wine (or something similar but cheaper if you're serving a pricey bottle) in your dish that you pour in your glass for a match that's guaranteed to please.

QUAIL IN ROSEHIP SAUCE

These little birds are really flavourful, pretty cute, and no more difficult to prepare than chicken. Quail is a game bird, now farmed more often than hunted. It also tends to be one of the less expensive and easier-to-find game birds around. The difference between cooking quail and cooking a chicken is that in order to maintain moisture, a quail should be served medium to medium rare. You can also serve a whole quail per person depending on the size, or split one bird into two if it's larger. Rosehips are a fruit from the rose, which need to be cooked in order to be consumed. You'll find them most often in the form of jams and jellies, as well as teas and powders. Health food stores and gourmet food shops are your best bet to find a jar of the jelly you need here. **Serves 6**

6 quail, approximately 12oz (335g) each

Salt and pepper to taste

1 tablespoon (15ml) unsalted butter

1 tablespoon (15ml) vegetable oil

1/2 cup (125ml) toasted, roughly chopped
    macadamia nuts for garnish

2 cups (500ml) mixed organic greens for garnish

Sauce

1 cup (250ml) red wine (Tempranillo's
    a good one)

1 tablespoon vegetable oil

1 tablespoon (15ml) rosehip jelly

1/2 fresh vanilla bean, scraped

1 whole star anise

2 tablespoons (30ml) white onion, finely diced

1/2 cup (125ml) fresh raspberries

Salt and pepper to taste

- Preheat oven to 350F (180C).

- Pat quails dry with a paper towel. Season with salt and pepper.

- Set a large skillet over high heat and add the oil and butter. Allow skillet to heat for 30 seconds. Place the quails skin side down in the pan and cook for 3–4 minutes, until a crispy golden brown skin forms. Flip the birds and cook for another 2 minutes. Place pan in the preheated oven and cook for another 6 minutes.

- Pull the quail from the pan and set on a tray. Cover the tray with foil.

- You're going to using the same pan the quail was cooked with (so you can max out on all the flavour the quail left in there) to make the sauce. Place the pan over medium heat and warm up a tablespoon of oil. Add your onions to the pan and soften the onions for about 3–5 minutes. Pour in the red wine and use a wooden spoon to scrape the bottom of the pan and release the caramelized bits left over from the quail. Continue to stir as you add the rosehip jelly.

TIP

What are tannins?

Tannins are more about how a wine feels in your mouth rather than how it tastes, and they are mostly found in red wines. When red wine is made, the grapes are crushed, and the skins and seeds (and sometimes stems) are left in with the juice to extract colour and flavour. Tannins come from those skins, seeds, and stems. The longer the period of skin contact and the thicker the grape skins, the more tannin a wine develops. Now think about the last time you had a glass of red wine, or better yet, grab yourself a glass right now and take a sip. If you feel a drying, puckering, or astringent sensation in your mouth, your wine has tannins. You can get a similar experience from strongly brewed tea or biting into a grape seed. Not all red wines have tannins and like most wine characteristics they vary from grape to grape, region to region, and year to year. Wines like Cabernet Sauvignon (and blends like Bordeaux or Meritage) have lots of tannins, especially when they're young. On the other hand, lighter reds like Pinot Noir and Gamay Noir have little or no tannin.

- Turn down heat to medium low and add the scraped vanilla bean, star anise, and the raspberries. Allow the mixture to cook for 3 minutes. Season to taste with salt and pepper. Remove from heat and strain the sauce into a bowl through a fine mesh strainer.

- To plate the dish, place a quail in the centre of a plate and drizzle with the rosehip sauce. Garnish with macadamia nuts and fresh greens.

WINE MATCH – **Tempranillo**

Though quail is a game bird, the flavour and texture are quite delicate, so it's important to choose a red wine that isn't going to overpower with heavy tannins. Tempranillo, and specifically a Rioja from Spain, works beautifully with this dish. The sauce is the star, and the wine mirrors all of its elements – they both have flavours of raspberry, vanilla, and spice. Of course, if you follow our cooking with wine trick and use the same wine for your sauce that you serve with the dish, you'll have a match made in heaven.

SEARED PEPPERED CARIBOU LOIN WITH SASKATOON BERRY SAUCE

I have a good friend from Saskatchewan who introduced me to the hometown berry with so much affection that I felt like the earlier years of my life were empty. It tastes kind of like a dirty blueberry, but that's because it has an earthier flavour that does take a little getting used to. In a dish like this though, it's absolutely perfect, it's not too sweet and is a natural extension to the gaminess of the Caribou. Serves 6

2 lb (1kg) caribou loin, silver skin removed

Coarse salt and pepper to taste

1 tablespoon (15ml) olive oil

1/2 cup (125ml) red wine

1 tablespoon (15ml) Saskatoon berry preserve,
*   good quality*

1/2 cup (125ml) game, veal, or beef stock

- Season the caribou with salt and pepper and drizzle with half of the olive oil. Give the caribou about 1/2 an hour to come to room temperature.

- Preheat oven to 425F (220C).

- Place a large cast iron or heavy bottomed skillet over medium-high heat. Allow the pan to heat up for about 2 minutes. Add the remaining oil to the hot skillet.

- Put the caribou in the pan and allow it to cook for 3 minutes (without moving the meat) until a caramelized crust is formed. Flip the caribou and cook the other side for 3 minutes as well, until the same caramelized crust forms.

- Put the skillet into your preheated oven for 5–6 minutes for medium rare doneness.

WINE MATCH – **Bordeaux**
(Meritage/Cabernet-Merlot)

Red Bordeaux (the Cabernet-Merlot blend) works with the caribou for two reasons – body and taste. Caribou is a rich, big-flavoured, fill-your-mouth kind of meat, and Bordeaux is a full-bodied, fill-your-mouth kind of wine. Plus the tannins in the wine are smoothed out by the protein in the meat. As for the taste, the ripe, juicy berry flavour of the wine matches the berries in the sauce. And the sauce has a splash of red wine in it, so use a Cabernet-Merlot in the recipe to make your pairing bang-on.

- Pull the caribou from the oven and move it to a plate. Don't clean the pan yet, save it for the sauce you're going to make. Loosely cover the meat with foil and allow the meat to rest at least 5 minutes before you slice into it.

- Meanwhile make the sauce. Place the used skillet over medium-high heat. Add the wine and use a wooden spoon to scrape the caramelized bits from the bottom of the pan.

- Add the berry preserve and whisk until the sauce is blended well.

- Add the stock, turn down the heat to medium low and cook for about 3–4 minutes; at this point the sauce should be slightly thickened.

- Pull it from the heat and season to taste with salt and pepper.

- To plate the dish, carve the rested caribou loin across the grain of the meat into 1/4 inch slices and drizzle with Saskatoon berry sauce.

TIP

Tips on tannins:

Pairing a tannic wine with red meat high in protein (like beef or lamb) will smooth out the tannins and make it easier to taste the flavours of the wine.

Tannic wine + spicy food or fishy flavours is a big no-no, they just don't work together. Fish paired with tannic wine gets overpowered by the wine and creates a metallic aftertaste. And spice in food is intensified instead of cooled.

Tannins act as a preservative in wine, helping the wine last longer after it's been bottled. Ever opened an old wine like a Bordeaux and noticed lots of sediment in the bottle? As a wine ages, the tannins fall from the wine and collect as sediment in the bottle.

Though some people don't like tannins, they can add an interesting dimension and texture to wine, also allowing it to age better than wines without tannins. Paired with red meats and strong cheeses, wines with tannins shine.

VENISON LOIN WITH BLACKBERRY LAVENDER SAUCE

When I think of a deer walking through the woods I picture it eating blackberries. I would if I were a deer. So it only seems natural that the two would want to see each other again in a pan. When cooking nearly any game meat rare to medium-rare doneness is how you will extract the most flavour, and moisture. When overcooked it becomes tough and dry. Here is where a trusty meat thermometer can be your new best friend. If you don't own one already, I strongly suggest you pick one up. They are really inexpensive and can save you numerous headaches, especially when cooking a really nice piece of meat such as this one. You can easily switch up the port for a full bodied red wine and, if you want to try something other than lavender and keep the blackberry element, you can leave it out and just bump up the amount of thyme by an extra sprig. You'll end up with a pretty different dish, but it will still work really well. Serves 6

1 rack of venison, cut in half, bones
 Frenched (cleaned) (6–8 bones)
2 tablespoons (30ml) olive oil
1/2 tablespoon (7.5ml) mixed peppercorns,
 crushed
Coarse salt, to taste

Sauce
1 cup (250ml) ruby port
1 cup (250ml) veal or beef stock
2 teaspoons of dried lavender
2 sprigs fresh thyme
3 tablespoons finely chopped shallot
1 cup (250ml) fresh blackberries
Salt and pepper to taste

- Preheat oven to 425 degrees F (230 degrees C).

- Drizzle venison loin with 1/2 tablespoon (7.5ml) olive oil and rub all over both racks. Rub the crushed peppercorns over the meat and sprinkle with course salt. Allow the racks to sit out at room temperature for 30 minutes.

- Heat a large ovenproof skillet over medium-high heat. Add the remaining oil for 30 seconds or until the pan is hot and almost smoking.

- Place the two venison racks, fleshy side down into the hot skillet. Allow to cook for 3–4 minutes or until a deep caramelized colour and crust is achieved. Flip the racks over to achieve similar results on the remaining side.

- Pull the skillet from the stovetop into the preheated oven for 8–9 minutes for medium rare or until a meat thermometer reaches 125F.

- Pull the venison from oven and pop onto a tray. Tent the meat loosely with a piece of foil and let it rest for 10 minutes. Save the skillet to make sauce.

TIP

What does "legs" mean?

Take a glass of wine and gently swirl it around the glass. See the wine that clings to the inside then slowly drips down? Those are the legs of a wine (also known as tears) and they actually look like legs. Easy to see, but what do they mean? They are neither a sign of age nor quality. All they really tell you about a wine is the texture – how the wine will feel in your mouth once you take a sip. If the wine drips down very slowly in a thick stream (long legs), the wine will feel thicker and richer in your mouth, either from high alcohol or from sweetness (think over-the-top, blockbuster Zinfandel or sweet, rich Icewine). If the wine drizzles down quickly (short legs), the wine will be lighter in texture (like Pinot Grigio or Sauvignon Blanc).

- Place the skillet over medium-high heat for up to 1 minute. Add the port and scrape the bottom of the pan using a wooden spoon to release the caramelized brown bits left from the meat.

- Add veal stock, thyme, shallots, lavender and half the blackberries. Reduce to medium-low heat. Simmer the sauce for around 6 minutes, until it has a chance to thicken.

- Place a fine mesh strainer over a medium saucepan. Remove the skillet from heat and pour the sauce into the strainer, pressing gently with a spoon to release all liquid. Move the saucepan over medium-low heat and bring it to a simmer. Season to taste with salt and pepper. Add remaining blackberries to the sauce and keep warm.

- Slice venison rack into chops by evenly slicing the meat between each bone of the rack. Spoon the warm sauce on a plate and top with venison chops.

WINE MATCH – Zinfandel

Okay, just writing about this wine and food match is making my mouth water. Zinfandel is a big, honkin' wine that needs something big on flavour and texture to pair up with it. Venison and other red game meats have a ton of flavour built right into them before you add seasonings and sauces, and this sauce is really big on taste too, so a full-bodied California Zin is just the thing to bring everything together. The wine has dark berry flavour and brambly, floral notes that flawlessly mirror the blackberry and lavender in the sauce – perfection!

WARM DUCK BREAST SALAD WITH HAZELNUT DRESSING

Duck seems to intimidate a lot of people, but it is no more difficult to cook than a steak. You just have a little more time for a larger glass of wine as you prepare it. The trick with this bird is to cook it on a lower heat than you normally would to sear meat. You need to slowly melt the fat, which you'll pour into a heatproof bowl and save for two good reasons. One, you don't want to deep-fry your duck breasts and two, you can save the fat for cooking. It's has such an intensely savoury flavour you can use it for future cooking adventures. In a good butcher shop you can buy rendered duck fat, which chefs covet, especially when cooking potatoes. Potatoes and duck fat, when combined, create culinary magic. With a little patience and some serious duck fat payback, you'll see how easy it all is. **Serves 4– 6**

2 large whole boneless duck breasts, skin on

Salt and pepper

1/2 cup (125ml) hazelnuts in skins

3 tablespoons (45ml) golden raisins

1 medium celeriac (celery root)

1 large crisp apple

Salt and pepper

Vinaigrette

3 tablespoons (45ml) vegetable oil

3 tablespoons (45ml) hazelnut oil

2 tablespoons (30ml) sherry vinegar

Squeeze of lemon juice

Honey to taste

- Preheat your oven to 350F (180C). Lay the hazelnuts on a baking sheet (with a rim) and roast for about 10 minutes, or until they are toasty and golden. Pull them out of the oven. Using a clean kitchen towel rub the skins off the nuts, roughly chop them and set aside.

- To prepare the breasts, start by removing the tenderloin, the small, loose strip of meat on the back of the breast. Flip the breasts over and with a sharp knife score the skin about 1/8 inch deep, without cutting into the meat, first in one direction and then in an opposing 45 degree angle, to create a checkerboard crosshatch. Cutting the skin like this helps the fat to render out when you are cooking it, which helps you get a lovely sear on the breast.

- Generously season the breasts on both sides with salt and pepper. Cover and refrigerate for a minimum of 4 hours or overnight.

- Preheat your oven to 450F (230C).

- Heat a heavy skillet over low heat until hot and then add the duck, skin-side down.

Contd . . .

- Cook the duck uncovered, over medium-low heat, without turning, until most of the fat is rendered and the skin is golden brown. Expect this to take about 25 minutes.

- Spoon off the fat as it starts to accumulate in the pan so you don't deep fry the duck. Once you have a thin crispy sear, flip the duck over and slide the pan into your oven.

- Cook the duck breasts for 6–8 minutes or until a thermometer reads 125F (52C) for rare or 135F (57C) for medium rare.

- Pull the pan out of the oven, transfer to a plate and tent with foil. Allow the meat to rest for 10 minutes while you put together the rest of the salad.

- Cover the raisins with boiling water and let them soak for 5 minutes so they plump up. Drain them and set aside.

- Whisk together all of the vinaigrette ingredients in a small bowl, and set aside.

- Peel the celery root and cut into thin matchstick-sized pieces. Toss into a medium bow. Mix some of your dressing in, along with the raisins. Cut your apple in small matchstick pieces, adding to the celery root mixture as you go to prevent the apple from turning brown.

- Add the hazelnuts in at the end of your salad assembly.

- To serve the salad, place a mound of the salad onto each of the plates. Carve your duck breast quite thin. Lay the breast slices over the salad and drizzle any good ol' duck juices that are on your cutting board over the dish. Serve immediately.

WINE MATCH – **Pinot Noir**

I think this has to be one of my favourite pairings in this book. First of all, I'm obsessed with Pinot Noir and duck and how their flavours work together. Pinot Noir not only complements the flavour of duck, but it also has enough acidity to balance off the vinaigrette and the earthy notes in the wine are in harmony with the rich, toasty hazelnuts. Try it and see if my obsession is justified.

COQ AU VIN

I don't speak French but I'm pretty sure this means Chicken in Wine. That sounds good enough to eat! This dish is a classic French stew of chicken, bacon, mushrooms and onions. It's cooked in this recipe in Côtes-du-Rhône wine. That is where the stew originates from and seems appropriate but any medium-bodied red wine would do the trick. I adore this stew served with roasted or mashed potatoes. **Serves 4**

3 lb (1 whole chicken carved when raw)
  chicken parts, skin on and bone in
Salt and pepper to taste
2 tablespoons (30ml) vegetable oil
2 tablespoons (30ml) olive oil
1 1/2 cups (375ml) pearl onions, peeled
  (see page 214)
2 cups (500ml) whole small-sized button
  mushrooms, cleaned
1 cup (250ml) celery, chopped medium dice
1 1/2 cups (375ml) Côtes-du-Rhône red wine
2 cups (500ml) chicken stock
1 bay leaf, fresh or dried
2 sprigs fresh thyme
8 baby carrots, cut in half lengthwise

- Preheat oven to 350F (180C).

- Pat the chicken dry with clean paper towels. Season chicken on both sides with salt and pepper.

- Add half of the vegetable oil to a large ovenproof skillet or casserole baking dish and heat over medium-high heat for about 1 minute. Place half of the chicken, skin side down, into the hot pan. Allow the chicken skin to sear and cook until golden brown and crispy, approximately 3–5 minutes.

- Remove the chicken from the pan and place on a paper towel-lined tray. Add more oil to the pan and continue to cook the remaining chicken.

- Remove the pan from the heat and drain out the excess chicken fat. Set the reserved skillet over medium heat and add the olive oil. Allow the oil to heat for 1 minute.

- Add the pearl onions and sauté, stirring occasionally until onions are lightly browned, approximately 2–4 minutes. Reduce heat to medium low and continue to sauté for approximately 5 minutes.

- Increase heat to medium and add the mushrooms. Sauté until brown, about 5 minutes.

- Add celery and for sauté 1 minute.

Contd . . .

- Pour the wine into pan with the vegetables. Use a wooden spoon to scrape up all the brown bits from the bottom of the pan and reduce heat to low.

- Add the chicken stock, bay leaf, thyme, season with salt and pepper and bring to a simmer.

- Add the seared chicken to the skillet and top with the carrots. Cover the pan with a lid or foil and place into the preheated oven for 20 minutes.

- After 20 minutes, remove the lid or foil from the chicken and cook for another 15 minutes. Remove the pan from the oven and serve with good helpings of sauce covering chicken and vegetables.

WINE MATCH – **Southern Rhône blend (Grenache/Shiraz/Mourvèdre)**

Coq au Vin is classic French cuisine so we've gotta go French with the wine as well. A French Burgundy (Pinot Noir) is the traditional choice for this dish but I love a good Grenache-based blend with it instead. Pick a simple but spicy Côtes-du-Rhône for a wine that works well both in the dish and alongside it. It's medium-bodied and has lots of fruity flavours that stand up to the intense and rich flavours and textures in the dish. And of course, we're cooking with it, so if it's on your plate and in your glass, you know it's gonna work.

SPICY THAI CHICKEN WINGS WITH MANGO SALAD

I don't know too many people who don't crave chicken wings. These are sticky and spicy and incredibly easy to prepare. The nice thing about them is you bake rather than fry them, which is less hassle in the kitchen and a little less work at the gym. The mango salad takes minutes to whip off and is perfect for cooling down your palate as you go back for more! **Serves 6**

20 chicken wings, arm of the wing intact

1 teaspoon (5ml) cracked black pepper

2 teaspoons (10ml) freshly grated ginger

1 tablespoon (15ml) freshly chopped garlic

1 tablespoon (15ml) grated palm sugar
  (brown sugar can sub in here)

1 tablespoon (15ml) soy sauce

2 tablespoons (30ml) vegetable oil

2 tablespoons (30ml) lime juice

1 tablespoon (15ml) garlic chili paste
  or more to taste

6 lime wedges (optional garnish)

Cilantro leaves to taste (optional garnish)

- Pat chicken wings dry with paper towel and place in a large glass bowl.

- In a separate bowl combine pepper, ginger, garlic, palm sugar, soy sauce, vegetable oil, lime juice and chili garlic paste and stir to evenly combine. Add the wings and toss evenly with the marinade. Place the wings in the refrigerator and allow them to marinate for a minimum of 2 hours and a maximum of overnight.

- When ready to bake the wings, preheat the oven to 400F (200C).

- Place the wings on a baking tray and bake for 20 minutes, turning them halfway through. Wings are done when they look shiny, golden brown and have a bit of a crispy edge around them.

- Serve with your favourite hot sauce and garnish with cilantro and lime wedges if you so desire.

Contd . . .

Mango Salad

This mango salad takes minutes to whip off and is perfect for cooling down your palate! **Serves 6**

3 medium ripe mangos

2 teaspoons (10ml) minced garlic

2 tablespoons (30ml) roughly chopped
    fresh cilantro

2 teaspoons (10ml) finely chopped fresh ginger

Juice of 1 lime

Sugar to taste (if desired)

- Remove the peel from the mango and cut into strips slightly larger than matchsticks. Add to a medium glass bowl and combine with remaining ingredients to evenly distribute the flavours. Season to taste with sugar. Chill well before serving.

WINE MATCH – **Grenache**

This is party food gone gourmet and there's no other wine I'd rather drink with these spicy little wings than a juicy, jammy Grenache. It works really well with the chicken wings because its ripe, juicy berry flavours mellow out and cool down the intense spicy flavours of the marinade without big tannins that would interfere with the spice of the dish. The low tannin is also important in pairing a red wine with a white meat like chicken – it has a nice, smooth feel in the mouth that works well with lighter meats. Want something that you can chill down and drink cold? Go for a Grenache-based dry rosé – it'll be perfect.

SLOW ROASTED SHREDDED CHICKEN WITH TOMATOES, BASIL AND FETTUCCINI

Slowly roasting the tomatoes sweetens them up while infusing the chicken with tomato and garlic flavours. The basil lays over the meat, perfuming everything and crisping up just a little. Cooking the chicken on the bone boosts the flavour of the meat which leeches into the vegetables. Once you let this dish cool, you shred the meat off the bone and re-mix it into the tomatoes, creating a meaty, colourful sauce. These flavours, bound together with a little olive oil, always satisfy my soul, especially in the early fall when the market is full of crazy coloured plump tomatoes. All that's needed is a bottle of wine and good company. **Serves 6**

6 chicken legs, thighs and drumsticks
  separated
Salt and freshly cracked black pepper
2 cups (500ml) basil leaves picked and
  roughly chopped
4 cups (2 pints) cherry tomatoes (various
  colours if you can find them), halved
3 ripe plum tomatoes, quartered
1 garlic bulb, cloves separated and peeled
1 1/2 teaspoon (7.5ml) red chili flakes
Olive oil
1 1/2 lb (675g) fettuccini

- Preheat your oven to 350F (180C).
- Pat your chicken pieces dry with a paper towel and season them with salt and pepper on both sides and rub with some of the olive oil.
- In a big bowl toss together the tomatoes, basil, red chili flakes and garlic, drizzle with some olive oil and season lightly with salt and pepper.
- Add half of the tomato mixture to the bottom of an ovensafe pan, large enough to lay the chicken pieces flat.
- Lay the chicken pieces on top of the tomato mixture, trying not to overlap them. Scatter the other half of the tomato mixture over top and around the chicken pieces.
- Slide your chicken into the oven for about 1 1/2 hours, stirring gently once, to move around the tomatoes. You want the chicken to be practically falling off the bone.
- When the chicken is done, pull the pan from the oven and allow to cool slightly.

Contd . . .

- Once you can handle the chicken, pull the pieces from the pan. Remove the skin and shred the chicken pieces back into the tomatoes, throwing out the bones as you go. Toss the meat and tomatoes together and give the mixture a taste. Season with salt and pepper.

- Warm gently in the oven at 200F (100C) while you prepare the pasta.

- Bring a large pot of salted water to a boil. Add your pasta and cook until al dente. Drain the pasta and pour the noodles into a large bowl.

- Toss with the tomatoes and shredded chicken and top with some generous gratings of Parmesan cheese.

WINE MATCH – **Dolcetto**

Dolcetto is known for its food-friendliness and I love pairing it with pasta dishes that feature tomatoes as one of the main ingredients. The wine has crisp, refreshing acidity that is perfect to off-set the acidity in tomatoes, and it's light enough that it won't overpower the chicken. Dolcetto is made in the northern part of Italy – if you can't find it, try its older sister Barbera for an earthier, slightly fuller bodied alternative, or go for good ol' Valpolicella.

BREAST OF CHICKEN STUFFED WITH BOURSIN CHEESE AND PROSCIUTTO IN A BALSAMIC REDUCTION

Chicken breasts make the greatest pockets for all sorts of flavour. Boursin cheese is on the top of my list of favorite things. It's a triple cream cheese that has been infused with garlic and fine herbs. The texture is silky and the flavour intense. Combined with salty, chewy prosciutto, the tender, mild chicken breast and the tangy balsamic reduction, this dish will have your taste buds working overtime. Boursin cheese can be found in most grocery stores in the "special" cheese section or in most local cheese shops. **Serves 4**

4 large skinless, boneless chicken breasts

1/2 cup (125ml) Boursin Cheese, at room temperature

8 thin slices prosciutto

2 tablespoons (30ml) olive oil

1/2 cup (125ml) corn meal

Salt and freshly ground black pepper to taste

1 cup (250ml) chicken stock

1/2 cup (125ml) balsamic vinegar

4 cloves garlic, sliced

1 bay leaf

1 tablespoon (15ml) fresh lemon thyme leaves

2 tablespoons (30ml) unsalted butter, cold and cubed.

- Pat the breasts dry with paper towel. Cut each one open like a book, trying to make sure you don't cut all the way through.

- Spread 1/4 of the Boursin onto inside of each breast.

- Lay 2 slices of the prosciutto on top of the Boursin and fold the one side of the breast over the other, pinching the ends closed so you don't lose any filling.

- In a bowl big enough to add a chicken breast to, measure out the corn meal. Season the outside of the chicken breast with salt and pepper. Coat the outside of the chicken with the cornmeal and set aside.

- Preheat your oven to 200F (100C).

- Heat your heavy skillet over medium heat and warm the olive oil for a minute or two. Brown your chicken breasts on both sides.

- Add the chicken stock, vinegar, garlic, bay leaf and fresh lemon thyme to the pan. Simmer everything together for about 10 minutes, give the breasts another turn half way through for even cooking. Pull them from the pan and keep them warm in the oven.

- Turn up the heat on your skillet and bring the sauce to a boil until the sauce has a nice flavour and has thickened, about 5 minutes.

- Whisk in your cold butter cubes and give the sauce a taste.

- To serve, place a breast on each plate and drizzle with your sauce.

WINE MATCH – **Barbera**

Prosciutto has a salty, smoky flavour and chewy texture that is meant for the bubbly goodness of Prosecco, but this dish demands the satisfying richness of a red, so Barbera is the ideal solution. This wine has a fresh backbone of acidity that cuts through the prosciutto, yet it's not too heavy for light chicken breast meat and the herbaceous flavour of the Boursin. It's also a good foil for the sweet reduced balsamic. If you must go white, try Prosecco or go for Riesling with just a touch of sweetness.

CHICKEN B'STEEYA PIE

B'Steeya is a traditional Moroccan pie, filled with chicken, ground almonds and lots of spices. It's sweet and intensely savoury. The different textures – flaky pastry, crunchy almonds and tender chicken – create complete satisfaction; but on top of all that, visually this is a good lookin' main course. The key to any pie, sweet or savoury, is to make sure that you are really happy with the filling before you go ahead and bake it off. It's good to try it before you stuff the pastry. **Serves 6**

1 large chicken breast on the bone, split, skin
removed, about 1 1/2 lb (675g)

8 chicken thighs, skin removed, bone in
(about 2 lb) (1 kg)

2 tablespoons (30ml) vegetable oil

1 medium onion, chopped

2 cloves garlic, peeled and smashed

1/4 teaspoon (1.25ml) turmeric

Pinch of saffron

1 large cinnamon stick

1/2 teaspoon (2.5ml) ground ginger

1/2 teaspoon (2.5ml) salt

1 cup (250ml) parsley leaves, chopped

1/2 cup (125ml) coriander leaves, chopped

3 eggs

1/4 cup + 1 tablespoon (60ml + 15ml) icing sugar

Freshly ground black pepper

2 tablespoon (30ml) freshly squeezed lemon
juice

1 tablespoon (15ml) preserved lemon, pulp and
pith removed and peel finely chopped or
2 tablespoons of lemon zest, finely grated
(optional)

Contd . . .

- In a large sauce pan with a lid, warm the oil over medium heat, add the onion, and cook gently until soft and translucent, 5 minutes.

- Toss in the garlic, turmeric, saffron, cinnamon stick and ginger, stir it all together and keep cooking for another 2 minutes. If the spices start to stick, add a tablespoon of water to keep them from burning.

- Add the chicken, salt, chopped parsley, coriander and 1 1/2 cups (375ml) of water. Cover and simmer for 40 minutes until the chicken is cooked. With tongs, pull the chicken from the broth and let it cool.

- Bring the leftover liquid to a boil to reduce by half, about 10 minutes. Remove cinnamon stick and lower the heat.

- In a small bowl, whisk eggs with 1 tablespoon (15ml) of the icing sugar and the pepper. Pour into the hot liquid and cook gently to scramble the eggs.

- Add the lemon juice. Once the eggs are cooked transfer the mixture into a large bowl.

- Shred the chicken into chunks and discard the bones. Add the chicken to the egg mixture, along with the preserved lemon (if you are using) and check the seasoning.

- In your food processor blitz the toasted almonds, remaining icing sugar and cinnamon until blended.

- Preheat the oven to 375F (220C).

Contd . . .

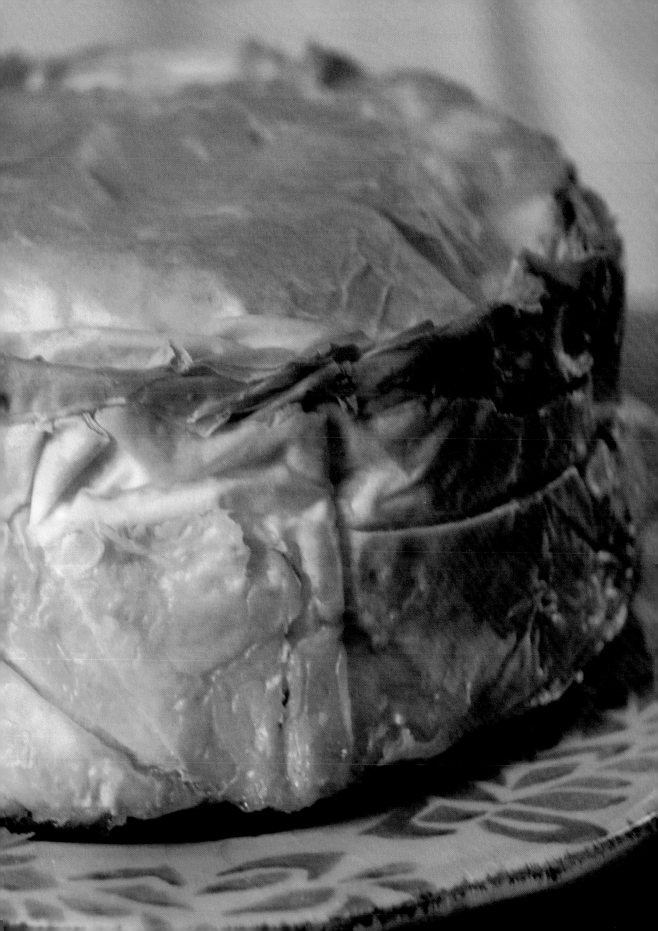

1/2 cup (125ml) chopped almonds, toasted

1 teaspoon (5ml) ground cinnamon

12 sheets phyllo pastry

1/3 cup (90ml) unsalted butter, melted

Icing sugar and cinnamon for top of pie

- Butter a 9-inch cake pan (preferably with removable sides if you have it). Dampen a towel and cover your phyllo sheets to keep them from cracking as you work. Pull out 3 sheets of phyllo at once. Brush each lightly with melted butter and layer them on top of one another. Carefully pick up the prepared phyllo and line your cake tin. Trim edges carefully using a small paring knife.

- Sprinkle half the mixture of almond and sugar over the phyllo sheets. Now pull out 3 more sheets of phyllo and do the same thing, lightly buttering each and layering them. Pop these on top of the almond mixture and again trim the phyllo to fit the pan. At this point add all of the chicken filling, spreading it evenly over the phyllo.

- Make a third pile of three buttered phyllo sheets and lay on top of chicken mixture. Sprinkle rest of the almond mixture over phyllo and finish pie with a final stack of 3 buttered sheets. Tuck the edges of pastry into the cake pan.

- Brush top of the pie with more butter and bake for 25–30 minutes, until pastry is golden and crisp.

- Sprinkle with cinnamon and icing sugar before serving.

WINE MATCH – **Pinot Noir**

This pie is filled with spicy Moroccan-inspired flavours including cinnamon and nutmeg. It's these spices that inspire me to pair Pinot Noir with this dish. See, Pinot often has a sweet spice flavour to it, something that reminds me of clove or cinnamon, so it plays off these flavours perfectly. It also has nice, crisp acidity that not only cuts through the rich pastry, but also plays off the tart preserved lemon. Wanna be more adventurous? Try a spicy but soft Shiraz from Australia – the jammy fruit flavour will play off the savoury flavours in the pie for a nice contrast.

ROAST HALIBUT WITH MUSSELS AND CHORIZO

In this recipe I'm breaking one of the sacred rules – cook with the wine you drink – but that's what rules were made for. In this case, the white wine is going to balance out the intensity and heat of the chorizo sausage, but the flavour of the sausage is going to turn this dish into a red wine match. Chorizo is a super flavourful Spanish or Mexican sausage made with garlic, chili powder and pork. It's a bright orangey red in colour and adds a smoky heat to nearly anything it's cooked with. The flavours in this dish are really gutsy. The mussels make a sublime stock, which blends the smokiness of the chorizo and the sweetness of the roasted peppers. The texture of the tender halibut just soaks it all in. The end result is a bold and meaty fish dish with some serious visual appeal. **Serves 4**

1 tablespoon (15ml) extra virgin olive oil

4 oz (112g) chorizo, cut lengthwise in half then crosswise into 1/4-inch thick slices

1 medium cooking onion, cut in half then crosswise into 1/4-inch thick slices

2 cloves garlic, peeled and finely diced

1 each sweet red and yellow pepper, roasted, peeled, seeded, cut in 1/4-inch thick strips

4 plum tomatoes, peeled, seeded and diced (juice reserved, see tip)

Pinch smoked paprika

Salt and pepper

2 tablespoons (30ml) extra-virgin olive oil

4 thick halibut filets (5 oz, 140g each)

Salt and pepper

2 tablespoons (30ml) extra-virgin olive oil

20 mussels, de-bearded (See page 130 for prep.)

1 sprig thyme

2 cloves garlic, finely chopped

4 sprigs Italian parsley, leaves only

1/2 cup (125ml) dry white wine

2 tablespoons (30ml) unsalted butter, cubed and cold

Salt and pepper

- Put a large pan over medium-high heat and warm 1 tablespoon (15ml) of the olive oil. Throw the chorizo into the pan and brown the sausage for about 4 or 5 minutes. Once the chorizo is cooked pull it from the pan with a spoon and drain it on a paper towel lined plate. Set aside.

- Now toss the onions and garlic into the same pan. Cook, making sure to give them a stir until the onions are soft and sweet, but here we are trying to make sure the onions don't get any colour, so if they start to brown a bit just turn down the heat and cook a little more slowly, this should take about 8–10 minutes.

- Now add the tomatoes and any juice, the smoked paprika and the chorizo. Add a little salt and pepper and cover the pan with a lid. Turn down the heat to low and simmer for 10 minutes.

- To cook the mussels, heat 1 tablespoon (15ml) of olive oil in a sauté pan that has a lid, over high heat.

- Add your mussels to the pan, and the thyme, garlic and parsley and toss all this together, letting it cook for about a minute. Now pour in your white wine and cover the pan. Turn the heat back down to medium and steam everything until your mussels have opened up, 3–4 minutes. If there are one or two that didn't open, throw those guys out.

> ## TIP
>
> To peel a tomato, get a little pot of salted water on and bring it to a boil over high heat. Cut a little X in the bottom of each tomato. Get a bowl of ice water ready beside the stove. Once the water is boiling, add the tomatoes and cook for about 30 seconds until you see the peel at the ? starting to curl back. With a slotted spoon, transfer the tomatoes to the ice bath and cool for another 30 seconds. As you pull the tomatoes out of the water peel the skins back and discard.

- Move your cooked mussels to a plate and keep warm. The juices from the mussels and the wine are a perfect sauce so you need to strain all the liquids into a blender and toss out the solids. With the motor running on the blender, add your cubed cold butter in batches. It will thicken your sauce and give it a super impressive shine.

- Pour this into a little saucepan and keep it warm over super-low heat.

- Add the pepper mixture to a separate pan and start to warm over low heat.

- To cook the halibut, put a large sauté pan over medium heat. Add a tablespoon of olive oil to the pan and let it get hot. Season your halibut on both sides with salt and pepper. Slip the halibut into the pan and cook for about 4 minutes. Flip it over and cook it on the other side for about 3–4 minutes. The fish should feel firm to the touch.

- To put this dish together, divide the warmed pepper mixture among 4 warm, wide bowls. Put your halibut fillet on top and lay 4–5 mussels around the pepper/fish mound. Drizzle your lovely sauce over everything and serve.

WINE MATCH – **Tempranillo**

Okay, I know you're all thinking I'm crazy – putting a fairly full-bodied wine with a fish as light as halibut. Trust me on this one. Matching wine is more about the dominant flavours on the plate rather than the protein and this dish is full of spicy Chorizo sausage. The fish is quite light in texture and flavour and there's even more seafood with the mussels, but the Chorizo, paprika, and tomatoes all give this dish enough oomph to raise it to red wine levels. I love Tempranillo with it because I find the acidity in the wine is a nice balance to the tomatoes. Look for something that hasn't been aged too long in oak – this adds too much tannin and richer flavours for an overpowering wine. Reds from Rioja, Spain are a great way to go, especially with "Crianza" on the label, which is the lowest level of oak aging in this region.

GROUPER WITH PORCINI, TOMATO, AND OLIVE SAUCE

Grouper, part of the sea bass family, is a firm, meaty fish with mild flavour. One thing to note with grouper is that you always remove the skin before starting to cook, as it has a strong unappealing taste. Picholine olives are a new obsession of mine, they are a green olive that has been brined with coriander and Herbes de Provence. The flavour, if you like olives, is fresh and lovely and addictive. If you can't find them, or eat them all before starting to cook, substitute regular green olives. **Serves 4**

4 large pieces of dried porcini mushrooms

1 tablespoon (15ml) extra-virgin olive oil

2 large cloves garlic, peeled and finely diced

1 large shallot, peeled and finely diced

4 large, very ripe tomatoes, peeled, seeded,
   and cut into large dice

Fine sea salt, to taste

Freshly ground black pepper, to taste

3/4 cup (175ml) Valpolicella or other
   light red wine

2 tablespoons (30ml) fresh oregano, chopped

1 tablespoon (15ml) small capers, drained

1 teaspoon (5ml) chopped anchovy fillets

8 picholine olives, thinly sliced around the pit

4 tablespoons (60ml) vegetable oil

4 7-oz (200g each) grouper fillets

2 tablespoons (30ml) chopped fresh
   Italian parsley

- Soak the porcini mushrooms in warm water for 20 minutes. Drain the mushrooms through a paper towel to get rid of any sediment. Save 1/4 cup (60ml) of the liquid. Chop mushrooms and set aside.

- In a large pot, warm the olive oil over medium heat. Add garlic and shallots to the pot and sweat them out until the shallot is soft, about 3 minutes.

- Add the chopped porcini to the pot and mix it all together, cooking for an extra minute.

- Pour in the wine and bring to a boil.

- Add tomatoes with a good cracking of black pepper, but not salt at this point, the anchovy, capers and olives will add quite a bit of saltiness to the sauce. Turn heat to high and bring everything to a boil.

- Stir in the oregano, capers, anchovy, olives and the mushroom liquid. Turn down heat to low and simmer for 20 minutes, stirring the sauce occasionally.

Contd . . .

- Place a large skillet over high heat and get a tablespoon of oil to the almost smoking point. Season both sides of grouper with salt and pepper. Without crowding, put as many pieces of fish as will comfortably fit in the pan and sauté until browned on the bottom, about 2 or 3 minutes. Flip the fish and cook on the other side until cooked through, about 3 minutes more.

- To serve, spoon some sauce into 4 warm wide bowls and place the grouper over each, and the chopped parsley scattered over the fish.

WINE MATCH – **Valpolicella**

The main thing to keep in mind when you're pairing red wine with fish is that you want to avoid anything that has a lot of tannins. Tannins and fish don't mix. You also want the dish to be robust enough to fare well with red wine, and if it's not a meaty fish like salmon or tuna, the flavourings should be on the bigger side. This dish falls into the latter category, with earthy porcini mushrooms, tart tomatoes, and red wine as an ingredient in the sauce. I've chosen Valpolicella as the pairing and it works on all these levels. Plus the Italian-inspired ingredients in the dish (porcini, tomatoes, and olives) suggest an Italian wine. Make sure to use Valpolicella for the sauce as well to make your match even better.

PAN ROASTED SALMON WITH RED WINE LENTIL SAUCE

"It is, of course, entirely possible to cook without using wine. It is also possible to wear suits and dresses made out of gunny sacks, but who wants to?"

—MORRISON WOOD, FROM *WITH A JUG OF WINE* (1949)

Salmon is a rich fish but the acidity of the wine and the earthiness of the lentils balance out both flavour and texture. The appeal to me is the simplicity of this dish. It has a good number of ingredients, but the flavours are really clean. Du Puy lentils are French and you can usually find them in health or gourmet food stores. They are a little tighter than your average green lentil and have a bit more of a pop to them once they are cooked. They are sometimes also called French lentils. Because the lentils are the star of the show, it's important that they be good quality. You also need good wine for the sauce, the same grape you're going to drink with it. **Serves 4**

3 tablespoons (45ml) grapeseed or canola oil

1/2 cup (125ml) peeled, finely diced carrot

1/2 cup (125ml) peeled, finely diced onion

1/2 cup (125ml) peeled, finely diced celery

4 large cloves garlic, peeled and finely diced

1/4 cup (6oml) double smoked bacon
    chopped into 1/4-inch dice

3 sprigs fresh Italian parsley, + 3 tablespoons
    (45ml), chopped

3 sprigs thyme

2 bay leaf

1 cup (250ml) Du Puy lentils, rinsed under
    cold water and picked through for pebbles

2 cups (500ml) Pinot Noir or other red wine

4 cups (1 litre) chicken stock

Fine sea salt to taste

Freshly ground black pepper, to taste

4 tablespoons (6oml) unsalted butter

4 5-oz (140g) salmon fillets, as even in
    thickness as possible, skinned

- Warm 1 tablespoon (15ml) of grapeseed oil in a medium saucepan over medium-low heat. Add the carrot, onion, celery, garlic and bacon and cook gently until the vegetables are tender, probably about 5 minutes.

- Add the lentils to the pan and the sprigs of thyme and parsley, bay leaf, wine and the chicken stock along with a few good cracks of black pepper. Bring it all to a boil, then lower the heat and let everything simmer. The lentils will give off a bit of a foam so skim that off every now and then. Cook until the lentils are tender, about 20 minutes. Lentils cook at pretty significant degrees of time, based on how old they are, so give them a try after about 20 minutes of cooking. Once they are nice and tender, but not mushy, season with salt and pepper to taste. You can make this dish the day before up to this point. Refrigerate and warm up later when you need them.

- To serve this dish, you need to reheat the lentils and sauce and preheat your oven to 45oF (23oC). Stir the butter and the chopped parsley into the lentil sauce.

Contd . . .

- Put a large skillet over high heat. Add a tablespoon of oil and let warm through for 30 seconds or until it's about to smoke.

- Season both sides of salmon with salt and pepper. Put the fillets into the pan and sear until golden brown; it will take about 2 minutes before you should even poke at the fish. Flip fish over and put sauté pan into oven. Depending on how done you like your salmon, and how thick each piece is, check after 3 minutes. Just peek between the natural layers of the fish with a knife. The salmon should be completely cooked through in 6 or 7 minutes.

- Pull from the oven and set aside.

- To put it all together, spoon the lentils onto 4 plates, making sure that each plate also receives a good amount of sauce. Lay the salmon over the bed of lentils and serve.

WINE MATCH – **Pinot Noir**

Pinot Noir and salmon have become a new classic pairing, a good example of the broken rule that only white wine can go with fish. That's because salmon is a meaty fish with lots of oils that can handle a red wine, and Pinot Noir is generally low in tannin and medium in body so it doesn't overpower. This dish is particularly suited to Pinot because of the smoky bacon, red wine sauce, and earthy lentils. Go for a new world Pinot Noir (think California) to get a fuller style of wine – this dish can handle it.

GRILLED PICKEREL WITH FRESH GREEN BEANS AND SMOKED BACON CREAM

Pickerel come from the pike family. They are lean, firm and Canadian. The bacon cream adds a serious hit of rich smoky flavour to this dish which is freshened by the green beans. You could also use asparagus or fiddleheads, depending on what is in season. **Serves 4**

Bacon Cream

3 thick slices of double smoked bacon,

    cut into smaller strips

2 cloves garlic minced

1 tablespoon (15ml) fresh rosemary, chopped

5 tablespoons (75ml) sherry

1/3 cup (60ml) chicken stock

2/3 cup (120ml) 35% cream

Salt and pepper to taste

The Fish

4 6-oz (170g each) pickerel fillets

1 tablespoon (15ml) olive oil

1 teaspoon (5ml) unsalted butter

2 good handfuls of fresh in-season

    green beans, cleaned and de-stemmed

Salt and pepper to taste

- In a sauté pan over medium heat, add the bacon and sauté until crisp.

- Add the garlic, rosemary, and sherry to the pan.

- Sauté for an extra minute or two and then add the chicken stock and bring to a boil.

- Reduce the chicken stock by half, about 3 minutes.

- Turn down heat to low and stir in cream. Continue to simmer the sauce for about 8–10 minutes.

- Pass the sauce through a fine mesh strainer or a cheese cloth and into a clean pot. Keep warm over very low heat while you cook the fish.

- Preheat your grill or grill pan to medium-high heat. Season fish on both sides with salt and pepper and rub with the olive oil.

- When hot, grill the fish fillets for 2–3 minutes on each side or until cooked through. Pull fish from the grill and keep warm.

- In a medium sauté pan over medium heat, add some butter and melt until it gets foamy. Toss in your green beans and season with salt and pepper. Cook, giving the beans a good toss or two, until the beans are bright green and tender, about 2 minutes.

- Pull pan from the heat and pour in the bacon cream. Stir until the sauce has just come to a simmer.

- To plate, divide the green beans between the 4 plates. Gently place your pickerel on top and spoon bacon cream sauce over the whole thing.

WINE MATCH – **Gamay Noir**

Gamay is a light style of red wine and its food-friendly personality begs to be tried with unusual pairings. This dish is a great example. My first inclination was to put it with an oaky Chardonnay, which totally works if you want to go white. But there's something about the sherry and smoky bacon that whispers "red wine" in my ear. Pickerel is delicate so a big red is out of the question, but a light, fruity Gamay proves to be just the ticket. It has the perfect balance for this dish.

BAROLO BRAISED LAMB SHANKS WITH ROSEMARY

If you've never tried rapini before, this is a great way to start. Rapini is a super-flavourful green related to both cabbage and turnip that has enough personality to not get lost beside the rich, earthy lamb. Gorgonzola is a traditional Italian cow's milk blue cheese, which has a creamy texture and a lot of good stinky flavour, which somehow sweetens the flavour of the rapini ever so slightly. The lamb shanks, as they cook, become sticky and fall-off-the-bone tender while infusing with the herbs, wine and citrus. All of these elements on the same plate will make your guests and any Italian grandmother's heart swell with adoration. Serves 6

2 tablespoon (30ml) olive oil

6 lamb shanks

Salt and pepper to taste

1 1/2 cups (375ml) chopped Spanish onion,

4 garlic cloves, whole

1 tablespoon (15ml) tomato paste

2 cups (500ml) Barolo (or other red wine made from Nebbiolo grapes)

1 cup (250ml) veal stock (use beef stock instead if you like)

3 sprigs rosemary

Zest of 2 large navel oranges

Steamed Rapini with Gorgonzola

1 lb (454g) fresh rapini, washed

2 oz (56g) fresh Italian Gorgonzola cheese sliced into 6 equal pieces

Salt and pepper to taste

- Preheat your oven to 325F (160C).

- Put a large ovenproof roasting pan over medium high heat and add the olive oil. Let the oil heat up for about 30 seconds.

- Season the lamb shanks with salt and pepper and put them in the hot pan.

- Brown the meat without moving the shanks for about 3 minutes. You want a deep caramelized colour before you turn them over. Repeat with the remaining shanks and as you finish each, transfer to a plate and set aside.

- Turn the heat on the roasting pan down to medium and add the onion and garlic. If you need to, add a little more oil to the pan. Cook, stirring constantly until the onions have become slightly translucent.

- Add tomato paste and stir using a wooden spoon.

- Add the wine and use the same spoon to scrape up any brown bits from the bottom of the pan.

WINE MATCH – **Nebbiolo**

Alrighty, first things first – Barolo is a region where Nebbiolo is the grape grown to make the wine. So yes, we are following the rule of drink what you cook with. Generally speaking, most Barolo is pretty pricey, so I hope you can handle pouring some into your pot – I promise it's well worth it for the final, insanely delicious result. Barolo is incredibly flavourful and rich, and it's a perfect choice for lamb in just about any preparation. But braised shanks are possibly the best cut for this wine – so flavourful and meaty. I can't wait for you to try it! PS – the wine is also fantastic with the pungent but creamy Gorgonzola on the rapini.

TIP

Why do you let wine age, and how do you know which ones?

Some wines are meant to be aged and others are meant to be drunk young. But how can you tell which is which? Unless you know the ins and outs of wine, grape varieties, different regions and climates, and the importance of vintage, it's pretty tough to know whether or not you should hang on to a wine for a while before you drink it.

But why age a wine anyway? Most of the wine produced today is meant to be drunk immediately or within a couple of years of the vintage – they are at their prime now. But you can still find wines that actually taste better once they've had time to hang out in the bottle for a bit longer. For example, the red wines of Bordeaux tend to be very high in tannin in their youth. As they get older, the tannins fall out of the wine as sediment and the wine is smoother and softer, allowing you to better enjoy the flavours of the wine. So, does that mean that all wines that have lots of tannins in their youth can age well? Unfortunately, no. In addition to tannins, a wine also has to have a good concentration of fruit and balance of acidity to be able to age well. It's tricky to know which wines have all these things, so go check the tips listed below and ask the experts.

And yes, you can go overboard in aging a wine. When a wine has been kept too long, the fruity aromas and flavours start to fade and you end up with a sort of flat-tasting wine. My tip when it comes to aging wine – better to drink too soon than too late. If you open a wine that seems like it should have aged a bit longer before being opened, pour it in a decanter and let it breathe for a few hours. It'll open up and mellow out a bit, similar to how a wine slowly develops in the bottle.

Here are a few tips to help you figure out which wines you should age:

Check the back label – more and more wines are offering tasting notes, food pairings, and other useful information on the back label, including when the wine will be at its prime.

Ask the experts – many wine or liquor stores have well-trained staff that are familiar with their products and can give you advice on when the wine should be drunk.

Read up – if you are looking for a special wine to lay down for a few years, go online and read up on what's in stores now that could last for awhile.

- Add the veal stock, rosemary sprigs and orange zest. Bring everything to a simmer.

- Return the lamb shanks to the pan and cover with foil or a well fitted lid. Put the pan into the oven for about 2–3 hours. After 1 1/2 hours, pull off the lid from the lamb. The lamb is done when the meat is so tender it nearly falls off the bone.

- Pull the roasting pan from the oven and allow it to cool for 5 minutes. With tongs, pull the lamb shanks out of the braising liquid and onto a baking tray with sides (to catch any run off juices). Cover the meat loosely with foil.

- Pour the braising liquid through a fine mesh strainer into a clean saucepan. Bring the liquid to a boil over high heat and reduce for 5 minutes, or until the flavour of the sauce has intensified. Set aside.

- Put a vegetable steamer over high heat. Add the rapini and cover with a lid until the rapini turns a bright green colour and a knife inserted into the stalk, goes in easily, 3–5 minutes.

- To serve this dish, put the warm lamb on a large serving platter and drizzle liberally with the sauce. Pull the rapini from the steamer and sprinkle with salt and pepper. Plate with the lamb and top with a slice of Gorgonzola cheese.

MEDITERRANEAN LAMB STEW

Tender pieces of lamb that have been slowly infused with garlic, wine, tomato, and fresh herbs is always going to be a hit recipe in my mind. We're breaking on the rules here, using white wine in the stew. The white in this case, lightens the dish slightly but the lamb keeps it a red wine match. You are welcome to replace the white wine with the red if you already have some opened. Or better yet, try it both ways and decide for yourself. Serves 6

3/4 cup (180ml) fresh orange juice

5 cloves garlic, thinly sliced

5 tablespoons (75ml) coarsely chopped fresh mint leaves

2 tablespoons (30ml) extra virgin olive oil

1 1/2 tablespoons (22.5ml) dried oregano

1 bay leaf

2 teaspoons (10ml) freshly ground black pepper

2 lb (1kg) boneless lamb shoulder, cut into 1 1/2-inch cubes

2 tablespoons (30ml) olive oil

2 tablespoons (30ml) unbleached all-purpose flour

2 cups (500ml) dry white wine

1 1/2 (375ml) cups beef stock

2 tablespoons (30ml) tomato paste

2 cups (500ml) carrots cut into 1-inch chunks

2 cups (500ml) white navy beans, cooked

2 cups (500ml) diced and seeded ripe plum tomatoes, canned or fresh

1 cup (250ml) kalamata olives, pitted

Finely grated zest of 2 oranges.

- In a bowl large enough for all the lamb, mix together orange juice, garlic, half the mint and the olive oil. Add lamb and toss until well coated. Cover the bowl and marinate at room temperature for two hours.

- Preheat your oven to 350F (180C).

- Pull lamb out of the marinade, and set both aside.

- In a large Dutch oven, heat 1 tablespoon (15ml) of the olive oil over medium heat. Brown the lamb in small batches. On the last batch you can add all the lamb back to the pot. Sprinkle the flour over the lamb pieces and give everything a good stir for 2 more minutes or until the flour is cooked off.

- Pour your wine into the pot and scrape up all the brown bits from the bottom of the pan. Once the wine has started to simmer, add your leftover marinade, beef stock and tomato paste. Toss in the carrots and bring to a simmer.

- Pop on a lid, or cover with aluminium foil and transfer to the oven to bake for 40 minutes.

- After 40 minutes, pull off the lid and add the cooked beans to the stew. Continue to braise, uncovered, for 15 minutes longer.

- Stir in tomatoes and olives. Cook 10 minutes more.

- Pull pot from the oven. Ladle stew into 6 bowls and garnish with leftover mint and grated orange zest.

WINE MATCH – **Malbec**

For lamb, this is actually a light, fresh dish. The tomatoes, beans, and white wine do the trick, and the mint and orange zest garnish bring it up even more. But it is still lamb, and lamb needs a flavourful red wine to go with it. Malbec is a great choice for this dish because it has big, bold flavours, but it's mellow and easy-drinking, with full body and a smooth texture (go for Argentine Malbec for this style). Malbec is robust enough for lamb, but soft enough for the lighter ingredients.

MARINATED LAMB WITH GREEN OLIVE RELISH

Lamb and olives are such a good team. The heavy earthiness of the lamb is lifted and contrasted by the tangy olives. The relish is a nice change from sauces and contributes a lot to the texture of this dish. Finding a good butcher really does make life a whole lot easier. For example, you are about to make this impressive recipe and you need a leg of lamb, boned and butterflied. You can ask you butcher to do it for you. Butterflying a piece of meat means to cut through the centre, taking your knife almost – but not quite – through. Your meat should then open up like a book or a butterfly. It's easy enough to do on your own but why not save yourself added steps. Serves 4

For the lamb

1 leg of spring lamb, about 5 lb 2.25 kg,
    boned and butterflied

6 garlic cloves, peeled and roughly chopped

3 tablespoons (45ml) chopped fresh
    rosemary leaves

1/2 teaspoon (2.5ml) coarsely ground
    black pepper

2 tablespoons (10ml) lemon juice

1 tablespoon (15ml) sea salt

2 tablespoons olive oil

Olive Relish

1 large shallot, finely chopped

1 tablespoon (45ml) white wine vinegar

3/4 cup (180ml) green olives

1/2 teaspoon (2.5ml) finely chopped lemon zest

1 teaspoon (5ml) chopped fresh thyme

1 tablespoon (15ml) chopped fresh parsley

1/4 cup extra-virgin olive oil

- In a small bowl mix together the chopped garlic, rosemary and pepper. Rub the mixture into the cut side of the meat. Place the meat in a shallow dish and pour the lemon juice and olive oil over top. Rub it all into the meat with your hands to make sure the whole piece is coated. Cover up the dish with plastic wrap and either marinate it at room temperature for 4 hours or in the refrigerator overnight. Either way, turn it over a couple of times to keep coating the meat.

- Roll the meat back to its pre-butterflied shape and tie it closed with butcher's twine.

- Preheat an oven to 400F (200C).

- Preheat a large heavy bottomed skillet over high heat. Add some oil to the pan and allow to heat through for 30 seconds until just before smoking.

- Pull the meat from the marinade and pat it dry with paper towel. Season the meat with salt. Carefully place meat into the pan and sear until a caramel crust appears. Turn the leg and repeat until all sides have been seared.

Contd . . .

- Slide the skillet into the oven and roast until a meat thermometer reaches 125–140F (52–60C), depending on your preferred doneness, 35–45 minutes. For medium rare lamb, pull it from the heat when a thermometer reaches 125F (60C). When the lamb is cooked, pull from oven, cover loosely with foil and allow to rest for at least 10 minutes.

- To make the green olive relish, let the chopped shallot sit in the white wine vinegar for a minimum of 15 minutes. The acidity of the vinegar will soften the flavor and texture of the shallots.

- While you're waiting for that to happen, rinse, pit and finely chop the olives. In a small bowl, combine the chopped olives, lemon zest, thyme and parsley with the olive oil. Add the vinegar and shallots to the relish just before serving.

- To serve, slice the lamb and top with the relish.

WINE MATCH – **Zinfandel**

I am a self-professed olive nut. The only problem is, they're not super wine-friendly so I never could sit around snacking on olives and sipping a big red wine. Until I tried this dish with a big, bold Zinfandel and realized I could! Angie and I ran a cooking class together when we first tried this pairing and it was such a hit that we had to share it with you. The Zinfandel is full-bodied with big, mouth-filling flavours that are perfect for the lamb. The green olive relish worried me with its tart, briny flavours but Zin has a shot of acidity that's just enough to balance it.

VEGETABLE PHYLLO ROLL WITH RED PEPPER COULIS

This is such a beautiful dish – the colourful tender vegetables rolled up in crispy phyllo pastry are perfect with dressed salad greens for a light lunch or a really impressive first course. This dish is nice heated up the next day, but as with most phyllo dishes it's best to serve it within a half an hour of pulling it out of the oven. After that the Phyllo begins to lose its crispiness. This is also a really visual recipe, so when chopping the ingredients try to keep them all around the same size. Serves 6

Filling

1 cup (250ml) chopped cooking onion

2 cups (500ml) peeled and diced carrot

1 cup (250ml) diced red bell pepper

1 cup (250ml) diced zucchini

2 cups (500ml) sliced button mushrooms

3 tablespoons (45ml) chopped fresh basil

1/4 cup (60ml) grated Parmesan cheese

Salt and ground black pepper to taste

2 tablespoons (30ml) olive oil

For the Phyllo

1 cup (250ml) good quality bread crumbs

2 cloves garlic, finely chopped

1/4 cup (60ml) melted unsalted butter

10 sheets phyllo dough

2 tablespoons (30ml) poppy seeds

For the Red Pepper Sauce

1 jar (125ml) roasted red peppers
(packed in oil rather than a brine)

Salt and pepper

- In a large skillet, heat the olive oil on medium heat. Add the onions and sauté for 5 minutes or until they are translucent.

- Add carrots, toss with the onions and cover the pan. Cook for about 5 minutes, giving the occasional stir.

- Add the bell peppers and zucchini, stir altogether and cover once again, cooking for another minute.

- Add the mushrooms and a little salt and pepper. Give a good stir. This time we want to cook until the mushrooms release their juices and become tender. This will take about 7–10 minutes.

- Drain the vegetables and season with salt and pepper again if it's needed.

- Stir in your chopped basil and grated Parmesan.

- In a bowl, mix together the breadcrumbs and the finely chopped garlic. Melt your butter on very low heat. Throw some parchment paper down on a cookie sheet.

- Preheat your oven to 350F (180C) and very lightly dampen a clean kitchen towel.

- Beside your work space have your vegetable mixture, a clean pastry brush in your melted butter, your breadcrumb mixture, and your phyllo laying flat with your lightly dampened towel laying on top to keep it from becoming brittle.

Contd . . .

- Take 2 sheets of the phyllo (don't separate them) and lay them on your work space. If there are any wrinkles in it, smooth them out. Lightly brush top of the phyllo with the melted butter.

- Sprinkle about 1/4 of the garlic breadcrumbs over the sheet. Repeat the layers: 2 sheets of phyllo, melted butter, bread crumbs, until the phyllo and bread crumbs are used.

- Spread your lovely little vegetable mixture evenly over top, leaving about 1 inch frame of phyllo around the vegetables on all 4 edges.

- It's now time to roll. Tuck in both short ends by folding them inward. Taking the long side farthest from you, gently roll towards you. You are making this look like a jelly roll.

- Carefully pick up your phyllo package and place it on the parchment-lined baking sheet with the seam side down. Brush the top and sides with the remaining melted butter and sprinkle with poppyseeds on the top.

- Pop it in the oven and bake for around 35 minutes or until it is golden in colour and a little puffy looking.

- While the phyllo is cooking, make the easy red pepper sauce. In a food processor, add the drained red peppers and blend until smooth. While still blending, slowly add the oil reserved from the jar until the sauce is at a pourable consistency. Taste and add salt and pepper if you feel it needs it.

- Strain this sauce through a fine mesh strainer into a bowl and using the back of a spoon push through all the meaty parts. This will give you a beautiful silky looking sauce. Using about 2 tablespoons (30ml), drizzle onto the serving plates.

- Now, if the phyllo is ready it will be piping hot out of the oven, so give it 5 to 10 minutes before you attempt to cut into it.

- With a bread or serrated knife, cut 2-inch thick slices on a bias, place it over the sauce, and serve.

WINE MATCH – **Cabernet Franc**

When Angie first told me about this dish, I was sure that a tart, flavourful white would be the best pairing but as soon as I tasted it I knew I was wrong. The finely diced veggies turn into an earthy, almost sweet filling that begs for a red wine, and the red pepper coulis made the choice simple – Cabernet Franc. The wine has a vegetal, bell pepper flavour to it that mirrors the ingredients in the dish, especially the coulis, and it's just medium in body, so not overpowering. If you want something cold to drink with this dish, try a dry rosé – even better if you can get your hands on one made from Cabernet Franc grapes.

PARMESAN PANKO BREADED BABY LAMB CHOPS

Man alive these are good! One of those "less is more" dishes. There aren't a lot of ingredients, and they are pretty straight forward, so I say claim it early and make them your specialty. What happens here is that the cheese and bread crumb coating adds a crust to the chop with a ton of flavour and a contrasting texture to the tender meat. The flavours are clean, the texture is crisp! All you need is a glass of wine! **Serves 4**

8 single-rib lamb chops, bone ends trimmed of fat and meat, (about 1/2 inch thick)

1 cup (250ml) finely grated Parmesan cheese

2 large eggs, lightly beaten

1 cup (250ml) panko or regular bread crumbs

1 cup (250ml) vegetable oil for frying

Salt and pepper to taste

2 lemons, quartered, for garnish.

- In a shallow dish, mix together the grated Parmesan and the breadcrumbs.

- Pour lightly beaten eggs into a second shallow dish.

- Holding onto the bone, dip each chop into the eggs, covering both sides. Hold up the chop and give it a little shake to lose any excess egg.

- Coat each side of chop in the breadcrumb/cheese mixture. Again, shake to lose any excess coating.

- As you finish each chop, transfer it to a large plate and let it sit at room temperature for an hour. Letting the chop sit for a period of time helps the coating adhere to the meat.

- Heat a large skillet over medium-high heat with 1/2 cup (125ml) vegetable oil. Just before the pan is about to start smoking, add the chops, giving each one about 1/2 inch of space between them. Cook each side for 4 minutes before moving, to keep the coating intact. Flip the chop once it's golden brown and cook on other side for the same period of time.

- As you cook the chops, gently transfer them to a paper towel-lined tray to soak up any extra grease. If cooking the chops in batches, add more oil to pan and allow one minute to come up to temperature before adding the new batch of chops, or they will be really greasy.

- Season the chops with salt and pepper as soon as you've put them on the paper towel and serve immediately with lemon wedges.

WINE MATCH – **Super Tuscan**

It's dishes like these that get me extra-excited about wine and food matching, when before I'm even done reading the title I already know what wine is going to be a fabulous pairing. For these tasty little chops, a Super Tuscan is the way to go. These are wines made in Tuscany from grapes like Cabernet Sauvignon, Merlot and Syrah, quite often blended with some native Sangiovese. The result is a big, intense, spicy wine with classic Italian acidity – perfect for the crispy-coated chops with rich lamb flavour and pungent, salty Parmesan for a little Italian twist. Super Tuscan not your thing? Go for an Aussie Shiraz or a big, bold California Cabernet Sauvignon.

LINGUINI WITH DUPUY LENTILS, CREAM CHEESE AND SWISS CHARD

This is one of my all time favourite pasta dishes. Earthy lentils cooked in broth with a hint of cumin, covered in a rich cream cheese sauce, and blended with swiss chard makes you feel healthy and decadent all at the same time. It works beautifully with a glass of wine, and a simple tomato salad.
Serves 6

3 cups (750ml) vegetable or chicken broth

1 cup (250ml) Dupuy lentils, rinsed and drained

1 teaspoon (5ml) cumin seeds

1 lb (454g) swiss chard, coarse stems removed

2 tablespoons (30ml) olive oil

1 large onion, chopped

2 cloves garlic, minced

1/2 teaspoon (2.5ml) crushed red pepper flakes

12 oz (335g) dry linguini

6 oz (165g) cream cheese, cut into cubes

- In a 5–6 quart saucepan over high heat, bring 2 cups (500ml) of the broth to a boil.

- Toss in your lentils and cumin. Reduce heat to low, cover with a lid and simmer until the lentils are tender to bite. This could take anywhere from 15–30 minutes depending on how old the lentils are. If after cooking there is still liquid in the pan, drain it and keep the cooked lentils in a bowl nearby.

- Meanwhile, cut the chard stems and leaves crosswise into 1/4 inch strips, keeping stems and leaves separate.

- In a pan, warming over medium heat, add your oil, onion, garlic, red pepper flakes and chard stems. Cook, stirring often, until the onion is lightly browned (about 10–15 minutes).

- Add the chard leaves and cook until the leaves are bright green and limp, about 2 minutes. Add lentils and remaining 1 cup (250ml) broth; cook just until hot (about 3 more minutes). Season to taste. Set aside and keep warm

- In another large pot, bring a good amount of salted water to boil. Add your pasta and cook until tender to bite (this usually takes about 7 or 8 minutes.) Drain the pasta well and place in nice big bowl.

- Acting quickly, while everything is nice and hot, add your lovely lentil mixture and cubed cream cheese to the steaming pasta. Mix lightly and serve immediately.

WINE MATCH – **Barbera**

I have to confess I was a little stumped when Angie proposed this recipe. Creamy but mild cheese, earthy lentils, and bitter greens with pasta. Hmmmm. But I love a challenge and I love pasta so I didn't mind doing a bit of experimenting. After several bowls and several wines, the results were clear – Barbera proves to be the winning match. Not only does it offset the bitterness of the greens, it brings out the earthiness of the lentils, and that streak of bright, crisp acidity in the wine is tamed by the rich cream cheese.

PROSCIUTTO AND RICOTTA EGGPLANT CANNELLONI

These are a refreshing twist on the expected cannelloni since we are using the tender eggplant and the salty prosciutto in place of the pasta. The creamy ricotta is a fresh vehicle for the garlicky pesto. All the flavours melded together create one delicious dish. These take very little time to whip up, and one or two make a really nice first course or you can serve three or four per person for a full main. All you need is a lovely salad and a glass of you know what. **Serves 4**

A good solid tomato sauce, store bought
* or homemade*

1 garlic clove, roughly chopped
1/2 cup (125ml) basil leaves, tightly packed
1/3 cup (90ml) pine nuts
1/4 cup (60ml) olive oil
1 lb (454g) ricotta
Salt and freshly ground black pepper

2 large eggplants
16 slices of prosciutto
Olive oil for frying

- To prepare the stuffing of the cannelloni, in your food processor whip together the garlic, basil, and pine nuts while you drizzle in the olive oil. Season to taste with some salt and pepper.

- Stir in ricotta a couple tablespoons at a time until you are happy with the ricotta/pesto combination.

- To prepare the eggplant, slice it lengthwise about 1/8 inch thick. You need about 12–16 slices, depending on how many cannelloni you want to give each person.

- In a large skillet, heat about 1/4 inch of oil to almost smoking. Fry the eggplant slices for about 1 minute each side or until golden. If oil isn't hot enough, the eggplant will just soak up the oil and get soggy, so if it looks like that might be happening, just wait another 30 seconds before trying again.

- Drain the eggplant on paper towel as you fry. You'll probably need to add extra oil as you go. Don't forget to give added oil time to warm up.

- Preheat your oven to 300F (150C)

- On the stove top, warm tomato sauce on low.

- When you're done frying, lay a piece of the prosciutto along the eggplant and about 2–3 tablespoons (30-45ml) of the filling on the widest end (the bottom). Roll eggplant up to make a tube full of cheese and pesto. Set into a casserole dish. Keep going until you've filled all the fried eggplant slices. Drizzle tomato sauce over top and pop into the oven until everything is warmed through.

WINE MATCH – **Dolcetto**

This dish is filled with ingredients that need a tart red wine that's not too heavy – I picked Dolcetto but other wines in the same category would also work (like Gamay Noir, Barbera, or Valpolicella). Dolcetto has an almost bitter tang to it on the finish which gets tamed down with the salty prosciutto and the smooth, creamy ricotta. And the acidity in the wine balances the tomato sauce and cuts through the prosciutto so both the wine and the food taste better together than they each did on their own – the sign of an amazing match!

How to read a wine label

So, you're in the wine store and want to try something different. You are face to face with a wall of wine – so many choices! So much wine, so little time! Not to worry. I'm sharing with you a few easy tips to help you decipher wine labels and make your next wine store experience fun instead of scary.

Ok, the first thing that we need to talk about is **region** vs. **grape**. Just to keep us all sufficiently confused, sometimes winemakers label their wine by the region and sometimes by the grape. Generally speaking, many Old World countries (think European countries like France, Italy, and Spain) label their wine based on region, whereas most New World countries (like Australia, Chile, Canada, and the United States) label by grape. Bordeaux, Chablis, Côtes-du-Rhône . . . these are all wines of France, but none of these is a grape. Bordeaux and Côtes-du-Rhône are blends and Chablis is actually just Chardonnay. To make things even more confusing, labeling by region isn't always the rule in France. You can often buy a Merlot, Syrah, or Viognier from the south of France that will have the grape listed right on the label. So, how's a blossoming wine lover to know? Here are two things to try:

Learn the basics – like I said before, there is never a rule of either region or grape in any one country. If you get to know some of the more common region names and what the wine inside the bottle tastes like, your wine shopping experience will be much easier. And the best way to do that is to experiment – try new wines every now and then instead of ol' faithful, or go to a wine tasting featuring a region you're not familiar with.

Check the back label – often the mysteries on a front label (e.g. Chinon) will be decoded on the back label by listing the grapes (e.g. 100% Cabernet Franc), what it tastes like, and what foods to pair with it.

Another thing that will help you in deciphering wine labels is **learning the lingo**. Just like seeing "AAA" on a package of Canadian beef or "free range" on a carton of eggs, wine has its own language that is meant help you understand what's in the bottle. Here are a few common buzzwords you might come across:

Appellation – on French labels you might see *Appellation d'Origine Controlée* (AOC), on Italian labels, *Denominazione di Origine Controllata* (DOC), and on Spanish labels *Denominación de Origen* (DO). When you see any of these on a label, it's a clue that the wine may be labeled by region instead of by grape. Appellations are officially defined growing regions that have rules on grape varieties, geographical boundaries, alcohol levels, and other regulations. And they're labeled by region because that was the traditional way wine was sold, making it especially easier for vintners who used a variety of grapes to make up their wine.

Estate bottled – this means that the grapes used to make the wine were grown, vinified, and bottled on the premises of the winery. It's often interpreted as a sign of quality because the winery has control over the entire wine-making process. It also tells you that the wine is actually from the region it says it is, whereas some wines can have imported grapes from other regions blended in. That doesn't mean that a wine without "estate bottled" on the label isn't any good – they could be amazing, you just might not know the grapes' origins and other details about how it was made. Some vintners actually don't even grow any of their own grapes – they specialize in the winemaking and leave grape-growing to the experts, leaving them the freedom to choose the best grapes from year to year.

Old vines or *vielles vignes* – the exact meaning of this is fairly unregulated since old vines could be 40 years old at one winery and 100 years old somewhere else. But what the winery is trying to tell you is that the grapes used to make this wine came from vines that are mature, which also means they produce fewer grapes that are more concentrated in flavour than those from younger vines. It's meant to be another term of quality.

Unfiltered – there are two things to remember about this. First, if a wine is unfiltered, you may have some sediment or other bits in your wine. This isn't a bad thing, just something to keep in mind when you are serving it (you may want to decant, or at least pour carefully and slowly). Second, it means that the wine has been handled less, and the less fussing with the wine, the more flavour and aromatics.

Reserve – again, this is a term that is not very regulated and could mean any number of things. But in general, wineries are saying this is their better class of wines, not the regular stuff. In some countries like Italy, *riserva* means that specific aging and other winemaking provisions have been met.

Now you have some key words under your belt, you are ready to hit the wine store. And just before you head out, here's a quick rundown of the important things you'll find on a wine label:

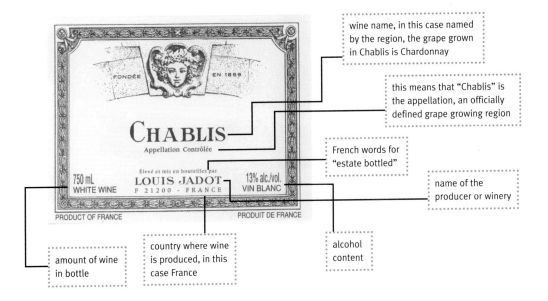

wine name, in this case named by the region, the grape grown in Chablis is Chardonnay

this means that "Chablis" is the appellation, an officially defined grape growing region

French words for "estate bottled"

name of the producer or winery

amount of wine in bottle

country where wine is produced, in this case France

alcohol content

And last but not least – when in doubt, **ask someone** who works in the store. A good wine store will have staff trained to know about the products they sell (just like a good grocer, fishmonger, or butcher) and should be able to help you out.

Screw Cap – Good or Bad?

There are three main types of closures for wine packaged in bottles – natural cork, synthetic cork, and screw cap. We all know and love the romantic tradition of popping a cork on a bottle of wine. But the natural cork isn't all it's cracked up to be, for a couple of important reasons. First of all, they're made from chunks of cork tree bark, which can only be harvested every seven or so years. The bark then needs to cleaned, dried, and processed, which is costly and time-consuming. Cork trees are also a natural resource, supplies of which are waning, especially in the face of the ever-growing wine industry. All these things add up to one big factor – natural cork is expensive and in short supply. The other biggie is that about one in twelve bottles sealed with natural cork are "corked" (tainted with TCA, a bacteria that makes your wine taste moldy and flat). Imagine if you were a baker, and every twelfth loaf of bread you made you threw right in the garbage? That's the frustration that winemakers face in using natural cork.

Synthetic corks are a great alternative, though they can often be a bugger to get out of the bottle. And then there's the screw cap (also called a "Stelvin" closure). It's too bad about the bad reputation screw cap wines have – a lot of people right away think it's a cheap wine. But they're actually the best closure out there. Because a screw cap provides such a good seal, the wine inside the bottle is almost always exactly as the winemaker intended it to be – no oxidization and no cork taint. Screw cap is also really convenient because you can store your bottles upright and you don't need a corkscrew.

So all in all, though we love the traditional cork, we should open our eyes to the benefits of the screw cap. We'll be seeing more and more of it on the shelves as wine producers (especially in New World regions like New Zealand and Australia) jump on the screw cap wagon.

ACT 4

Ending your meal with an amazing wine and dessert match often proves to be the highlight of the meal, so play around! This section outlines the basic styles and options out there for dessert wines and what kinds of desserts they go with, so you're all set to go.

Serving Wine with Dessert

One of the saddest things I see all too often at the end of a meal is diners continuing to drink their dinner wine with dessert. Ever noticed how your Cabernet Sauvignon doesn't taste as good next to the lemon meringue pie as it did with the steak? That's because dinner wines belong with dinner, and dessert wines belong with dessert. So relax, take a break before dessert and finish your dinner wine.

There's one thing that I'll repeat over and over again in this section – if you're serving wine with dessert (which I strongly encourage) make sure it's at least as sweet as the dessert you're having. Just like with any kind of wine and food matching, keeping them in balance is important. If your wine is dry and your food is sweet, the sugars are out of balance which means your wine is going to taste bitter.

If you're worried because you don't love super-sweet wines, please give it a chance – pairing sweet wines with dessert actually makes the wine taste less sweet – and again, that's because the sugars are in balance. Many dessert wines are sold in half-bottle (375ml) sizes, and you only need to serve an ounce or two in a small glass, so it's perfect for experimenting.

Asti

When I think of Asti, I think of my sister. This was her first favourite wine, and to this day, she and her hubby enjoy a bottle alongside a bowl of popcorn while watching a movie. Sounds weird, but you should try it – it's actually pretty good!

Asti is a fun, light, fizzy wine from Italy, and it's the perfect introduction to dessert wines because it's simple and delicate. There are two versions to look out for – Asti Spumante and Moscato d'Asti. Both made from the Moscato Bianco (White Muscat) grape in the Piedmont region of northern Italy, the former is easier to find on store shelves whereas the latter is rarer and only has a slight fizz to it (it actually comes in a regular wine bottle with a regular cork).

Let's start with Asti Spumante, a sweet, sparkling wine that's inexpensive, widely available, and perfect with simple fruit desserts. I love this wine for its party-friendliness – all you need is a chocolate fountain, some fresh fruit, and few bottles of Asti – I guarantee you'll have happy friends.

Moscato d'Asti is the more refined older sister of Asti Spumante, which garners a teeny bit more respect and is not as widely distributed. It's an aromatic semi-sparkling wine called frizzante in Italian (about half as much fizz as other bubblies) that works both as a light dessert wine but also can be nice as an apéritif or with brunch.

Gentle and light on the palate, these wines are intended for pure and simple pleasure, with fruity, fragrant, musky aromas and flavours of honeycomb, wildflowers, herbs, peach, and sweet vanilla.

The great thing about this wine is that unlike lots of other dessert wines, Asti is low in alcohol. There are many ways in which dessert wines get their sweetness, but this is the most straightforward of them all – for Asti, the fermentation is simply halted early, leaving behind lots of the natural sugars of the grape juice. And since only a bit of the sugar ferments, the alcohol level is relatively low (like 5 or 6%). And that's why this is a great brunch wine – you don't want too much of a buzz that early in the day! Or do you?

Aromas & Flavours
Light, fruity flavours of peach, apricot, and tangerine
Fragrant aromas of wildflowers, honeycomb, and herbs
Ranging from slightly to very bubbly, but always light and sweet

Food Ideas
French toast with fruit and maple syrup
Fruit based desserts
Custard desserts

My recommended region for Asti is:
Piedmont, Italy

Banyuls

Two words – Banyuls and chocolate. If you're a chocolate lover, this is the one wine and dessert match that you have to try.

Banyuls is a sweet dessert wine made from Grenache grapes in the Banyuls region in southwestern France. It's part of a group of wines called *Vin Doux Naturels* (see page 322) which translates to "natural sweet wines." Similar in style to port, this wine is both sweet and high in alcohol because part-way through fermentation, Banyuls is fortified using a super-high-strength grape spirit, which is a fairly neutral-tasting wine that has been distilled to up the alcohol to sky-high levels (were talking around 80 to 95%).

Once the wine has been fortified, it spends some time under the heat of the summer sun, giving the wine a "baked" quality, with flavours of raisin, dried cherry, and chocolate. Some are bottled (these have more of the dried fruit flavours) and other see some oak-aging, during which deliberate oxidization occurs. Banyuls made in this style develops flavours of caramel, coffee, and walnut.

But what Banyuls is famous for is its mouth-wateringly delicious partnership with chocolate. The raisiny-berry flavours and its unctuous texture stand up perfectly to the richness of chocolate – something that many wines can't do. And the high sugar levels in the wine work with both bittersweet and sweeter versions of chocolate. If you can't find Banyuls, also look for Rasteau (from the Rhône) and Maury or Rivesaltes (from Languedoc, near Banyuls) as alternatives. Then go out and buy some chocolate!

Aromas & Flavours
Deep, rich dried cherry and raisin flavours
Nutty, chocolate, "baked" notes
Full body with rich port-like texture

Food Ideas
Dark chocolate

My recommended region for Banyuls:
Banyuls, France

Brachetto

If it weren't for the alcohol, Brachetto could easily be confused with cream soda. The first time I tried it, that's exactly what I thought of – sweet, fizzy wine with a ruby colour, pink mousse, and creamy-berry flavours that brought me back to my childhood instantly.

Brachetto is made in a zone in Italy called Acqui (in the northern Piedmont region) so it's labeled "Brachetto d'Acqui." It's made in very small quantities so you don't see a lot of it in stores, but it's a fun, unique wine to pick up if you do happen to come across it.

Brachetto is a red grape and the wine it makes has typical raspberry and cherry flavours, but it also has a perfumey, rose petal aroma and sweet vanilla notes. It's made in the frizzante style, which means it isn't quite as bubbly as a Champagne or a Prosecco would be, but you still see the mousse as you pour it, and you'll feel the fizz in your mouth. Though it's sweet, it's also light in texture, with very low alcohol levels, which makes it ideal with lighter desserts like fruit salad but also an amazing partner with a chocolate hazelnut brownie.

Aromas & Flavours
Intense, sweet aromas and flavours of rose petal, raspberry, cherry, and vanilla
Ruby-red colour with low alcohol and sparkling, refreshing bubbles

Food Ideas
Dark or bittersweet chocolate
Hazelnut desserts
Chocolate-dipped strawberries
Fruit salad

My recommended region for Brachetto is:
Brachetto d'Acqui from Piedmont, Italy

Framboise

Okay, this is pretty straightforward – *framboise* means "raspberry" in French, and that's what this is – raspberry wine. So I'm bending the rules here a bit – this is the only non-grape-based wine in this book, but it's just so damn good that I had to include it.

Imagine eating a spoonful of your grandma's homemade raspberry jam. Add some alcohol and that's what Framboise tastes like – mouth-filling, unctuous, and bursting with fresh, sweet raspberry flavour. My grandmother made raspberry jam, but she also made raspberry wine (yup, my Baba was super-cool), and every time I have Framboise, I remember tasting tiny sips from the giant pails of it she would keep in her basement.

There's nothing too complicated about this wine – it's made in just the same way that many other dessert wines are made. The fresh raspberries are fermented in steel tanks just like grapes, then the wine is fortified to stop the fermentation while it's still sweet, which boosts the alcohol level. Framboise is made by fruit wineries all over the place so just keep an eye out – there's lots made in Canada, the United States, and in France.

Framboise is very versatile, and once opened it lasts quite well in your fridge if you want to keep some on hand. Perfect for sparkling wine cocktails (just add a bit to the bottom of your flute and top with bubbly), you can also pour it on ice cream for an insanely good dessert, or pair it with chocolate anything for a meal ending to remember.

Aromas & Flavours
Intense, jammy raspberry aromas and flavours
Rich, unctuous texture

Food Ideas
Rich, dark chocolate desserts
Poured over vanilla or chocolate ice cream
Chocolate truffles with raspberry filling

My recommended regions for Framboise are:
Regions all over Canada and the United States
France

Icewine

Icewine – the nectar of the gods, and the pride of the Canadian wine industry. This prestigious, expensive wine is what put Canada on the wine map, though its origins begin in Germany. As the name implies, Icewine is made from frozen grapes. But these frozen grapes are special. Because of the popularity and cachet that Icewine has, wine producers around the world have tried to cash in on the craze by throwing grapes in the freezer, then making wine out of them. Unfortunately for them, it's not the same thing. Let me explain.

Icewine is extremely sweet, and the only reason that it's not cloying or downright intolerable is because it's also got lots of acidity. In a great Icewine, the sugar and the acid balance each other out which makes for a wine experience unlike any other. But achieving this perfect sugar-acid balance isn't as simple as freezing grapes.

The true way of making Icewine is to leave the grapes on the vine until the temperatures drop to a certain level (in Canada, regulations require that the air be -8C (17F) or colder while the grapes are harvested and crushed). By leaving them on the vine, the grapes continue to develop their aromas and flavours through the fall months and into the winter, adding to the amazing intensity of the final wine.

But developing the right acidity in the grape is the key, and this comes naturally in cool climate wine regions where sunny days allow the grapes to ripen and colder temperatures at night boost the acidity. Along with the right climate, you have to use the right grapes, which not only have to have lots of natural acidity but also must be hardy enough to last into the winter months. Riesling is the traditional choice, but Vidal and Cabernet Franc also work well. Germany invented this brilliant winemaking technique with their *Eiswein* made from Riesling grapes, but Canada has proven to be the country that in just about every vintage, it gets cold enough to make this liquid gold.

Now we all know Icewine is good. But you're probably wondering why it's so bloody expensive. Well, besides the fact that many people are willing to pay the price (so why wouldn't you charge it?) it's also very costly to make. Wineries take a huge risk in leaving their grapes on the vine past regular harvest time – Icewine crops are usually about 5% to 10% of normal yields for a number of factors. Rot and rain are but two of the problems that are encountered.

It's also labour intensive to make it. First, the vines usually need to be netted to protect them from birds and other wildlife that like eating grapes. Plus, when that key temperature of -8C (17F) is reached, it's usually the dead of night. The grapes have to be hand-picked, so wineries often have a team of workers on-call who will jump out of bed on a moment's notice to get going on the harvest – and they don't come cheap. On top of that, the grapes have to be crushed while maintaining the same cold temperatures, so grape presses are set up outside in the vineyards to make it happen. This is the key step that makes Icewine what it is – frozen grapes means that the water content in the grapes is frozen, so when they are crushed, all you get is syrupy, thick, concentrated juice and that's what is fermented to make Icewine. So needless to say, jumping through all these hoops costs mucho deneiros.

Icewine, although it can be dessert in a glass all on its own, pairs beautifully with fruit and custard-based desserts, but one of my favourite ways to enjoy it is with a plate of really strong, aged cheeses, nuts, and dried fruit – it's heavenly.

Riesling Icewine

Riesling is the traditional grape used for Germany's Eiswein, and it's also often used in Canada as well. Riesling's racy acidity is the perfect foil for the intense sweetness of Icewine, and its mineral flavours add an interesting complexity, especially as the wine ages (Riesling Icewine tends to be the most ageworthy of them all, sometimes lasting over a decade in the bottle while still maintaining is trademark acidity).

Aromas & Flavours
Fruit flavours of apricot, peach, and honey
Complex mineral notes that develop as the wine ages
Intensely sweet, unctuous texture, and bracing acidity

Food Ideas
Fruit or custard desserts
Strong, pungent cheeses
Rich pâtés and foie gras

My recommended regions for Riesling Icewine are:
Niagara, Canada
Germany, where it's labeled Eiswein

Vidal Icewine

Canadian winemakers chose Vidal as an Icewine grape because of its remarkable hardiness against the elements, which is vital for the grapes to survive until their very late harvest. And while somewhat simpler, Vidal has lots of similarities to the aromas and flavours of the classic Icewine grape Riesling. This is the grape you'll see most often in Canadian Icewine, both for its hardiness and exceptional flavours, but also because it makes a less expensive Icewine (when compared to Riesling or Cabernet Franc) so it's more accessible to consumers.

Aromas & Flavours
Intense orchard and tropical fruit flavours like apricot, peach, mango, and passionfruit
Rich, honey-like texture with a long, luscious finish

Food Ideas
Fruit or custard desserts
Rich cheesecake with fruit topping

My recommended region for Vidal Icewine is:
Niagara, Canada

Cabernet Franc Icewine

Cabernet Franc is a red grape, which sets this Icewine apart. Red Icewine is rare, expensive, and a real treat. The Cabernet Franc grape is hardy, but struggles to survive through cold winter temperatures, making yields very low and prices of the final wine very high. Cabernet Franc Icewine is an experience – intense berry flavours, with a rich, luscious texture and a long-lasting finish that makes your mouth water.

Aromas & Flavours
Sweet but tart berry flavours of strawberry and raspberry
Strawberry-red hue
Luscious, mouth-filling texture

Food Ideas
Dark or bittersweet chocolate
Chocolate-dipped strawberries and rich berry desserts

My recommended region for Cabernet Franc Icewine is:
Niagara, Canada

Late Harvest Wines

A huge portion of dessert wines out there are harvested late in the growing season, so this is a bit of a tricky section. Here I'll cover wines that are simply picked past the regular harvest time without other special ways of developing different flavours (like the "noble rot" of Sauternes and Tokaji Aszú).

I think this is my favourite style of dessert wine, not only because it's often less expensive, but also, it's less sweet and I'm a wine and cheese girl for dessert so I don't need a high level of sweetness in my dessert wines for cheese pairing, just a bit. So late harvest wines fit the bill.

A late harvest (LH) wine can be any wine that has been left on the vine past regular harvest times. Wine producers do this to allow more sugars to develop in the grapes by giving them more time in the sun. It's a tricky process, because the longer you leave the grapes on the vine, the bigger the chance that you lose the right balance of acidity and sweetness in the resulting wine. And sweet wine without the right acidity just ends up being cloying.

Often, leaving grapes on the vine past harvest also lets them start to raisin, or shrivel, which develops unique qualities in the wine, and also helps concentrate the sugars and flavours, which is the whole point of late harvesting in the first place.

Late harvest wines are made around the world. The United States, South Africa, Australia, and Canada all make lots of late harvest wines. In the Old World, Germany and Alsace, France are the pioneers of this style. In Germany, Rieslings classified as Spätlese, Auslese, Beerenauslese, and Trockenbeerenauslese are all late harvest wines (from driest to sweetest, the last two also undergoing noble rot which I'll discuss in the Sauternes section on page 329). In Alsace, you'll find wines labeled *Vendage Tardive* which translates to "late harvest." The main grape used for this in Alsace in Gewürztraminer, but you'll also see Vendage Tardive Pinot Gris, and the rare Riesling and Muscat. In Canada, you can find dozens of different late harvest wines produced, most often from the Riesling and Vidal grapes (which are also used for Icewine, the latest of late harvests).

No matter what the grape, late harvest wines are rich, full of flavour, although often fresh, and sometimes quite delicate with floral and citrus character, plus the other flavours and aromas expected from the particular grape in question. Late harvest wines are lovely with a cheese plate because their rich texture mirror the creamy textures of cheese, and the sweet fruit flavours contrast the salty, pungent cheeses. But they also pair well with fruit desserts of all kinds, desserts made with honey, or rich foie gras.

Aromas & Flavours
Flavours of honey, raisins, and ripe apricot and citrus
Delicate floral aromas
Medium body with good acid/sugar balance

Food Ideas
Fruit desserts, especially flans and tarts
Custard desserts
Honey and spice cakes

My recommended regions for Late Harvest wines are:
United States, South Africa, Australia, and Canada
Germany, where it's labeled Spätlese, Auslese, Beerenauslese,
  and Trockenbeerenauslese from driest to sweetest in style
"Vendange Tardive" wines from Alsace, France

Madeira

Madeira is a fortified wine named for the Portuguese island where it's made. We've all heard of port, the famous fortified wine of Portugal. Madeira is its island cousin – similar in some ways, but with its own unique aromas and flavours resulting from how it's made and the grapes used to make it.

What Madeira wine is today came about by accident. Originally, Madeira was a light, acidic wine but to ship it to the New World, it passed through the tropics. On this journey, the barrels of wine baked in the blazing sun, and as a result, developed a softness, depth of flavor, and pleasant burnt quality that became the qualities now sought after in Madeira wine. The winemakers then started doing it on purpose at the winery before shipping, and the result is a unique wine that lasts for decades without losing its flavours and quality (century-old Madeira is not uncommon). Since it's already been through so much with oxidization and cooking, it's tough enough to weather age in the bottle.

There are four major types of Madeira: Malvasia (also known as Malmsey), Bual (or Boal), Verdelho, and Sercial, the latter two being drier. These are all named after the grapes used to make them. The interesting thing about Madeira is that especially for the sweeter styles, there are hardly if any primary fruit flavours – they're more molasses, caramel, burnt sugar, nutty flavours, with rich texture and a long finish. You will also sometimes get some dried fruit flavours like raisin, fig, and date, and in the drier styles (Verdelho and Sercial) you'll get apricot and marmalade flavours as well.

Like port, Madeira is good friends with a nice cheese plate, but I also love it with sweet, nutty desserts like the caramel fondue you'll find in Angie's recipes in this section. The drier styles (Verdelho and Sercial) can even be chilled slightly and served as an apéritif.

Aromas & Flavours
Sweet flavours of molasses, caramel, burnt sugar, and roasted nuts
Dried fruit flavours of raisin, fig, and date
Rich texture and long finish

Food Ideas
Caramel or nut based desserts
Strong, blue-veined cheeses
Plum pudding
Pecan pie

My recommended region for Madeira is:
Madeira, Portugal

Marsala

Marsala is known as a cooking wine, and although it's great in the kitchen, it also has its place at the table. Made on the west coast of Sicily, Marsala is a fortified wine that's named after its city of origin. Indigenous grapes Cataratto, Grillo, and Inzolia are fermented and fortified, then the sugar level is increased either by adding a sweet wine or boiled down grape juice.

Most Marsala is inexpensive and perfect for adding its distinctive flavours to sauces and desserts. But if you can get your hands on a quality one, it can be complex and delicious. As a dessert wine, look for one that is labeled "semisecco" or "dolce," the latter being the sweetest. The simplest (and most common) of Marsalas will be labeled "fine" which means it's been aged for less than one year, so for a more interesting style, look for any of the following labels, each referring to a progressively longer aging process: Superiore, Superiore Riserva, Vergine, Solera, Vergine Stravecchio, and Vergine Riserva.

Aromas & Flavours
Sweet flavours of honey, caramel, marmalade, and spice
Earthy notes of truffle and soil

Food Ideas
Milk chocolate desserts
Italian desserts that feature Marsala as an ingredient

My recommended region for Marsala is:
Sicily, Italy

Muscat

Although Muscat is a grape that can be made into both dry and sweet wines, I decided to include it in the dessert section because I think it shines in sweeter styles. You also tend to see a lot more dessert style Muscats in wine stores than the drier table wines.

If you've never tried Muscat before, think of it as a lighter, less perfumed version of Gewürztraminer. It's still very floral, but doesn't have quite the intensity of its Alsatian friend. Dessert wine Muscat is made in countries all over the world, all in varying styles:

Portugal makes Moscatel de Setubal, a sweet fortified wine

Spain uses Muscat in some of its sweet styles of sherry as well as in other fortified wines in various regions across the country

Moscato Bianco is used in Italy to make Moscato d'Asti and Asti Spumante, sweet bubbly wines

The United States (California in particular) uses Orange Muscat and Black Muscat for lusciously sweet, rich wines

Australia (especially the hot region of Rutherglen) uses Muscat to make its famed "stickies," sweet wines made using a method similar to that used to make Spanish sherry

Greece produces sweet Muscat wines on a handful of its islands

Besides all of these versions of sweet Muscat, some of the best and most well-known examples come from the Rhône Valley and Languedoc regions in France. There, a group of sweet wines known as *Vins Doux Naturels* are made, many from the Muscat grape. They are made by fortifying partially fermented wine with a high-alcohol grape spirit to create strong wines that are boldly perfumed and intensely sweet. Appellations include Muscat de Beaumes de Venise (in the Rhône) and Muscat de Saint Jean de Minervois, Muscat de Frontignan, Muscat de Mireval, Muscat de Lunel, and Muscat de Rivesaltes (in Languedoc).

Aromas & Flavours
Intensely perfumed aromas of orange blossom, jasmine, and other flowers
Sweet citrus like marmalade
Rich texture and full body

Food Ideas
Lemon cheesecake
Chocolate mousse
Citrus-based desserts

My recommended regions for Muscat dessert wines are:
Any of the regions listed above, especially Muscat de Beaume de Venise, France;
Rutherglen, Australia, and California, U.S.A.

Oloroso Sherry

Oloroso means "scented" in Spanish – a good name for a wine that has big, giant aromas that jump out of the glass at you. In the first section of this book, I tried to explain that there are other sherries out there, ones that weren't dark and sweet and rich. But now that we're back on the subject, let me introduce you to Oloroso.

Oloroso is completely unlike the Fino, Manzanilla, and Amontillado sherries in Act 1. In fact, Oloroso is made in an entirely different way. Unlike the drier sherries, the winemakers don't allow flor (the layer of yeast) to grow at the surface of the wine during fermentation. And no flor means that the wine is exposed to air which causes oxidization. So instead of being fresh and clear, Oloroso becomes darker and stronger and is often left for many decades to develop during the aging process.

Oloroso can be either dry or sweet. I like the sweet ones, because the deep, nutty, "baked" aromas and flavours that develop during its long aging process are complemented by sweetness, creating a wine that's aromatic and can be dessert in a glass. If you'd like to pair Oloroso with food, try it in place of a tawny port – nut-based desserts, cheese plates, and dried fruits all pair up nicely with sweet Oloroso.

And here's a tip, it you ever want to splurge and are lucky enough to find it, try out Pedro Ximenix (a.k.a. PX) – it's an insanely sweet, nutty sherry similar but more over-the-top than Oloroso. If you like 'em sweet, PX is for you.

Aromas & Flavours
Sweet and rich aromas and flavours like fruitcake – nuts, raisins, figs, toffee, and almonds
Rich texture and full body

Food Ideas
Nut-based desserts
Strong cheeses
Desserts with dried fruit

My recommended region for Oloroso Sherry is:
Jerez, Spain

Port

My first port experience was with a buddy I'd known since high school. We were getting close to the end of our university years and he came back to town to catch up with old friends. We met up and he brought a bottle of port, which we sipped on slowly for hours while we laughed and reminisced. I was not into wine at all at that time, but it was easy to drink – sweet and smooth with rich flavours that reminded me of fruitcake. Too easy to drink, in fact, because I also remember having a bad headache the next day.

Port is the famous fortified wine of Portugal. My first port was a tawny, but it comes in many styles from simple, berry-scented Ruby port, expensive and complex Vintage port, late bottle vintage, and a range of others, including the nutty tawny port.

But let's start at the beginning of the port story. The British have always been big wine drinkers. They love their wine, and historically, they got their wine from French vineyards. But throughout the years, there were times when politically, it wasn't cool to buy wine from France, so they looked elsewhere, and they liked what they saw in Spain and Portugal. Portugal made red wines blended from their many indigenous grapes that were an acceptable substitute for their beloved French *claret*. But these Mediterranean countries presented a problem – the wine had to be shipped on boats up through the Atlantic Ocean to reach England. Under the hot sun, the wines cooked and were unpalatable by the time they reached British soil.

But the Brits are smart cookies. They knew that higher-alcohol booze shipped just fine, so they spiked the Portuguese wine with grape brandy to make it more stable. This solved the shipping problem and soon, this rich, high-alcohol wine became not just a convenience for better shipping, but a wine that pleased the English palate.

Port grapes are grown along the banks of the Douro river in Portugal. There, the weather is hot, the sun is blistering, and the grapes (a blend of indigenous varieties such as Touriga Nacional, Touriga Franca, Tinta Roriz – also known as Tempranillo in Spain – and a handful of others) are harvested super-ripe and full of sugar. The fermentation begins just like regular table wines, but partway through, while there is still lots of natural sugar left in the wine, a high-alcohol grape spirit is added. This "fortification" stops the fermentation by killing the yeast cells, leaving a wine that is both sweet and high in alcohol.

Here's where the wines can go in a number of different directions. **Let's start with ruby port,** the simplest of the red ports. These wines are aged usually for three years or less in oak casks, then filtered and bottled. They are full-bodied and deeply coloured, and some of the least expensive ports on the market. Unlike many ports, they are ready to drink once bottled, with no aging required, and they have simple, fruity flavours of berry and plum with a long, sweet finish. You can also get reserve ruby ports that have been aged in casks for up to five years before bottling for a richer, better-quality wine.

Tawny port is next up, my first and my favourite. This style has been matured in oak for at least seven years, which leaves the wines soft, smooth, and an amber colour, hence the name "tawny." They're often labeled with an "indication of age," meaning that though the wine could be a blend from various years, the final product is something that fits the typical characteristics for a 10-, 20-, 30-, or over 40-year-old tawny port. Tawnies are concentrated and complex in flavour, and that's because they've spent such a long time in oak casks which not only allows a slight amount of oxidization (oak is porous) but also imparts many aromas and flavour from the wood. You can expect notes of walnut, coffee, chocolate, caramel and the spicy fruitcake that I recognized as a novice wine drinker, all complementing the dried or stewed berry flavours from the grape.

Vintage ports are some of the most expensive and long-lived wines in the world. They are made only in the best years, when producers agree that the highest quality of wines can be produced. The wine will only contain grapes from that particular vintage (whereas most other ports are blended from various years) and they are bottled when only two years old. They are rich, full, and tannic at first, but they slowly mature in the bottle, usually for at least a decade if not several, before they reach their peak. Because it ages in the bottle, there is usually quite a bit of sediment at the bottom, so using a decanter is a good idea. And here's a tip for you bargain-hunters out there – look for wines labeled "LBV" or "late bottle vintage." These are wines that are similar in style to vintage ports but aren't from declared years. They're richer than ruby ports but not as complex as vintage ports, a good value for a delicious wine.

Another unique style of port to look out for is white port. This wine is made from white grapes, and has a light golden colour, low acidity, and nutty, honey flavours. They can range from dry to sweet (the style is listed on the label) and can be served as an apéritif (the drier styles) or with light, fruity desserts. It's also often served on the rocks with soda and lemon, the perfect patio cocktail.

Ruby Port Aromas & Flavours

Rich fruit flavours of berry and plum

Sweet, simple, and high in alcohol

Food Ideas for Ruby Port

Dark chocolate desserts

Strong, pungent cheeses

Chocolate chip cookies

My recommended region for Ruby Port is:

Douro Valley, Portugal

Tawny Port Aromas & Flavours

Tawny, amber colour

Aromas and flavours of dried fruit, plum, roasted nuts, and caramel

Smooth, mouth-coating texture

Food Ideas for Tawny Port

Pungent washed rind, aged, and blue-veined cheeses

Nut-based desserts

Plum pudding

Banana cake

My recommended region for Tawny Port is:

Douro Valley, Portugal

White Port Aromas & Flavours

Tropical and citrus fruit flavours balanced by notes of nuts and honey

Rich golden colour, can range from dry to sweet

Food Ideas for White Port

Salted, roasted almonds

Tart citrus-based desserts

Mild, fresh cheeses

My recommended region for White Port is:

Douro Valley, Portugal

Recioto Della Valpolicella

Valpolicella is a region in Veneto, Italy, where a range of red wine styles are made using the same grape blend – Corvina, Molinara, and Rondinella – three indigenous grapes that work together to create ripe cherry-flavoured wines. In Act 3 we covered off the three dry styles but I saved the sweet one for the dessert section.

Recioto is made in exactly the same way as Amarone (see page 211). The best grapes of the region are hand-picked and set aside to dry over a period of a few months – this grape-drying is called *passito* or *appassimento* and you'll often see these terms right on the wine label. As the grapes dry, their water content evaporates, but the sugars remain and the flavours concentrate. These dried, raisiny grapes are then fermented, which produces a wine with intense flavours and port-like texture. Here's where Amarone and Recioto differ – for Amarone, the wine is fermented to dryness, which means that you get a full-bodied wine with a high alcohol level. Recioto is made in a sweet style, so the fermentation is interrupted to leave some residual sugar in the wine.

This wine is luscious and intense, with aromas and flavours of dried fruits, jammy cherry, and sweet spice. I love this wine on its own – dessert in a glass I like to say – but paired with a cheese plate or something chocolaty it is truly divine.

Aromas & Flavours
Aromas and flavours of ripe, jammy cherry, dried fruits like raisin and prune,
  sweet spice, and smoky coffee

Food Ideas
Gorgonzola and other blue-veined cheeses
Desserts that feature chocolate or berries

My recommended region for Recioto is:
Valpolicella in Veneto, Italy

Sauternes

Sauternes is one the most famous and respected of dessert wines around the world. It's a golden sweet wine named after the region in which it's made. Sauternes is in Bordeaux, France, where two main grapes are grown for its wines – Sauvignon Blanc and Sémillon. These are the same grapes that make the dry white Bordeaux wines, but in the misty, cool, sunny vineyards of Sauternes, something special happens.

Now hang on to your hats – the thing that makes Sauternes special is mold. I know, I know, "special" isn't quite the word you'd use for mold, but let me enlighten you. The mold of Sauternes is called *Botrytis cinerea* or simply "noble rot." And there's good reason for calling it noble. Botrytis thrives in the conditions in Sauternes – damp, misty mornings, and dry, sunny afternoons – and attacks the grapes, sucking out the water and concentrating the sugars in the shriveled grapes. The noble rot also leaves behind its own mark, a distinctive honeyed flavour that's hard to describe in words but is easy to smell and taste in wines that have it.

The wine made from these dehydrated, botrytis-affected grapes is golden, sweet, intense, and flavourful. Aromas and flavours include honey, caramel, tropical fruit, and toasty, nutty notes from oak-aging. Sauternes is classically paired with foie gras, the rich, fatty duck or goose liver, but I love it with strong blue cheeses like Roquefort, or with sweet, tropical fruit desserts. A wine experience unlike any other.

Aromas & Flavours
Sweet and luscious with full body
Flavours of honey, caramel, and tropical fruit
Toasty, nutty notes from oak-aging

Food Ideas
Rich custard-based desserts
Foie gras
Roquefort cheese
Crepes Suzette

My recommended region for Sauternes is:
Sauternes, France
TIP – check out wines from Barsac, a region close to Sauternes that makes similar but less pricey wines

Tokaji Aszú

This is the Sauternes of Hungary. If you've ever had Sauternes from France and loved it, then you've got to try Tokaji Aszú. Hungary isn't exactly known for their wine, but that doesn't mean what they make isn't great. And if anything, their prized wine is Tokaji. Interestingly, though Sauternes is more famous, Tokaji Aszú was made for centuries before the French version developed. It's all in the marketing.

Just like Sauternes, the grapes used to make Tokaji are attacked by noble rot or botrytis. but here's where things start to change. For Tokaji, the botrytis-affected grapes (there are four different grapes that can be used, but the main one is Furmint) are pounded into a paste which is then added to grape juice to ferment. The amount of paste added to the juice is measured in "puttonyos" which is what you'll see on a label of Tokaji, and indicates how sweet (and usually how expensive) the wine will be – the higher the number of puttonyos, the sweeter the wine is.

Aromas & Flavours
Intensely sweet and richly textured
Amber-coloured with aromas and flavours of nuts, caramel, and honey

Food Ideas
Roquefort and other blue-veined cheeses
Foie gras
Buttery, spiced desserts
Desserts with hazelnuts

My recommended region for Tokaji Aszú is:
Tokaji, Hungary

Vin Santo

I love this dessert wine because the first time I had some, I was told I should dunk my biscotti into it. I'm serious. How fun is a wine that you can dunk cookies in?? Like Oreos in milk, how can you not love it!?

Vin Santo is the "the wine of the saints," named as such because once the grapes are picked, they are dried for several months (a method called *passito*), and the fermentation doesn't take place until around Easter time, hence the reference to saints. Regardless of saints or Oreo cookies though, this wine is special and delicious. Because the grapes are dried out before they are fermented, the flavours and sugars are concentrated, which makes an intensely flavoured and sweet wine.

Vin Santo (sometimes also called Vinsanto or Vino Santo) is amber-coloured, made from Malvasia and Trebbiano grapes, and traditionally from Tuscany in Italy. It is rich and sweet, with aromas and flavours of raisin, fig, and tart marmalade. It has a full bodied texture and fairly high alcohol.

The tradition is to serve Vin Santo with biscotti, dipping the cookies into the wine to soften them before biting in. It's a wonderful tradition, and I encourage you to try it. Dunking cookies into your wine is liberating.

Aromas & Flavours
Rich, sweet, and full bodied in texture
Aromas and flavours of raisin, fig, nuts, and tart marmalade

Food Ideas
Biscotti
Nut-based desserts
Citrus tarts

My recommended region for Vin Santo is:
Tuscany, Italy

BITTERSWEET CHOCOLATE TART WITH ALMOND CRUST

I'm a girl who loves chocolate and who believes those who say they don't aren't telling the truth. If you are the same, this dessert may both improve and ruin your life. This rich, ultra silky chocolate filling, cradled in a crispy, nutty pastry thrills me every time I make it. This recipe is one that your guests will talk about for the rest of your life . . . in a good way. Serve with a small scoop of vanilla ice cream or even better, a small scoop of raspberry gelato. Serves 6 to 8

Pastry

2 cups (500ml) toasted almonds

1/3 cup (90ml) sugar

3 cup (750ml) all purpose flour

1 cup (250ml) unsalted butter –
   room temperature

1 large egg

1 teaspoon (5ml) vanilla

Chocolate Filling

3/4 cup (180ml) 35% cream

1/3 cup (90ml) 10% cream

7 oz (200g) good quality bittersweet
   chocolate, finely chopped

1 large egg, lightly beaten

- In a food processor purée the almonds on pulse until they have the consistency of a graham crumb (watch not to get too excited about blending them or you will make almond paste).

- Add sugar and flour to your almonds and continue to blend until fine.

- Add your butter, egg, and vanilla and blend to incorporate all ingredients. Don't be shy to pull off the lid and scrape the sides and corners with a spatula. If the pastry is too dry, add a tablespoon of water.

- Divide your dough into 2 equal pieces, wrap them tightly in plastic. You can freeze one for later and refrigerate the other for 30 minutes before using.

- Grease and flour a 10-inch pie plate.

- On a lightly floured surface, roll out your dough to 1/8-inch thickness. Lay it in your prepared pie tin. If there are any holes in the pastry, patch them with other little pieces of dough. Pop this fella in the freezer for 15 minutes to give it a good chill.

- Preheat oven to 350F (180C). Bake your tart shell for 10–15 minutes or until golden brown. Allow to cool.

- Reduce oven temperature to 275F (135C).

Contd . . .

TIP

What does fortified mean?

Fortified wines, including port, some sherries, Madeira, Marsala, and many others are wines that have been "spiked" with something high-alcohol, like brandy, as part of the winemaking process. Originally this was done because the wines lasted longer that way in less than ideal storage conditions. Partway through the fermentation process, while there was still some natural sugar left in the wine, brandy or another high-alcohol grape spirit was added. This not only killed the yeast cells (which stops fermentation), but it also increased the alcohol level. Higher alcohol and sugar levels both act as preservatives so the wine would travel better when shipped overseas. Over time, people developed a taste for this sweeter, more potent style of wine and now the process of fortification continues more for that reason than for its preservation benefits. Because they're sweet and high in alcohol (usually around 20%) it's drunk in smaller quantities before or after a meal. See the beginning of Act 4 (page 312) for more detailed information on specific fortified wines.

- Put both creams in a small saucepan and bring them to a simmer over moderate heat. Remove your pan from the heat and immediately add the chocolate stirring constantly until melted and the mixture looks silky and smooth. Cool to room temperature.

- Whisk in your egg to the cooled chocolate, until well blended.

- Pour the filling into the cooled tart shell.

- Bake in the centre of a preheated oven until the filling is slightly firm but still trembling just in the centre, 15–25 minutes. You need to keep an eye on it since everyone's oven temperatures vary.

- Place on a rack to cool for 1 hour before cutting it.

WINE MATCH – **Banyuls**

I said it before and I'll say it again – Banyuls + Chocolate = Heaven. I'm not the biggest chocolate fan (I know, I know – Angie doesn't believe in that) but this dessert is to die for, and when you put Banyuls with it, there's an even bigger pay-off. That's because the rich, sweet, berry-flavoured wine is the all-time best partner for dark chocolate – they balance each other and bring out the best in their respective flavours. If you can't find Banyuls (it's sometimes hard to find) you could also try a sweet Oloroso Sherry, a Ruby Port, or Recioto della Valpolicella.

ANGEL FOOD CAKE WITH LEMON CURD AND FRESH FRUIT

This dessert reminds me of summer afternoon parties. Angel food cake with fruit is the perfect light dessert to have after a big meal. The classic lemon curd adds an element of class and richness that ties the whole thing together. Curd can be made up to a week in advance. Making angel food from scratch is really pretty easy. It is important to note that plastic and glass bowls tend to deflate the egg whites as you beat them. For the best results, stick with stainless steel and remember, these egg whites are going to quadruple in size so make sure your bowl is nice and big. **Makes 16 portions**

For the cake

10 egg whites, at room temperature

1 1/4 teaspoons (6.25ml) cream of tartar

1/4 teaspoon (1.25) salt

1 teaspoon (5ml) vanilla extract

1/2 teaspoon (2.5ml) almond extract

1 1/4 cups (310ml) sugar

1 cup (250ml) cake flour sifted

For the Lemon Curd

Zest of two lemons

2/3 cup (90ml) granulated sugar

5 egg yolks

1/2 cup (125ml) fresh lemon juice

Pinch of salt

1/2 cup (125ml) unsalted butter, melted

4 to 6 cups (1 to 1.5 litres) fresh fruit such as
   strawberries, raspberries, blueberries,
   peaches, etc, sliced and sprinkled with
   a little granulated sugar to bring out
   the juices.

1 cup (250ml) 35% whipping cream,
   whipped until soft peaks form, with a little
   sugar and a couple of drops of vanilla
   to taste

Lemon Curd

- To make your curd, blend the lemon zest and sugar in a food processor,.

- Next, add in the egg yolks, lemon juice and salt. Give the processor a couple of good pulses to combine them.

- With your processor running, add your melted butter through the feed tube until it's all really well combined.

- Once you're done grab a spatula and scrape it all out into a stainless steel saucepan.

- Cook your filling over medium-low heat, stirring constantly with a wooden spoon, until thick, 4–5 minutes. You never want this to boil or to look like it's going to boil. The curd is cooked when you pull the wooden spoon out, hold it so that the sauce can run, and draw a line with your finger through the curd on the back of the spoon. If the line holds and your curd doesn't run into it, you, my friend, are done.

- Pull your thickened curd from the heat and allow it to cool before you put it in a container and pop it in your fridge.

Contd . . .

Angel Food Cake:

- Preheat your oven to 350F (180C).

- In a bigger stainless steel bowl than you think you will need, beat the egg whites, cream of tartar, and salt with an electric mixer until they form soft peaks. You'll know what this is, if you pull the beaters out of the eggs and they form little peaks that kind of flop over on the top.

- Add your vanilla and almond extracts and gradually add the sugar, beating until the whites are stiff, but not dry and shiny.

- Sift the flour onto the egg whites.

- Using a rubber spatula, gently fold in the flour trying to keep the air in the egg whites.

- Gently spoon your mixture into an ungreased 10-inch non-stick tube pan, and bake until a toothpick inserted in the cake comes out clean, 40 minutes.

- Invert your pan and let the cake hang out for about 2 hours so it's completely cooled. When you're ready, loosen the cake by running a knife around the edges and turning it out onto your serving dish.

- Serve with your lemon curd, whipped cream and fresh cut fruit.

WINE MATCH – **Asti**

The beauty of this dessert is that it's light and airy, with tart, refreshing fruit flavours. So we need the same kind of wine – something that won't overpower the delicate nature of this dish. And Asti is absolutely perfect – it's very light in body, with delicate bubbles and a sweet, peachy flavour. The texture and bubbles will keep the wine fresh enough for the tart lemon curd and not too heavy for the cake. And there's nothing better than a glass of Asti with fruit, so enough said. If you can find Moscato d'Asti, go for that but if not, Asti Spumante will work too.

LEMON POPPY SEED CUPCAKES WITH CREAM CHEESE ICING

Everyone loves a tasty cupcake. Lemon cake with crunchy poppy seeds and tangy cream cheese icing is a perfect dessert for so-called non-chocolate lovers in your life. When it comes to cream cheese icing I prefer to keep mine more cream cheese and less icing sugar, but feel free to adjust the amount of sugar to your taste.   30 cupcakes

1 1/2 cup (375ml) unsalted butter, softened

2 1/2 cups (625ml) granulated sugar

7 eggs

1 1/2 tsp (7.5ml) vanilla

3 3/4 cup (875ml) unbleached flour

2 1/2 tsp (12.5ml) baking powder

3/4 tsp salt (3.75ml)

1 cup (250ml) milk, room temperature

1 1/2 tsp (7.5ml) lemon zest

1/3 cup (80ml) poppy seeds

Glaze

1 1/2 cup (375ml) icing sugar

1/4 cup (60ml) fresh lemon juice

Icing

12 oz (335g) cream cheese, softened

1/2 cup (125ml) unsalted butter, softened

4 cups (1 litre) icing sugar

- Preheat your oven to 350F (180C).

- Line a 30-muffin tin with cupcake liners or butter and flour them.

- In a large mixing bowl, beat together the butter and the sugar until they are light and fluffy.

- Continue beating and add your eggs one at a time making sure you mix each one in well before the next egg is added.

- Add in the vanilla and set this mixture aside.

- In a different bowl, mix together the flour, baking powder and the salt. In thirds you are going to add 1/3 of the dry mix to the butter mixture, alternating with the milk.

- Once you have finished that, with a rubber spatula, gently fold in the lemon zest and the poppy seeds.

- Divide the batter into the muffin tins and bake for 20–25 minutes or until a toothpick inserted comes out clean.

- With a little whisk or a fork mix together your sugar and lemon juice.

- When the cup cakes come out of the oven, gently poke the tops of them 6–8 times with a toothpick.

Contd . . .

- Brush the glaze on while they are still warm to the touch and allow them to cool completely.

- Beat the cream cheese and butter with an electric mixer on medium high until it's nice and smooth and gradually start adding the sugar. I find for the best icing you need to beat it longer than you think for a light fluffy result.

- Finish the cupcakes by spreading the icing on top of each one. Pop these fellas in the fridge to help the icing set up.

- If you want an added decorative flare to each little cake, garnish the top with fine citrus zest or a sprinkling of poppy seeds.

WINE MATCH – **White Port**

This dessert's a bit tricky when it comes to wine matching. We've got a light cupcake, tart but sweet citrus flavours, and rich, creamy icing. My first pick is White Port – its sweet honey flavours pair up nicely with the icing, and the nuttiness of the wine picks up on the poppy seed flavour. If you can't find White Port, a late harvest Riesling or Vidal will do the trick nicely, or you could go with an Asti Spumante – a glass of bubbly and a cupcake – could a girl get any happier?

CHAI POTS DE CRÈME

The difference between *pots de crème* and *crème brûlée* is the burning of the sugar on the top. If you would prefer *crème brûlée* just dust the tops of these with granulated sugar and with a kitchen *brûlée* torch, or the broiler setting on your oven, lightly caramelize the tops just before serving. In this recipe we are using a *bain-marie*, or water bath. All that means is we are gently cooking the custard with the heat of the water, rather than dry cooking to avoid the custard scrambling or splitting.
Serves 6

1 cup (250ml) 35% cream

1 cup (250ml) whole milk

1 tablespoon (15ml) loose English Breakfast
    or Jasmine tea

1 cinnamon stick

8 whole cardamom pods

6 whole cloves

3 rounds of peeled fresh ginger,
    each 1/4 inch thick

1/4 tsp (1.25ml) grated orange peel

4 large egg yolks

1/2 cup (125ml) packed golden brown sugar

- Combine your cream, milk, loose tea, cinnamon stick, cardamom pods, cloves, ginger and orange peel in a medium saucepan. Bring the mixture to a boil. As soon as it starts to boil pull the pot from the heat, cover it with a lid and let it sit for 10–15 minutes while all the spices flavour up the milk.

- Preheat your oven to 325F (160C).

- You'll need 6 3/4-cup (180ml) ramekins which you'll put into a 13 x 9 x 2inch baking pan. This is a good time to heat up a kettle full of water.

- Using your fine mesh strainer or a cheesecloth, pour the milk mixture through into a clean bowl. You can discard the flavorings.

- In a bowl, whisk together the egg yolks, brown sugar. Gradually in a thin stream whisk in the milk mixture (the slowness of adding the cream is so the eggs don't freak out from the heat and curdle on you, so take it nice and slow.)

Contd . . .

- Transfer your custard mix to a measuring cup with a spout and pour your custard into the ramekins dividing equally. The ramekins won't be full but that's a good thing, you'll see when you put them into the oven.

- Slowly add your hot water to the pan until it has reached the halfway point up the side of the ramekins.

- Cover your pan with foil and poke with a fork, four or 5 times to allow some steam to escape.

- Carefully put this pan into the preheated oven making sure you don't get any water into your custards. Bake the custards until the outside has set and there is about a nickel size belly shake in the middle (about 30–35 minutes). Pull them out of the oven and with a tea towel, an oven mitt or some tongs, remove them from the water and cool for 30 minutes.

- Chill the custards in your refrigerator until they are cold. To make these for a dinner party you're going to want to give yourself a good 4 hour start to set properly but you can make them the day before as well if you like, just wrap them with plastic wrap.

WINE MATCH – **Late Harvest Gewürztraminer or Riesling**

Okay, this velvety smooth custard is rich and creamy but it has some unique flavours going on with the tea and all the spices. So we need a wine that's sweet and silky as well as spicy. Say that five times fast. The exotic fruit and spice flavour of Gewürztraminer are the perfect pairing. Remember, if the food is sweet, your wine needs to be at least as sweet, so look for a dessert-style Gewürz that has a high sugar level. If you can't find late harvest Gewürz, go for a sweet Riesling. Or for something extra-special, try Tokaji Aszú from Hungary. Its rich honey-like flavours would be a treat with this elegant dessert.

FLOURLESS CHOCOLATE CAKE WITH HAZELNUT MERINGUE

If you're a texture person when it comes to your food, this dessert will blow your mind. This is a silky, almost mousse-like chocolate cake with a chewy, crunchy meringue on top. The black and white contrast of the dessert wows before you even bite into it and exceeds all your expectations with flavour. I will warn you, it's super-rich so start with a smaller piece and then go back for seconds.

10 tablespoons (150ml) unsalted butter
   (plus some for buttering the pan)

1 cup (250ml) hazelnuts

3/4 cup (180ml) firmly packed brown sugar

6 large whole eggs, separated

4 large eggs, whites only

12 oz (336g) best quality bittersweet chocolate,
   melted and cooled to room temperature,
   plus 4 oz (112g) roughly chopped

1 tablespoon (15ml) vanilla extract

Pinch of salt

1 tablespoon (15ml) cornstarch

1/4 teaspoon (1.25ml) cream of tartar

1 cup (250ml) granulated sugar

- Preheat your oven to 350F (180C).

- Lightly butter a 9 x 3-inch spring form pan (this will help your parchment stay in place). Pull the bottom of the spring form out and trace it on a piece of parchment paper (I know this is irritating but trust me, you'll be thankful for it at the end). Cut out the circle and stick it down on the buttered side of the spring form base. Cut 2 or 3 strips of parchment wide enough that it peeks up over sides of the pan when you lay them down horizontally to line the inside. Put the pan back together and set it aside.

- Put hazelnuts onto a cookie sheet and pop in the oven to toast. When ready you should be able to smell the toasty nuttiness and the skins will have started to crack, about 10–15 minutes. While they are still warm put them in batches into a clean kitchen towel. Rub them well to remove the skins. Chop them up roughly and set aside in a bowl.

- Once the nuts are cooled, add your chopped chocolate and cornstarch to the same bowl.

- To make the cake batter, in a large bowl with an electric beater, cream together the butter and brown sugar until the butter is pale and smooth.

- Add the 6 egg yolks, one at a time (you see this a lot in baking because if you toss all the eggs in at once they ban together and refuse to blend into the other ingredients properly, so beat well after you add each yolk), and keep beating until mixture is light and fluffy.

Contd . . .

- Add your melted chocolate and vanilla and beat until it's all mixed together. Set aside.

- In a second bowl, toss in your 6 egg whites and your salt. You need to make sure your beaters are clean so now's a good time to give them a good rinse from the last bowl we beat.

- Kick your electric mixer into high gear and beat until soft peaks form, which should take a couple of minutes.

- With a big spatula fold in 1/3 of the egg whites into the chocolate mixture, mixing it thoroughly but trying not to knock the air out of your whites.

- Fold in the remaining beaten egg whites just until combined.

- Pour batter into prepared pan, bake 25 minutes.

- While that's baking it's a good time to make your meringue. Rinse out the bowl you did your last batch of egg whites in and dry it well.

- Toss in the remaining 4 egg whites and cream of tartar and beat the whites on high speed until they are just frothy.

- Slowly add the sugar and keep beating until stiff peaks form (when you pull out the beaters your peaks will hold their shape). This should take about 7 or 8 minutes.

- Gently fold in hazelnut mixture with your spatula.

- When cake is done pull it from the oven. Using an offset spatula (if you don't have one of these, they really do make your life a heck of a lot easier when baking), spread the meringue mixture on top of the cake, and put it back in to the oven.

- Bake it again until the meringue is lightly browned and crisp, 25–30 minutes.

- When done, put it on a cooling rack and let it slightly cool before you carefully pop open the spring form to release the sides of pan (note how the parchment arts & crafts pays off now!). Let it cool, about 30 minutes, before slicing and serving.

WINE MATCH – **Brachetto**

Your texture-metre is going to go through the ceiling once you try this dessert with Brachetto, the sweet and fragrant red bubbly from Italy. Silky, mousse-like cake, chewy-crunchy meringue, and fizzy wine dance on your palate all at once. Brachetto has a happy relationship with chocolate and hazelnut, they are all best buddies. But if you can't find Brachetto, try a port (either ruby or tawny) or Banyuls.

TIRAMISÙ

This traditional Italian dessert is simply creamy coffee decadence. It's insanely rich but tastes light as air and rounds out any meal beautifully. You can make this dessert up to one day in advance, but, if you are running short on time, pop it in the freezer for an hour or two to help it set up. It actually makes for a nice twist, giving it a bit of ice cream flair. Mascarpone cheese is a buttery, rich double cream cheese, the consistency of really thick sour cream but much more mild in flavour. You can find it at nearly any grocery store. Lady fingers, if you've never had them, are a meringue-like cookie, oddly enough, shaped like fingers. You can make them yourself or you can buy them in the cookie section from your grocer, which cuts the work of this dessert in half.   Serves 6

6 tablespoons (90ml) very strong espresso coffee

4 tablespoons (60ml) brandy or Marsala

6 large eggs, separated

8 tablespoons (120ml) icing sugar

16 oz (455g) of Mascarpone cheese

24 Italian lady fingers

2 oz (56g) of best quality bittersweet chocolate, finely grated

- In a large bowl, whisk your egg whites with an electric beater until stiff and glossy.
- In a small bowl, combine coffee and the brandy or Marsala and set aside.
- In another large bowl, with an electric beater, combine the egg yolks and icing sugar until the mixture turns pale and thick.
- Add your mascarpone and whisk to blend.
- With a large spatula, carefully fold your egg whites into the mascarpone mixture.
- In a 10-inch square baking dish, lay out 12 of the lady fingers. With a pastry brush, brush on the coffee mixture giving the lady fingers a bit of a soaking.
- Spread half of your mascarpone cream over the biscuits.
- Sprinkle with about one half of the grated chocolate and now top with a second layer of lady fingers.
- Again with your coffee mixture followed by the mascarpone cream.

Contd . . .

> ## TIP
>
> ### Why does wine "go bad" once the bottle is opened?
>
> Wine can last for years, sometimes decades when it's properly sealed and stored, but as soon as you open the bottle and the wine has contact with the air it starts to lose its freshness. Think about a piece of cut fruit or a glass of juice that has sat out on the counter overnight and how it smells the next day – sort of old and brown – that's from contact with the air and just like your 2-day-old bottle of wine, they've oxidized.
>
> As mentioned earlier, there are a couple of things you can do to keep your wine fresher for longer. First, if you're only planning on having a glass or two, put the cork back in the bottle right away. The longer the bottle is left wide open, the faster the oxidation will happen. This doesn't solve the problem altogether (since there's some air in the bottle where the wine used to be) but it helps. Second, always always always store your leftover wine in the fridge, even if it's red wine. The cooler temperature helps it taste fresher longer. And finally, try out some of the the gadgets I mention on page 174. Whites tend to last longer than reds, and after two or three days, save it for cooking.

- Save the last bit of chocolate to be sprinkled just before you serve it. Cover and refrigerate your tiramisù for at least 3 hours. This helps the cream to firm up and gives the lady fingers some time to absorb the coffee mixture a bit better.

- To serve this lovely dessert, cut your tiramisù into rectangular slices, pop them onto chilled dessert plates and sprinkle with remaining grated chocolate.

WINE MATCH – **Muscat**

Alright, let's see here. We've got coffee, brandy, mascarpone cheese, and chocolate. Lots of flavours means we need a wine that's super versatile. My recommendation for this one is a sweet Muscat. Muscat is luscious and rich, but has citrus and floral aromas and flavours. So while the texture and sweetness level mirror the dessert, the flavours of the wine contrast.

CHOCOLATE RASPBERRY CAKE WITH RASPBERRY COULIS

I am always on the hunt for a mind blowing chocolate cake recipe, because when you indulge, you should indulge well. So far, this one takes the cake for being incredibly moist and decadently chocolate. If you aren't a fan of raspberries you can make the cake all chocolate and serve it up with some vanilla ice cream. I, however, love the raspberry element and feel that these two ingredients were actually made to be together, which is why I melt in ecstasy with Stacey's wine pairing. A coulis is just a pretty name for a thick purée. In this case it's raspberries and simple syrup. It makes this whole dessert not only pop in your mouth but look incredibly stylish on your plate. **One 9-inch cake**

Ingredients

1 1/2 cups (375ml) light brown sugar, packed

1 1/2 cups (375ml) unbleached flour

1/2 cup (125ml) best quality cocoa

1 1/2 teaspoons (7.5ml) baking soda

3/4 teaspoon (3.75ml) baking powder

1/4 teaspoon (1.25ml) salt

3/4 cup (180ml) strong coffee

3/4 cup (180ml) buttermilk

1/3 cup + 2 tablespoons (110ml) vegetable oil

2 eggs (1 whole egg + 1 egg yolk)

1 teaspoon (5ml) vanilla

Chocolate Ganache

1/2 cup (125ml) heavy cream

1 tablespoon (15ml) unsalted butter

5 oz (140g) semi-sweet chocolate, chopped

- Pre-heat oven to 350F (180C).

- Prepare two 9-inch cake pans by brushing with oil and cutting a parchment circle to fit the bottom as well as a band of parchment to fit the sides.

- Whisk together the dry ingredients.

- In a separate bowl, whisk together wet ingredients until well blended. Add the wet to the dry and stir together until all ingredients have fully blended and you can't see any lumps of flour.

- Divide batter between prepared pans and bake for 15 minutes, until a toothpick comes out clean.

- Allow the cakes to cool before removing them from their tins and peeling off the parchment paper.

- While the cakes are cooling, heat the cream and the butter until it's just about to boil (you will see a frame of little bubbles around the pot). Pour the hot cream over the chopped chocolate and let it hang out for a couple of minutes. After 2–3 minutes, gently whisk until the chocolate is melted and smooth. Cool for a few minutes.

- If your cake has rounded at the top, grab a good long knife (bread knife would work best, and shave the top to flatten it out. If you are a little anal about the vision of your cake, do the same to the second cake to perfectly flatten the top.)

- Slowly pour warm chocolate ganache over top of cake spreading evenly with a pallet knife or spatula.

Contd . . .

- If you are garnishing with raspberries, now is a good time. They look great placed upside down and framing the outside of the cake, but use your imagination.

- Carefully place your cake on a plate and pop into the refrigerator so the chocolate can set.

- When you're ready to serve, grab your raspberry coulis (recipe follows), drizzle a nice amount on the plate and pop your cake slice on top.

Raspberry Coulis

Fantastic with this cake! If you have some left over, try it on pancakes, ice cream, over oatmeal, in yogurt. Where ever you think it works.

1 cup (250ml) fresh or frozen, and
   defrosted raspberries

1–2 tablespoons (15-30ml) of sugar, to taste

A few drops of fresh lemon juice, to taste

- In a blender or food processor purée the ingredients, adding a little sugar at a time to taste.

- With a fine sieve or cheesecloth, strain your mixture and discard the seeds.

- Transfer to a container, cover tightly and refrigerate until you are ready to use. It keeps well for a week.

WINE MATCH – **Framboise**

Every time I pair Framboise, an intensely flavoured raspberry wine, with any chocolate-based dessert, the crowds go wild. There's something about the jammy, unctuous berry wine that brings out the best in chocolate. The raspberry coulis in this dessert carries the pairing to a whole new level, with the wine mirroring the flavours in the coulis. You might find Framboise too intense on its own, but with this rich, chocolaty cake, it brings the wine into balance, making it seem less rich and sweet. If you prefer to stick with grape-based wines, get your hands on a Recioto della Valpolicella. Its berry flavours and rich sweetness work equally well with this dessert.

CARAMEL FONDUE

Man alive this is good! Fruit and lemon pound cake dipped in hot caramel is sexy and so freakin' delicious. This is one of those really versatile desserts. It's fun for kids (minus the cognac), it's sexy for a hot date, and it's incredibly social for a larger group. Everyone is dipping into the same pot and grabbing from the same platter. It's also a do-ahead dessert which is so important for any kind of entertaining. Keep the fruit plate colourful, the fondue hot and you'll keep your guests in awe for the rest of the night.

1/2 cup (125ml) sugar

2 tablespoons (30ml) water

1 1/3 cups (330ml) 35% cream

2 tablespoons (30ml) cognac

1 tablespoon (15ml) unsalted butter

Fresh strawberries, thinly sliced apples or pears, sliced bananas, fresh tangerine segments and lemon pound cake cut into pieces for dipping.

- Combine the sugar and water in heavy, medium saucepan. Stir over low heat until sugar dissolves. Turn up your heat and bring to a boil without stirring until mixture is deep amber color, occasionally brushing down sides of pan with wet pastry brush and swirling pan, this will take about 3 minutes.

- In another small saucepan on low heat warm up your cream. Add the warm cream to the caramel, but be careful when you do as sometimes the sugar spurts up and it's pretty hot at this point.

- Stir over medium-high heat until sauce is smooth and reduced to 1 1/4 (310ml) cups, about 5 minutes.

- Add your cognac and cook for 1 minute longer. Remove from heat. Add the butter and stir until it's melted. You can prepare the fondue to this point up to 8 hours ahead.

- Cover and pop it in the refrigerator until you are ready to use it. To bring it back to fondue life, re-warm the caramel over medium-low heat, without boiling.

- Transfer the sauce to small fondue pot or flameproof ceramic bowl. Set the pot over a candle or canned heat burner.

- Serve with strawberries, apples or pears, bananas, tangerine segments and pieces of lemon pound cake.

Lemon Pound Cake

If you end up with pound cake left over from your party, try toasting it and spreading with some preserves for breakfast or an afternoon snack. It's also pretty great grilled on the barbecue and served alongside the grilled fruit with mascarpone cream (see page 366). **Makes 1 Bundt pan cake**

Butter and flour for the pans

1 lb (454g) unsalted butter, softened

3 cups (750g) white sugar

6 eggs

4 cups (1 litre) flour

1 tablespoon (15ml) baking powder

1/2 teaspoon (2.5ml) salt

1 teaspoon (5ml) freshly grated lemon rind

1 cup (250ml) milk

2 teaspoons (10ml) vanilla extract

1/4 cup (60ml) lemon juice

- Preheat your oven to 350F (180C).
- Butter and flour bottom and sides of a bundt pan.
- In a large bowl, cream together butter and sugar with an electric mixer until mixture is light and fluffy.
- Add your eggs, one at a time to the creamed butter, beating well after each and set aside.
- Sift together the dry ingredients in a separate bowl.
- Mix together your milk and vanilla.
- To bring it all together, add one third of the dry and one third of the wet alternately to butter mixture, beginning and ending with dry.
- Mix by hand – enough so you can't see any dry flour.
- Spread your batter into the prepared pan. Bake the cake for 50–60 minutes, or until a sharp knife inserted all the way down comes out clean.
- Allow your cake to cool for about 10 minutes before turning it out from the pan and onto a plate. If you are using the cake for the fondue, wait until it has completely cooled before cutting into bite-sized pieces with a serrated knife. If you would like to do this ahead of your guests arriving, store cut pieces in an airtight container – but use the same day.

WINE MATCH – **Madeira**

There aren't many wine and food matches that actually taste like you're drinking the same thing that you're eating. But this one is just that. The caramel flavour of the dessert is the same as the caramel flavour of the Madeira. One is literally an extension of the other. Enough said . . . this is a perfect match!

BUTTERMILK PANNA COTTA WITH LAVENDER OIL

Delicate is the first word that comes to mind when I think about this lovely little dessert. The panna cotta is silky smooth and creamy fresh. The lavender oil is subtly scented to perfume the dessert. By drizzling the oil around the custard, with each spoonful you get just a little taste. I don't know why, but blackberries and lavender seem like relatives to me – the kind that bring out the best in each other when on the same plate. **Serves 6**

Panna Cotta

1 cup (250ml) buttermilk

1 tablespoon (15ml) powdered gelatin

2 cups (500ml) 35% cream

1/3 cup (80ml) sugar

3 teaspoons (15ml) grated orange zest

A pint of blackberries that have been sprinkled with sugar and lemon juice to taste – this is called "macerating" them

Lavender Oil

1 cup (250ml) grapeseed oil

1 tablespoon (15ml) dried lavender

- In a food processor, combine the sugar and the grated orange zest and blend.

- Pour 1/4 cup (60ml) of the buttermilk into a pot. Sprinkle gelatin over the buttermilk. Heat the buttermilk over low heat to dissolve the gelatin slowly, giving it the occasional stir. If the gelatin turns into a blob, reheat on low and whisk until it is distributed in the milk.

- In a separate pot add rest of the milk, the cream, and sugar/orange zest combo. Bring this to a boil but watch it carefully. Milk is a jerk and will boil over the sides of your pot the minute you aren't paying attention, so be ready to pull it off the heat and turn down the burner to medium low. Simmer this mixture for about 5 minutes.

- Pull this from the heat and gently whisk in the gelatin mixture. Cool, giving it the occasional stir, until it has come to room temperature.

- With some of the grapeseed oil, grease 4 1-cup (250ml) ramekins.

- Strain the custard through a fine mesh sieve into a large pitcher. From the pitcher, fill each one of the ramekins with the custard.

- Put the filled ramekins into refrigerator for 2–3 hours or until they have set.

Contd . . .

- To make the lavender oil, heat the grapeseed oil in a saucepan with the dried lavender over medium heat until you hear the lavender start to crackle. Pull the oil off the heat and allow to cool to room temperature. Strain out the lavender when you are happy with the intensity of flavour, I let mine sit for about 10 minutes. If you have one, put the oil into a squeeze bottle which will make it super easy to distribute around the custard.

- When you are ready to serve, pull the panna cotta out of the fridge and turn each out onto your dessert plates. Drizzle 1/2 tablespoon (7.5ml) of the lavender oil around the base of each. And a small dollop of the macerated blackberries either on top of the panna cotta or artfully on the plate.

WINE MATCH – **Vidal**
(Icewine or Late Harvest)

As a self-proclaimed non-dessert girl, I have to say that this recipe compels me to revoke my title. The distinctive tang of buttermilk and the elegant aroma of lavender make my heart melt. The only way this gets better is with the best – you need a glass of Vidal Icewine. It has a silky texture that is perfect for the panna cotta and its delicate floral notes marry well with the lavender oil. If Icewine is too pricey, go for something late harvest.

CHOCOLATE WHISKY PECAN TART

The flavours of boozy chocolate and gooey pecans makes this tart a favourite in my family. This pie is great served slightly warm with some cold whipped or ice cream, at room temperature, or nice and cold. Feel free to buy a frozen pastry crust and proceed, no one will judge you. There is just something so homey about making your own pie crust. I don't know who ever came up with the phrase "easy as pie" – I'm guessing one of those people who eats but never bakes. See page 358 for tips on baking the perfect crust. **Makes one 9-inch pie**

Pie Crust

*2 1/2 cups (625ml) unbleached
    all-purpose flour*

1 teaspoon (5ml) salt

2 teaspoons (10ml) granulated sugar

*8 tablespoons (125ml) very cold, unsalted
    butter, cut into pieces*

*6 tablespoons (90ml) cold solid vegetable
    shortening, cut into pieces*

5 to 6 tablespoons (75-90ml) ice water

Pie Filling

2 oz (56g) unsweetened chocolate

1/4 cup (60ml) unsalted butter

4 large eggs

1 cup (250ml) granulated sugar

1 1/4 cup (310ml) dark corn syrup

1 teaspoon (5ml) vanilla extract

2 tablespoons (30ml) whisky

2 cups (500ml) pecan halves

- In a mixing bowl, blend together the flour, salt and sugar. Add the cold cubed butter and the shortening.

- Working quickly, use a pastry blender or two knives to cut in the ingredients until the mixture has coarse crumbs, a few of the butter/shortening pieces can be about pea-sized but ideally most of them will be smaller than that.

- Sprinkle the ice water over the mixture about 1–2 tablespoons (15-30ml) at a time, tossing with cutter each time. (sprinkle, don't pour – if you pour the ice water into one spot you're not going to get the beautiful pie pastry we both know you have in you).

- When you can just gather the dough into a ball, you've added enough water. It's usually about 5–6 tablespoons (75-90ml).

- Transfer the dough to a chilled, lightly floured surface and with your hands, just push the mixture together to form a ball. If the dough is too dry to hold together, put it back into the bowl and add a few more drops of ice water.

- Lightly flour your hands and round out the ball of dough. Flatten it slightly to form a disc and slightly smooth the edges. Wrap it up in plastic wrap and refrigerate for a minimum of 30 minutes.

Contd . . .

TIP

Pie filling is generally straightforward but the pastry can be tricky. Find a recipe you feel comfortable with and keep it as your standby. A few helpful tips make pie pastry a whole lot easier. Usually you preheat the oven before you do any baking, but in this case we are going to keep your kitchen as cool as possible to help your pie pastry adventure, so leave it off until we are ready to blind bake the crust. Blind baking is when you bake the pie crust before filling it. You can buy pastry weights but a cheap and easy way to keep the bottom flat as it bakes is to line the pastry with aluminum or parchment and pour in a layer of dried beans. You can keep the beans after, and use them over and over. You need to pull them out for the last few minutes of baking so that the bottom can crisp. Another trick to great pie pastry is to pop your bowl, pastry cutter, cutting board (or whatever surface you roll on) and your rolling pin into the freezer for at least 20 minutes before starting. And remember, at the end of the day, it's just pie!

- Roll chilled dough out on a lightly floured surface to form an 11-inch circle. Transfer pastry to a 9-inch pie plate (try rolling it back over your rolling pin and unrolling it on the pie plate) and gently press into the bottom and sides. Trim the dough leaving 1-inch overhang around the plate. Fold overhang back toward the inside, and crimp the edge decoratively.

- Preheat your oven to 400F (200C).

- Prick the bottom of the pastry with a fork and line with aluminum foil, shiny side down.

- Fill plate with either pie weights or dried beans and bake for 6–8 minutes. Remove beans and foil.

- Pop the piecrust back into the oven for 2 minutes. Cool it slightly before adding your filling.

- Move your rack in your oven to the bottom third of the oven and adjust the temperature to 350F (180C).

- In the top of a double boiler, add your chocolate and butter and melt over hot water on a medium heat. Stir on occasion to help it melt evenly.

- Once the chocolate and butter have melted, pull top of double boiler from heat and allow to cool slightly.

- Spread your pecans out on a baking sheet and bake in the oven until they are toasted and fragrant, about 7–10 minutes. Set aside to cool as you make the rest of your filling.

- In a large bowl, beat eggs lightly just to break up.

- Add in sugar and corn syrup and beat again. Add the vanilla, the whisky and the melted butter/chocolate.

- Make sure it's all blended well together and gently stir in the pecans.

- Carefully pour filling into the partially baked crust. Aim for middle of the pie to avoid a big mess around your beautiful pastry. Pay attention as you pour, if the filling starts to approach your crust don't use all the filling otherwise it'll overflow when you bake it.

- Bake for about 40–50 minutes until the pie is soft to the touch. It should be slightly set on the outside with a slightly jiggly belly (think post-Christmas holidays). The filling will set up as the pie cools.

- Remove the pie from the oven and place it on a cooling rack to cool to room temperature or just slightly warmer if you like.

WINE MATCH – **Ruby Port**

Pair up a sweet ruby Port and you've got yourself a winner. The rich berry flavours in the wine are a nice contrast, but the wine is as sweet and intense as the dessert so it won't be overpowered. You could also try an Oloroso Sherry with this tart. The nutty flavours in the wine will really bring out the pecan flavour. And here's a fun tip – sub in your wine of choice in place of the whisky in the recipe for an even better pairing.

BANANA COCONUT CREAM PIE

This is a pie I've known since I was a kid. We kind of fell out of touch for a while but have rekindled our relationship. I love it's creamy, refreshing tropical taste. You will need a couple of hours at least to chill this pie for it to set up. If you are hoping to make it the day before, I suggest keeping the custard in Tupperware and popping into the pie crust and assembling the rest of the pie day of, otherwise you'll have a soggy pie crust. **One 9-inch pie**

Graham Cracker Crust

1 1/2 cups (625ml) graham cracker crumbs

1/2 cup (125ml) sifted icing sugar

6 tablespoons (90ml) melted unsalted butter

Filling

1/2 cup (125ml) all-purpose flour

2/3 cup (160ml) granulated sugar

1/2 teaspoon (2.5ml) salt

2 cups (500ml) homogenized milk

3 egg yolks

2 tablespoons (30ml) unsalted butter

2 teaspoons (10ml) vanilla

1 cup (250ml) of grated or flaked coconut

2 ripe bananas

extra granulated sugar

35% cream

confectioners sugar to taste

vanilla extract to taste

- Preheat your oven to 350F (180C).

- In a medium mixing bowl mix together the graham crumbs, the icing sugar and the melted butter. Once these are well blended, press the mixture into a 9-inch pie tin trying to get an even layer all over. Place an empty pie tin of the same size on top and press down firmly. Trim any excess crumbs that rise up over the sides of the pan and remove the empty tin.

- Pop your pie crust in the oven and bake it until it's golden. That should take about 10 minutes.

- Set up a double boiler with about 2–3 inches of water in the bottom, heating it up to a simmer. Over the water, stir and cook the flour, sugar, salt and milk for about 10 minutes until the mixture has had a chance to thicken.

- In a small bowl, beat the 3 egg yolks slightly with a fork. In a slow stream, pour about 1/3 of the hot milk mixture into the eggs while stirring the eggs; what you are trying to do here is warm the eggs up and trick them into not scrambling on you.

Contd . . .

- Slowly add the warmed egg-milk mixture back to the pot of thickened milk where you will continue to cook until it has thickened enough. You'll know it's thick enough when you pull a wooden spoon out of the custard and hold the spoon so the sauce can run off. If you draw a line with your finger on the back of the spoon and the custard doesn't run over the line, it's done. This should take about 10 minutes again.

- Remove the thickened custard from the heat and stir in the butter, the vanilla and the coconut. Blend it all together and set it aside to cool down some before you add it to your baked graham crust.

- Slice bananas and in one layer cover the top of the custard. Sprinkle bananas with a thin layer of granulated sugar and with a little brûlée torch caramelize the tops (if you don't have a brûlée torch, skip the caramelizing part – leave out the sugar and just move on to the whipping cream.)

- In a large bowl, using an electric beater, whip the whipping cream into soft peaks. Add the icing sugar and vanilla in small amounts until it tastes as sweet as you like.

- With a spatula, gently spread the whipped cream over your pie to desired thickness.

- In a skillet on stovetop over medium-low heat toast coconut carefully until golden. Sprinkle top of your pie with the coconut and pop the whole thing in your refrigerator for a minimum of 1 hour. Serve.

WINE MATCH – **Sauternes**

Something downright magical happens when you pair Sauternes with this dessert. The toasty coconut is highlighted by the oaky flavours in the wine; the banana brings out Sauternes' fruity side; and that rich, silky custard couldn't find a better friend than the honeyed texture of the wine. This truly is a pairing that will knock your socks off.

CITRUS ANISE BISCOTTI

"Biscotti" basically translates to "twice baked biscuit," which gives you, the baker of biscotti, the advantage of being able to store them for a couple of weeks. These are a great thing to have on hand if you have the type of household that has random guests appear,. They make a light and easy dessert. I also adore how versatile biscotti are. You can generally take a good recipe and play around with your favourite ingredients switching it up for various nuts, dried fruit, chocolate chunks and spices for flavorings. Liberate yourself. Design your own signature biscotti!   **Makes 3 dozen**

3 1/4 (810ml) cups all purpose flour

1 tablespoon (15ml) baking powder

1/4 teaspoon (1.25ml) salt

1 1/2 cups (375ml) sugar

10 tablespoons (155ml) unsalted butter, melted

3 large eggs

3 tablespoons (45ml) freshly grated lemon peel

1 tablespoon (15ml) ground anise seeds

1 large egg white

- Position your oven rack to the middle and preheat your oven to 350F (180C).

- Line a baking sheet with parchment paper.

- In a medium bowl, sift together your flour, baking powder and salt.

- In a larger bowl mix together sugar, melted butter, eggs, grated lemon peel and ground anise seeds. Add dry mixture to wet mixture and with a wooden spoon or spatula mix it all together really well.

- Divide dough in half. Lightly flour your hands and shape each mound of dough into a 13 x 2 1/2 inch wide log. Transfer both logs to parchment-lined baking sheet, about 2 inches apart.

- In a little bowl, whisk egg white until a little foamy. With a pastry brush, brush egg over tops and sides of the dough, to give your biscotti a really nice crust.

- Bake logs until golden brown (don't panic if they have spread out, this is totally normal). The first baking should take around 30 minutes. Pull them from oven and cool completely on a rack for 25 minutes, but leave oven on.

- Take logs from the rack and carefully move to a cutting board.

- Using a serrated knife, cut each log on a severe diagonal into 1/2-inch thick slices and place the slices, cut-side down, back onto baking sheet.

- Reduce temperature to 325F (160C). Bake biscotti for 12 minutes. Turn over and bake until just beginning to color, about 8 minutes more. Transfer to rack and cool.

- If stored in a tin or a tightly closed container, biscotti will often keep for up to two weeks.

WINE MATCH – **Vin Santo**

Alright, tradition is tradition so let's not mess around with it. As long as Vin Santo's been around, people have been dunking their biscotti into it. They work amazingly well together, especially with traditional flavorings like citrus, anise, or just straight-up almonds, Vin Santo complements biscotti in both flavour and texture. It's the adult version of Oreo cookies and milk.

MANGO TART

This is one of those super-easy desserts that looks incredibly labour-intensive, so your guests will think you have slaved all day. What I love about this tart is that it's light and tropical, and it has mangos in it – one of my favourite fruits – stacked on buttery, flaky puff pastry. Due to the fruit purée you are using as your base on this tart, it doesn't hold well for hours on end. Get the whole thing ready, store it in the fridge and bake it while someone pours the dessert wine. A hot, flaky tart with icy cold sorbet and a glass of sweet wine is the best possible way to end an evening.   Makes 4.

4 large ripe mangos

1 sheet of puff pastry

1 vanilla bean

Granulated sugar

1/4 cup (6oml) melted unsalted butter

- Take 2 mangos, peel them, roughly chop the meat and add to a saucepan.

- Carefully slice open the vanilla bean trying not to go through both sides, you just want to slice down the belly and open it up. Scrape all the black goo out of the bean and into the saucepan.

- Cook the mango-vanilla mixture covered on medium-low heat – slowly until the mixture becomes soft and puréed looking. Stir on occasion to prevent it from sticking. Once this has cooked, pull the pan from heat and allow to cool.

- Peel and cut off the cheeks of the other two mangos and thinly slice the cheeks lengthwise.

- With a 4-inch cookie cutter cut out 4 circles from the puff pastry. On each disc spread 1/4 of the cooled mango purée. Arrange the mango slices on top of disc to your artistic desire. I like to line mine up and lean them to one side.

- Brush the top of each tart with melted butter and sprinkle with about 1/2 tablespoon (7.5ml) of sugar.

- Pop these tarts into the fridge and let them set for approximately 20 minutes.

- When you are ready for them, have your oven preheated to 400F (200C), maybe start to preheat the oven as you sit down for your dinner.

- Bake them in your oven for around 12 minutes until they are golden brown.

- Serve immediately with vanilla ice cream or mango sorbet or anything else you can think of.

WINE MATCH – **Riesling (Icewine or Late Harvest)**

A sweet Riesling is an excellent choice for this tart because it delivers ripe fruit flavours as well as crisp acidity, which is perfect for mangos. If you can find Icewine, go for that, but a late harvest Riesling (including Beerenauslese from Germany) also works. Sauternes is another option, with its tropical fruit flavours, and honey-like texture.

STICKY TOFFEE PUDDING

I was in New Zealand when I tried this dessert for the first time. I couldn't believe I had been on the planet for so long without knowing about sticky toffee pudding! Warm, sweet, cakey pudding with hot toffee sauce poured over, absorbed and served alongside is decadence at its best. Even better, it's such an easy dessert to whip up, it's worth keeping the ingredients on hand. Just in case. Serves 6

The pudding

1 generous cup (250ml) of pitted Medjool
    dates (or dried dates if you can't find fresh)

1 teaspoon (5ml) baking soda

1 cup (250ml) boiling water

1 cup (250ml) all purpose flour

1 teaspoon (5ml) baking powder

1/4 teaspoon (1.25ml) baking soda

1/2 teaspoon (2.5ml) salt

1/4 teaspoon (1.25ml) ground cinnamon

1/3 cup (80ml) unsalted butter at room
    temperature

1/2 cup (125ml) sugar

2 large eggs

2 tablespoons (30ml) plain yogurt

Toffee Sauce

2 1/2 cups (625ml) 35% cream

2 cups (500ml) sugar

1/3 cup (80ml) corn syrup

1/2 cup (125ml) unsalted butter

- Preheat your oven to 350F (180C)

- Butter an ovenproof baking dish.

- In a small bowl sprinkle baking soda over dates and pour boiling water over both. Allow dates to soften for about 10 minutes. Drain and give them a whiz in the food processor to form a bit of a paste.

- In a separate bowl combine the flour, baking powder, baking soda, salt and cinnamon.

- In a third and final bowl, with a spoon, cream together the butter and sugar until pale yellow.

- Add the eggs and the flour mixture.

- Mix all together and stir in date purée and yogurt.

- Pour batter into prepared dish and bake for 30–35 minutes or until a knife inserted comes out clean.

- While the pudding is cooking, make your toffee sauce. Put the cream, sugar, corn syrup and butter into a saucepan. Stir occasionally over low heat until the cream is caramel in colour, about 15 minutes.

- This is cheating but it's pretty great. While the cake is still hot, poke it 4–5 times with a skewer. Pour some toffee sauce on top and allow to sink into the cake for 2–3 minutes. Serve in dessert bowls with more toffee sauce, vanilla ice cream if you like, and a pitcher of warm toffee sauce on the side.

WINE MATCH – **Tawny Port**

The name of the dessert speaks for itself – sticky and toffee. I choose a tawny port to complement these key elements – tawnies have a rich, nutty, caramelly thing going on and it's just the right match for this tasty dessert. Look for something at least 10 years old to really make this pairing special.

GRILLED FRUIT WITH MAPLE MASCARPONE CREAM

This is dessert simplicity at its best. Grilling fruit on the barbecue is satisfying on a hot summer day. In the winter, when you are craving the taste of outdoors, grab some tropical fruit and grill it all in your trusty grill pan for close to the same results. One trick for grilling fruit is to cut your fruit into nice large pieces. This will keep them from falling apart and will make the whole experience a lot less fussy. Mascarpone is buttery rich cheese with a super-creamy texture and a really mild flavour that adds an unexpected twist to the average whipping cream. Think about variety in colours and flavours when creating a platter of grilled fruit for your guests and have a blast with this light and beautiful dessert.

Fruit of your choice: pineapple, strawberries,
  bananas, peaches, plums, pears, etc.
A few drops of brandy
Sugar to taste

Mascarpone Cream
9 oz (250g) mascarpone
About 2 tablespoons (30ml) whipping cream
Maple syrup to taste

- Wash the fruit, and halve, pit or core if necessary.
- Place the fruit in a shallow serving dish, add a couple of drops of brandy if you like, sprinkle with some sugar (sweeten to taste). If the fruit is already very sweet, use less than you would with tart fruit.
- Preheat grill to high or grill pan to medium high.
- Cook the fruit without moving, just long enough to soften slightly but still keep their shape. It should take roughly 2 minutes on each side, depending on the fruit.
- Place the mascarpone in a non-reactive bowl and beat with electric beaters adding syrup and a touch of cream. Beat until smooth. Set aside.
- To serve, arrange the grilled fruit on a platter alongside a bowl of the mascarpone cream for dipping.

WINE MATCH – **Vidal (Icewine or Late Harvest)**

The flavours in this dessert can vary based on what kind of fruit you use, so choosing a versatile wine makes your life easier. Vidal is intensely fruity with a nice backbone of acidity, so it'll go with this dish no matter what fruits you've got on hand. Plus, the added Canadiana link of maple syrup and Vidal Icewine makes the pairing extra-special. If Vidal dessert wine isn't available in your area, try a Tokaji Aszú – it has lovely honey flavours that will complement the fruit and is rich enough for the mascarpone cream.

What the heck is a Sommelier anyway?

"Wine is earth's answer to the sun."
—MARGARET FULLER

I love wine. I love it so much that I managed to find a way to make a living at it. I guess my official title, as earned from completing my wine studies, is "Accredited Sommelier." Pretty fancy name for someone who loves wine a lot. So what the heck is a sommelier anyway?

The dictionary.com definition says "a waiter, as in a club or restaurant, who is in charge of wines." In bigger restaurants, sommeliers are often in charge of putting together the wine list, managing the wine cellar, and serving wines to guests in the restaurant. Funny that my title should be Sommelier then, considering I don't actually work in a restaurant.

But these days, the term "sommelier" has been stretched to cover more than just wine servers in restaurants. In my job, for example, I run wine tastings, teach wine classes, and write about wine (both in print and online). There are lots of other sommeliers I know who work as wine agents, at wineries, as wine writers, reporters, and columnists, and even running wine tours around the world (nice work if you can find it!).

So, you're into wine, trying different kinds, matching it with food, and you really love it. Does that mean that you should become a sommelier? Not necessarily. For most wine lovers, a wine appreciation class or two is just the ticket. There are lots of fun classes and tastings in which you learn all about wine, including the part I think is the most fun (and the most practical to know about) – wine and food matching.

But if you're seriously considering a career change, there are many routes you can take to become a sommelier. The most hands-on approach to learning about wine is working in a restaurant. I have lots of friends in the industry who worked in restaurants for years, starting as dishwasher, bus boy, server, and worked their way up the ladder. Being in a restaurant environment gives you constant exposure to food and wine, if you're paying attention. It also gives you the experience you would need to land that coveted sommelier position in a great restaurant with a killer wine list.

Hands-on experience aside, getting formal wine training is very important too. There are sommelier accreditation programs offered all over the place, some as part of college or university programs, and others run by independent institutions or associations. These courses vary from basic levels to the highest accreditations of Master Sommelier (there's only one in Canada right now) and Master of Wine.

Wine training usually consists of three different elements – informational, tasting and service. There is a lot to know about wine. Grape types, winemaking techniques, grape growing, soil, wine laws . . . the list goes on and on. The more I learn about wine the more I believe that it's a lifelong learning process . . . I'll never get to the end. But taking wine classes definitely gives you a good basis.

Tasting – my favourite part. And actually the best way to learn about wine (and I'm not just saying that because I like drinking it so much!). It's so much easier to remember things about a wine that you've tasted than it is having only read about them. Plus, it supports the whole informational aspect as well. If you read in a book that wine from a certain region tastes a certain way because of the soil the grapes are grown in, why not crack open a bottle of that wine and see if you can taste it?

The service part, finally, focuses more on the restaurant aspect. How to properly open a wine, how to serve it, how to handle challenging wine matching situations. Practical, hands-on stuff you need to know to work as a sommelier.

So there you have it, the low-down on being a sommelier. If wine is your passion, attend a wine tasting or enroll in a wine appreciation class. With some basic knowledge, you'll have a lot more fun with wine. And who knows, maybe one day your passion will turn you into the next Master Sommelier!

ACKNOWLEDGEMENTS

To Luella Klinck, who taught me what love can do to food
To Christopher Pinney, who taught me what food can do to love
To my family: Dan, Cathy, Shelley and Ian who seasoned it all

All thanks begin with Chris Knight. Had we never met, my life would not likely have avalanched in this direction. Thank you for your sometimes patience, your frequent sarcasm and your endless ambition. Ms. Metulynsky, without your ever present laughter in varied and generally crazy circumstances, your energy when I'm out of mine and your balance, I'm not sure this book would have ever been finished with the fun factor that it contained. You are an excellent adventure partner and I wouldn't want to share this book with anyone but you. To Pins, who took deep breaths, answered all my questions with patience and made me dinner. A lot. A great big thank you to Vanessa Poirier and Matt Whitehead, who turned my living room into a photo studio and busted their butts to try to make this the best darn book we collectively could. One last and important thank you to Sherry Bishop from *With the Grain*, who taught me that integrity makes food truly fun and intensely satisfying. — **ANGIE**

To my mom, Alla, always my biggest fan

I could write a whole other book on all the people I'd like to thank, but I'll try to keep it short. To my family and friends who watched me procrastinate, then listened to me complain about it, and who still remain my family and friends – thank you for your patience. To Sean, for pushing me in the right direction – I never would have left my desk job, and I never, ever would have auditioned for a TV show – thank you for your faith in me. To Vanessa – thank you for the photos, to Matt for helping make them look so good, to Andrew for making us beautiful, and to the rest of the folks at Knight Enterprises who probably took care of all sorts of nitty-gritty we'll never know about. And last but not least, to the two people who made this book the experience that it was: Chris Knight, thank you for the amazing opportunity, for inspiring me, for firing me up, and for helping me find my voice; and of course to Angie MacRae – my partner in crime and my friend – thank you for always being on Team Stacey. We laughed, we cried, we shopped, we drank, and somehow . . . we wrote a book! — **STACEY**